_Kath_

# MARY PICKFORD
## Sweetheart of the World

From working in flickers for five million dollars a day to amassing a million dollars a year, this is the incredible story of literally the first movie star. Mary Pickford's eighty-year life is packed with _romance_ (her love affair, marriage and divorce from Douglas Fairbanks make more recent explosive showbiz unions pall by comparison), _accomplishment_ businesswoman supreme, she rose to be founder-head of United Artists and controller of a vast self-made fortune), _glamour_ (her every move was chronicled for her legions of fans), and _tragedy_ (two scandal-ridden divorces, the deaths in rapid succession of her brother, sister and mother, and her own exile and illness).

Robert Windeler's is a moving and powerfully entertaining biography, rich in atmosphere and anecdotes about an era and a star whose place is unique in the history of the movies.

# MARY PICKFORD
## Sweetheart of the World

Robert Windeler

**A STAR BOOK**
*published by*
W. H. ALLEN

A Star Book
Published in 1975
by W. H. Allen & Co. Ltd.
A division of Howard & Wyndham Ltd.
44 Hill Street, London W1X 8LB

First published in Great Britain by
W. H. Allen & Co. Ltd. 1973

Printed in Great Britain by
Richard Clay (The Chaucer Press), Ltd., Bungay, Suffolk

ISBN 0 352 30046 9

TO MY MOTHER
AND FATHER

And everyone else who used
to go to the movies

# Preface

HE had acted in her last film a decade before I was born. And by the time I got to Hollywood in 1966, to cover the entertainment world first for *Time* magazine and then *The New York Times*, she had abdicated from all society. Mary Pickford wasn't part of *my* Hollywood. And until 1971 most of even her landmark movies were unavailable for viewing. Thus, when I started this project almost four years ago, it was almost from ground zero. Almost, but not quite.

Part of my early growing up was spent in a small town on the Passaic River in northeastern New Jersey, which was used by D. W. Griffith and other early directors as a location for their movies—everything from *The Perils of Pauline* to authentic-looking westerns. And Mary Pickford, who had starred in two of Griffith's films made there, was somewhat of a local legend. *They Would Elope*, a delightful chase comedy made entirely in town, was the first Mary Pickford film I ever saw. It was at a local historical pageant in connection with New Jersey's tercentenary.

Throughout my research and writing on this book I've consistently had to answer two questions. The first, 'Why Mary Pickford?' has to be answered by the book itself. The second, 'Why you?' is a little more difficult. When I was approached, I took on the project immediately, in a large part, I confess, to further my own education in and appreciation for silent films. But I also confess that the more I became involved the more my fascination with the woman herself took over. And incredibly, no one had undertaken her life story.

Because of Mary Pickford's condition and the erratic availability of her films, the story has taken me to many people and places in the last three years. I started almost as far from Hollywood as it is possible to go and still be in the movie-crazy world . . . in Moscow during the 1969 Moscow film festival. The Russians have preserved in their film archives many American silent films, including some of Mary Pickford's which have not survived in this country; *Rosita*, directed by Ernst Lubitsch and which she hated above all her other work, for example. The Russians don't claim to have invented Mary Pickford or even the movies, but they took 'Marushka' to their hearts on film in 1920s *Pollyanna* and in person in 1926 when she visited Moscow with Douglas Fairbanks, her second husband.

And in 1969, when Lillian Gish through an interpreter told an audience at the great hall in the Kremlin about the early days in American films and showed film clips of Mary Pickford and others, they responded to Marushka with affection again. Silent films never knew a language barrier. And Mary always said that they should have started with sound movies and evolved to silents, the simpler, purer and (she felt) higher art form.

The Mary Pickford story also took me to Toronto, where she was born and where she lived her first eight impoverished years; to Spain's Costa del Sol for interviews with Gwynne Pickford Ornstein, Mary's niece and closest living relative; to London for the 1971 and 1973 Mary Pickford retrospectives and to interview Mary Charlotte Fullerton, Mary's grandniece and namesake; home to New York to see an active then ninety-seven-year-old Adolph Zukor at the old Paramount Building, and to talk to Lillian Gish again; and of course back to Hollywood and Pickfair most of all.

I am grateful first to Mary Pickford for living the kind of life worth writing about and for occasionally breaking her secluded silence. I'm particularly grateful to Mrs Gwynne Ornstein and her husband George ('Bud'), and to Mary Fullerton and her husband Peter, not only for their generosity with time and stories about Mary Pickford, but also for allowing me the use of family photographs never before seen outside the Pickford family; to Douglas Fairbanks Jr, for his graciously shared memories and helpful research materials; to Charles 'Buddy' Rogers for his hospitality at Pickfair, his reminiscences and for his good work in preserving the Pickford films and legend (with the help of Matty Kemp). My thanks to Lillian Gish and Adolph Zukor for helping to make those very earliest days of movies come alive for me, and to Gloria Swanson, Clare Booth Luce and Colleen Moore, who remember so well.

Many others were instrumental in helping me organize the research, particularly John Springer and Dick Spittel. Jack Hamilton, former entertainment editor of *Look*, provided valuable unpublished notes and photographs from his personal collection that would have been otherwise unavailable. Barbara Baker of *Time-Life Books* and a former assistant picture editor for *Life*, assisted admirably on the photographic research. The public Libraries of Toronto, New York City and Little Falls, New Jersey, the American Film Institute and the British Film Institute provided invaluable help. Many books were helpful, among them Kevin Brownlow's *The Parade's Gone By*, Robert M. Henderson's *D. W. Griffith: The Years at Biograph*, *The Fourth Musketeer*, a biography of Douglas Fairbanks Sr, by Ralph Hancock and Letitia Fairbanks, Mrs D. W. Griffith's *When the Movies Were Young*, Colleen Moore's *Silent Star*, Mary Pickford's own *Sunshine and Shadow*, *My Rendezvous With Life* and *Why Not Try God?* The background work Robert Cushman did for the Los Angeles County Museum's Mary Pickford Festival in 1971 was excellent and very useful.

The sources then are myriad, but the conclusions are my own. And any errors in fact are mine. Any person whose business and private pursuits make them larger than life obviously spawns many myths and apocryphal stories that get told and retold and embellished. Mary Pickford herself tends to romanticize many aspects of the past. I have tried to ignore mere myths and cut through embroidery, to arrive at the truth. Some of that truth, as always with truth, is unpleasant. But I have been guided throughout this book by a statement made by Mary Pickford:

'Actresses should realize when they deliberately choose a public career they have no right to disappoint the public—and no right to privacy. As a toy of the public, that's part of the price.'

Robert Windeler
*New York*
*March 1973*

# Introduction

ICKFAIR, the white country house with a green-tiled roof, stands atop a hill on Summit Drive off Benedict Canyon in Beverly Hills, as it has for more than fifty years, a symbol of the Hollywood movie industry at its most glamorous. Mary Pickford has lived there since it was built as a wedding present from Douglas Fairbanks—the other half of its name—in 1920.

It is a large comfortable house rather than a grand, pretentious one and, where it once sat on twenty acres, Pickfair's immaculately-groomed gardens are now confined to ten acres, the rest having been sold off to builders by her third husband Buddy Rogers. But the estate looks out as it always did to the homes of John Barrymore and Rudolph Valentino, long since dead, and of Charlie Chaplin, exiled to Switzerland these twenty-odd years, and down as it always did on the rest of Beverly Hills and Hollywood.

The wall that Douglas Fairbanks had built around the place to keep the world away still stands and still does its job, although the tourists out looking for the houses where their favorite television and pop music stars live pause only briefly, if at all, outside the gates of this once-shimmering palace where in the 1920s all of Hollywood longed to be invited, and where the royalty of the real world once paid court.

A butler and five maids live in the guest house, and three gardeners come every day to tend the flowers, trees and grass. A chauffeur is no longer needed and the pool, where once the best-known names in the world splashed and where Douglas paddled a canoe, lies still these days, riffled only by the canyon breezes or an occasional stray leaf.

Inside the home little has changed in almost fifty years, except that it is as quiet as a museum. And that is precisely what Pickfair is; a museum in waiting. The priceless treasures acquired by its occupants at the height of their fame are carefully catalogued, and the mistress of the house wants them to stay where they have been and she has provided that they will.

In the front hall of Mary Pickford's home is an oil portrait of her as the golden-curled Gwendolyn of *The Poor Little Rich Girl*, her 1916 film masterpiece. Nearby is a cabinet containing a pink, white and gold porcelain tea service that Napoleon gave to Josephine in 1807, and Douglas Fairbanks bought for his wife in Venice and gave her in 1927. The 102 pieces of the set are in perfect condition, having survived even the great 1971 earthquake, which destroyed some other items in the house. On Pickfair's third floor in glass display cases are the silk tapestries, porcelain, jade and ivory treasures from China and Japan, given to Mary and Doug on their travels to the Orient in 1927. The costumes from her famous films, and two of her famous golden curls are also displayed.

In the first floor library are the Rodin pen-and-ink drawings (the Lesbian series) of disputed authenticity. In the ground floor Western bar, the most-used room in the house, are twelve real Frederic Remingtons in rare black and white paint only. And the silver, gold, jewelry and antique furniture—much of it French and Oriental—are in such quantity that only she knows for certain what's where and for what fraction of its value it can be insured.

On the second floor of the house in the large bedroom she has occupied since 1920 lies Mary Pickford, a woman past eighty who has outlived most of her memories. She chose to go to bed in 1965 after returning from a retrospective of her pictures in Paris. She was tired, she announced to her family and staff, she had worked hard all her life since she was five, most of those years getting up at five in the morning. She had provided well for herself and her loved ones, and she would not get up out of bed or leave the house again, except to go to the hospital.

She is not really physically sick, although she had a cataract operation in 1966. Her vision is still limited and necessitates very thick reading glasses. Her regular examinations at home and the hospital show that she is in reasonably good health for a woman her age. Her legs have atrophied from many years in bed and she can't walk very well. But 'late at night when she thinks I'm not looking she walks downstairs to look over the house and her belongings,' says Gwynne Pickford Ornstein, Mary's niece.

Her and Buddy's bedroom is dominated by the large bed she occupies, and which he has shared with her when he was in residence at Pickfair and not away at Mary's home in Palm Springs or elsewhere. A picture of her mother Charlotte hangs on one wall, and the Oscar she won for *Coquette* stands on the dresser. A nurse is always on duty during the day, and the butler, a Belgian named Tony de Vos, who often quits but returns almost immediately, literally dances attendance on her. He wakes her up around noon, brings a tray of light food and whiskey as needed. He talks to her in French, which she learned from a tutor in the car going to and from the studio, reminds her if it's an important holiday, like Thanksgiving or Christmas, sings songs and makes her sit up in bed to eat.

On good days she sits up for more than meals, she reads the newspapers which are preread at Buddy's instructions for potentially 'upsetting' stories and they may arrive quite cut up with offending articles removed; her mail is also read prior to her getting it by a secretary under Buddy's supervision.

3

Mary Pickford still has legal control of her considerable property, money and affairs. But her contact with the bank, her business managers and attorneys is erratic and when she is overwhelmed she summons her niece Gwynne, her sister Lottie's daughter, from the south of Spain to come home to straighten things out. As Mary's closest surviving blood relative, Gwynne is the only person who can pre-empt the ruling routine, and sometimes even she is relegated to the guest house instead of being given a room at Pickfair itself. Once Mary was so worried she even paid for Gwynne's round-trip plane fare, something the thrifty multi-millionairess is not in the habit of doing.

But Mary Pickford still loves Buddy Rogers in her way, although she cries out in the night for Douglas Fairbanks, and swears the next day that she has seen his ghost, sometimes along with that of her mother Charlotte, who, even more than Douglas, dominated Mary's life.

To a great extent Mary is the prisoner of her own vanity. She doesn't want to be seen by even her dearest friends and it is easier to avoid society by staying in bed. 'People remember me most as a little girl with long golden curls,' she explained. 'I don't want them to see me as a little old lady.'

She is extremely thin these days weighing about eighty-five pounds, and her hair, the most distinctive feature of her screen image, is thin, a mixture of white and reddish-brown wisps. She always wears a wig for her infrequent company. It has been so long since she has seen almost anyone outside the family that though at times she wants to, it becomes too much of an effort and she usually declines at the last minute. Sometimes even Gwynne and Douglas Fairbanks Jr, her stepson, can't see her every day they are staying at Pickfair and, although she used to be carried down to the living room to greet guests, this hasn't happened since 1969.

Gwynne's daughter, Mary Charlotte, was married in Novem-

4

ber of 1970 at Pickfair as Gwynne herself had been twenty-eight years earlier. Mary, who was determined to go to the wedding downstairs, had summoned the wig-maker and picked out her dress. At the last minute she couldn't go through with it, explaining that, if she did, the occasion would become Mary Pickford's return and wouldn't be Mary Charlotte Pickford Ornstein's wedding.

Mary's friends from early movie days who have survived along with her, like Lillian Gish and Adolph Zukor, don't come to visit any more as they used to. Her entertainment consists of infrequently watching television, talking on the telephone and reading. The *Runner's Bible* is constantly by her bedside, as is a tall glass of whiskey and water, from which she takes small sips throughout the day. She has kept some of her sense of humor, her Irish scrappiness, her competitiveness, her love for her art, her interest in charities and all of her sense of money and how not to spend it.

Recently a mutual friend of hers and Charlie Chaplin's came to see her. The friend indicated that Chaplin, her one time close friend and later bitter enemy, whom he had seen in London, had mellowed considerably toward Mary and actually asked how she was getting along. Mary on hearing this, pursed her tiny lips and spat through her teeth in a high old-lady voice: 'That's all very well but I still say he's a son-of-a-bitch.'

What Mary Pickford has lost is her will to participate in any kind of active life, which Lillian Gish and Gloria Swanson, her contemporaries still active in their seventies, lament. 'She has lain dormant too long,' said Matty Kemp, who with Buddy runs The Mary Pickford Company which is actively restoring and distributing her films. 'And what that leaves her with is memories.' Mary spends a great deal of time with memories and these memories are what this book is all about. Hers was an extraordinary life, unlike any other.

She, more than any other person (except perhaps her first

director, D. W. Griffith) brought motion pictures from nickelodeon novelty entertainment to sophisticated sound stories, and even, at their best, an American-fostered art form. She was literally the first movie star. And for more than twenty years when this century was much younger she was the best-known woman in the world.

Largely because of her own policy of buying her movies to keep them from being shown, at least three generations of moviegoers have grown up without an on-screen glimpse of Mary Pickford, the comedienne supreme and the little girl who started us all on our moviemania. The releases in 1971, 1972 and 1973 of some of her pictures through the American Film Institute and The Mary Pickford Company for festivals and commercial theaters in North America and Europe are starting to change that.

Mary is a Canadian by birth, English and Irish by ancestry, but her story is straight out of the American Dream. Her parents were impoverished, she grew up poor in Toronto, was half-orphaned when she was four, and driven by the surviving parent to succeed to the full extent of her God-given beauty and talent to make millions of dollars.

Starting in movies in 1909 for $5 a day she worked her way up to owning her own studio and $1 million a year ten years later. In 1919 at the age of twenty-six she founded United Artists with Griffith, Chaplin and Fairbanks.

No less than Thomas Edison, the inventor of the medium she now worked in, labelled her 'The sweetheart of the Americans', and her international following as 'America's Sweetheart', and 'the World's Sweetheart' enabled Mary Pickford to make acting, that low profession for women, the highest paid if not the highest in esteem. She made and kept more money than any other woman in the history of entertainment, and probably more—in the days of no or low income taxes—than any man, and thus became the Bank of America's Sweetheart, too. Her fortune, perhaps in excess of $50,000,000, surely represents the single

6

largest amount of money amassed by a woman by virtue of her own labors.

She even married the Prince, not once but three times. Her love affair with and marriage to Douglas Fairbanks rivals the great love stories of all time. Together they made movie stars socially acceptable, and as the King and Queen of Hollywood they entertained other kings and queens at Pickfair. Mary's first and third husbands were also handsome silent screen idols and there are grown women today who still grow weak at the mention of Buddy Rogers. But so great was her success and acclaim that he and Owen Moore were overshadowed by Mary Pickford, and even Fairbanks' career was enhanced by his marriage to her.

She pursued her movie career for twenty-four years, won an Academy Award for her first sound picture, and retired after she made her fourth in 1932, with over two hundred silent movies behind her, 'because I wanted to retire while I was at my peak,' she explained. It was also partly because her fans couldn't accept her as a grownup woman without the curls and talking in a high-pitched voice.

As an actress she was generally underrated in her day, and as an actress and comedienne she is underrated still. Because audiences responded to her as a golden-haired girl—or as a type or an image of what they wanted her to be—they didn't always see how convincing she was as the poor little rich girl, Rebecca of Sunnybrook Farm, as Stella Maris or Little Lord Fauntleroy. Even Mary's friend Lillian Gish told me she couldn't possibly pick a favorite from among Mary's roles. 'It was always Mary herself that shone through,' she said. 'Her personality was the thing that made her movies memorable and the pictures that showed her personality were the best.'

But as a poor little girl she was believable, brave but never over-suffering. As a rich girl she had dignity and humility. In both kinds of roles and in many others she played there was

7

strength, goodness but a hint of deviltry that saved the characters from cartoonery. And despite all the talented actors of both sexes in the world I will never be convinced that anyone but Mary Pickford could have played both a young boy and his mother at the same time, as she did in *Little Lord Fauntleroy*, and been utterly brilliant in both parts.

The eighty-year life of Mary Pickford is full of romance, accomplishment and glamor—but it also has a great measure of tragedy: two scandal-ridden divorces, the deaths in rapid succession of her brother, under the most sordid circumstances, sister, and mother who was the single most important influence in Mary Pickford's life, for good and ill; and Mary's own gradual retreat into self-exile. They too are part of this story.

# Chapter One

HE movies and the girl who became Mary Pickford were born in the same year, 1893. The revolutionary art form emerged from a Thomas A. Edison laboratory in Menlo Park, New Jersey, and Gladys Smith made her first appearance 800 miles away, in a six-room, two-storey brick house in Toronto.

In 1893 President Grover Cleveland reclaimed the White House in Washington after a four-year interregnum. In Denver ten-year-old Douglas Ulman (later Fairbanks) was already memorizing Shakespeare soliloquies; hanging around the opera house when road companies came through and sneaking in through the fire escape when he didn't have money for a ticket; and staging back-yard shows (when he wasn't climbing trees and rooftops and frightening little girls by such pranks as letting snakes loose in horse-drawn trolleys).

The Broadway Theater, to which young Doug aspired and which was sublimely unaware of the competitive threat taking shape across the river in Menlo Park, was in its Gay Nineties heyday. Maurice Barrymore and Julia Arthur starred in *Lady Windermere's Fan*, and *Charley's Aunt* had its American première, starring Etienne Giradot. *Liberty Hall* with May Robson and Henry Miller, *The Girl I Left Behind Me*, *A Woman of No Importance* and *The Second Mrs Tanqueray* were the major dramatic hits. Eleanora Duse made her American début in *Camille*, and musical

9

audiences made successes of *1492*, a quadracentenary rendering of Columbus's discovery of America, with Richard Harlow female-impersonating Queen Isabella, and of *Princess Nicotine*, with Lillian Russell and Marie Dressler. Henry Irving and Ellen Terry visited New York that year with the classics. Sarah Bernhardt, Minnie Dupree, Ethel Barrymore, Maude Adams and Lily Langtree were other ladies at or near stardom, and John Drew, Theodore Roberts and Herbert Beerbohm Tree were top leading men.

All of this seemed very remote from the world of John Charles Smith, whose parents had come to Canada from England, and his wife Charlotte Mary Catherine Pickford Hennessey, whose parents, both from County Kerry, Ireland, had met and married in Quebec. But it was in fact the very world that their first child and daughter would enter within five years.

John and Charlotte Smith lived at 211 University Avenue, Toronto, and there Gladys (so named for a character in a novel an aunt was reading at the time) was born 9 April 1893. The province of Ontario shows no record of her birth, which merely means that her parents and the doctor never reported it, such reporting not being required in Canada at the time. There is some evidence, including the insistence of surviving members of her family, that she was really born in 1892. And Mary Pickford always gave her birthdate as 8 April, having changed it to the day earlier in honor of her father who was born on 8 April 1869.

John Charles Smith, one of twelve children, was a charming, outgoing, somewhat dreamy man with a mustache, and gold-brown hair he gave to his elder daughter. He was short and delicate of build—and not always gainfully employed. He and his young dark-haired wife Charlotte ran a candy counter in a fish store, and at one point he worked in a theater as a stage hand pulling up scenery. Once he went to Western Canada for a few days and came back wearing a cowboy hat and talking in an Albertan nasal drawl about ranching and cowpunching, but nothing came of his scheme.

'Jack' Smith and his wife had two more children, a daughter

Lottie (from Charlotte) born fourteen months after Gladys, and John Charles Jr, born in 1897.

'In those days it was my father I loved,' Gladys recalled when she was in her sixties. 'I didn't really care so much about my mother. She was always too busy to play with me. But father could find time.'

Lottie was her father's favorite, however, and Gladys early experienced a jealousy of her younger sister that ended really only after Lottie's death.

Jack Smith obtained the candy and fruit concession on the *Chicora*, one of the steamships that ran across Lake Ontario from Toronto to Lewiston, near Niagara Falls. One day while stepping over a shaft near the paddle wheel to get off the boat, he hit his head on a pulley dangling overhead. It caused a blood clot on his brain, and he died a year later, at the age of twenty-seven. Gladys was four, Lottie (called 'Chookie' as a child) three and baby Jack just six months old.

Charlotte Smith, at the age of twenty-four a widow with three small children, for a time took over the boat concession. Gladys, quiet and well-behaved, would often go along and stay close by her mother, while Lottie and her girlfriends raced all over the boat, looking for trouble.

Gladys grew closer to her mother after Jack Smith died and soon the two younger children, who stayed close all their lives, combined against their older sister and mother, in deviltry more than outright defiance.

To keep her family going Charlotte Smith ran a penny candy counter in a fruit and grocery store on Queen Street. She was accounted a good seamstress and took in sewing at night. She also opened the house on University Avenue to boarders to take in extra money. But still the Smiths were poor, particularly with an invalid grandmother Hennessey to support. Friends and neighbors gave them meals when there wasn't enough food at home.

★ ★ ★

Thomas Edison, the invention and commercial success of the electric light bulb and the phonograph behind him, had experimented with moving images on a screen in a peep-show box as early as 1888, but it was his intention to combine them with his phonograph to produce moving talking pictures. When that proved impractical the inventor lost interest and left it pretty much to his assistant, William Kennedy Laurie Dickson, to develop the new form. In 1893 Edison built Dickson a laboratory for just that purpose. Dickson had applied for patents on what he called a Kinetoscope viewing device and a Kinetoscope photographic device. Edison's attorney didn't know what to call the new process, however, and treated it as an extension of still photography, which had been protected by patents since the late 1840s. This confusion led to twenty years of lawsuits and cutthroat rivalry between Edison's company and those that developed similar systems of projection.

In 1893, in the new lab Dickson developed on a continuous strip of film the first registered movie, *Record of a Sneeze*, which was copyrighted as a photograph. It was really a series of photographs which, when run through the Kinetoscope, would show a man, Fred Ott, in the act of sneezing. Fred Ott's Sneeze was given the movies' first public showing for money at the Holland Brothers Kinetoscope Parlor at 1155 Broadway in New York City on 14 April 1894.

\* \* \*

Gladys Smith was almost never a little girl, assuming at the age of five her father's place at the head of the family, and becoming its chief breadwinner before she was ten. Yet her health was delicate and she always had some ailment or other. She was also spoiled by her grandmother and Aunt Elizabeth, 'Lizzie', her mother's sister, who lived next door. Because of her illnesses and going to work young, Gladys only went to school for a total of six or seven months, spread over two years, in her entire life. It was at the McCaul Street School in Toronto. 'I never had any young companions my age except for my brother and sister,' she said. 'This matured me very early I suppose, but it cheated me of any real childhood.'

From an early age and throughout her life, Gladys Smith was acutely aware of the differences between her English (and Methodist) forebears and her Irish (and Catholic) ones. The Smiths never did become reconciled to her working in show business. Because of the religious split she wasn't even baptized Gladys Marie Smith until she was four and thought to be dying of black diphtheria and a visiting French-Canadian Catholic priest insisted on it. (After her father's death her mother also had her baptized a Methodist, to keep peace with her in-laws.)

Because she was ill so often she saw a great deal of a Dr G. B. Smith, head of the Children's Hospital of Toronto, and no kin. Charlotte Smith said he had saved little Gladys' life at least four times. Dr Smith and his wife were rich and childless and offered to adopt Gladys. Charlotte Smith left the decision up to her daughter, then seven. Mrs Smith and Gladys went to see the other Smiths but when the little girl realized that, although she could have a pony and ice cream whenever she wanted it, she couldn't share them with her mother and brother and sister she decided against the adoption and went home with her mother to Chookie and Jack. 'A determination was born in me that day that nothing could crush,' she remembered. 'I must prevent anything from breaking up my family.'

Most of Gladys Smith's childhood memories were of money, having it or lacking it: the first 75 cents her father ever gave her (she promptly turned it over to her mother), the time Lottie dropped a nickel down between two piano keys and Gladys was ready to use a hammer to get it out (waylaid only by her grandmother Hennessey), buying a rose-bud from the florist's whenever she could raise a penny—and talking him into giving her the

13

falling roses free, which she ate on the theory that she would absorb their good qualities.

When the Smiths, mother and children, all began to make money, they would keep it in one purse, of which Charlotte Smith kept charge. Even after millions of dollars were involved, Mrs Smith kept a shrewd eye on the family purse-strings until she died.

One particular Christmas, the first after her father died, did as much to send Gladys out to work as the near-adoption by the rich Smiths. Lottie and Gladys had asked Santa Claus for identical doll carriages with sleeping dolls, and Jack wanted a dancing bear. Mrs Smith had talked a toy shop manager into giving her the two carriages in exchange for a screen embroidered with chrysan-themums that she would work on nights, and by Christmas Eve she had the carriages but nothing to put in them.

In despair, Mrs Smith and Mrs Hennessey prayed for a miracle, which arrived in the form of ten dollars for each widow of Jack Smith's lodge, the Knights of Pythias. That provided the bear, the dolls and Christmas dinner, and she stayed up all night sewing dresses for the dolls. Gladys learned the story a few years later, and she resolved that keeping the family together was not enough—creature comforts would have to be provided.

As a girl Gladys would save up ten cents and rent a bicycle for an hour and eventually she had her own bicycle, an eighth birthday present from her mother, which she rode by the hour up and down the bridle path on University Avenue. 'Those were almost the only moments when I was a little girl,' she recalled sadly. And she remembered going to the fountain at Queens Park and drinking cold water from a copper cup on a chain. But she avoided most activities that would get her dirty and was perpetually distressed that Jack and Lottie had dirty hands and faces, despite her frequent washing of them.

'I was very timid and nothing of the tomboy I have portrayed so often on the screen,' Mary Pickford remembered. 'Skates in a Canada winter were as far as I dare venture. I was happier with the dolls I carried everywhere, even with me on the road.'

*     *     *

Toronto near the turn of the century was already a busy city of 250,000 people on the north shore of Lake Ontario. It was the capital of the province of Ontario and had been founded 100 years before as York. Quebec and Montreal were older but Toronto in the late 1890s was a commercial center and rapidly becoming a cultural one as well. There was—and there is today—an incredibly high proportion of home-owners, even among working men with modest incomes, whereas in virtually all other cities of its size people as poor as the Smiths would have been crowded into tenements.

The city then had well-managed theaters and public halls, a Grand Opera house, an Academy of Music. Toronto was prosperous, progressive, with low taxes and rents, cheap abundant labor, and free schools and colleges. It owed much of its cultural heritage to London but like all Canadian cities at the time looked across the border to the United States for leadership in most areas, including the theater. Little Gladys Smith was to begin the long parade of Canadians who had to come down to 'the States' to make it in show business.

*     *     *

'Those were anxious times, although we always somehow had enough to eat,' remembered Gladys as a bed-ridden woman nearing eighty. 'My mother was wonderful. I borrowed some of her courage and confidence—enough to last me all my life. Besides, a bit of financial anxiety in childhood isn't a bad thing, as long as plenty of love goes with it. It's likely to give a person an extra drive and ambition.'

15

Gladys was barely five when her mother reluctantly agreed to let the master bedroom to a married couple (it previously had been limited to single ladies). The husband was the stage manager of the Cummings Stock Company, which was producing *The Silver King*, a popular melodrama by Henry Arthur Jones about a mining magnate, at the Toronto Opera House. The play was best known for the line 'Oh Lord turn back thy Universe and give me yesterday'.

The boarders asked Mrs Smith if she would allow Gladys and Lottie to appear as extras in a schoolroom scene. Mrs Smith had some reservations about letting her daughters be involved with theater people and 'actresses who smoke', but she was sufficiently broke and sufficiently interested to meet members of the Cummings company back-stage, and sufficiently impressed with them to allow the girls to make their theatrical débuts.

Gladys had two parts, the first, in the first act, was as a school-girl who said one line about Cissy Denver, the Silver King's daughter: 'Don't speak to her girls, her father killed a man.' In the last act Gladys played the part of a boy, Ned Denver, son of The Silver King. She was instructed to sit quietly on stage while 'his' mother and father had a secret conversation. Instead Gladys built a set of blocks into a pyramid and proceeded to knock it down with a toy horse, stealing her first scene, as the audience laughed at the other actors' reactions.

Her mother's star boarder gave Gladys a lecture about spoiling other actors' speeches, but let her keep her invention in the scene in a less conspicuous place. Lottie played in the schoolroom scene and had no lines but did get to give Cissy Denver some candy and pat her on the back. The girls got about $10 a week each.

Ethel Clegg, a Toronto neighbor who sometimes wheeled Gladys around in her baby carriage, remembered going to the Smith house one day to take Gladys to her home for dinner. The younger girl was pinching her cheeks and poking them with a hairpin. When Ethel asked what she was doing, the five-year-old Gladys replied, 'I'm trying to make my cheeks red like Nellie Marshall's.' Miss Marshall was the actress in Valentine Stock Company, one of Toronto's best, who usually played an adventuress.

'Stage mother' is a term of derision applied to a woman who exploits her talented or merely attractive children and pushes her offspring into every form of show business, sometimes whether they want it or not. Her motivations are often complex, but can be simply the desire to make a lot of money through her child or to satisfy her own frustrated ambitions. It was an all-too-common phenomenon in the theater at the turn of the century, and even is today, but no one has ever lived the role more ardently than Charlotte Smith, who from this tiny beginning in Toronto in 1898 stayed with her elder daughter and managed her career until she herself died, a very rich woman, in 1927. Charlotte also lived and traveled with Mary Pickford and her husbands, and eventually even ran the company, United Artists, her daughter helped to found. 'To the very last day she lived, her word was law,' said Mary.

Since Mrs Smith had demonstrated no particular theatrical leanings, it is probable that she merely saw in Gladys and in the theater in general a permanent way out of poverty that had plagued her all of her life. Whatever the reason, Charlotte was hooked. And Gladys, already more than a little vain and a little ambitious, was her eager alter-ego.

The Cummings Stock Company went on to other projects and Gladys managed to get a role in a vaudeville show. Her spot was in a one-act play, *The Littlest Girl*, and she was put in a fairy-like costume in which she was carried on stage and passed from the one actor's arms to another's lap. There were no lines for her to speak. But she was paid $15 a week.

More importantly, however, on the same bill was Elsie Janis, who did an imitation of Anna Held, wore a knee-length dress and diamonds, and sang 'I Just Can't Make My Eyes Behave'.

Mrs Smith wasted no time, particularly after she heard Elsie was making $75 a week, in seeking out Elsie's mother for advice on how to make her own daughter a star. Mrs Janis advised taking Gladys to the teacher to see the best plays and actors and letting the girl be herself rather than copying someone else's style.

So little Gladys was taken to the theater as often as possible and set on her mother's or her Aunt Lizzie's lap, which had the dual effect of saving the price of a ticket and letting her see over everyone's heads. And when Mrs Smith heard from a neighbor, an electrician at the Princess Theater, that the superior Valentine Stock Company was doing another production of *The Silver King*, she marched Gladys and Lottie down to the theater to re-apply for their old parts in the Cummings Production.

Gladys, however, had decided that she wanted to play the bigger role of Cissy Denver herself, and the Valentine Company's casting director was willing to have her try. But Charlotte interjected, 'Oh, you can't trust her with lines'. Gladys convinced the casting director that she could learn the part, although she couldn't yet read herself, and she won it. Charlotte began that night reading the lines to her under a street lamp outside the theater, while waiting for the streetcar home.

Gladys Smith was a great success as Cissy Denver in *The Silver King*, and this led to a series of roles with the Valentine Stock Company, and with the Jessie Bonstelle Company in Rochester, New York. She signed as Little Eva in Harriet Beecher Stowe's *Uncle Tom's Cabin* while she was still suffering from pneumonia, arriving for her first rehearsal in a taxi provided by the company with her mother (her first taste of show business glamor and luxury), and bundled in blankets to keep warm. After that came *East Lynne*, and the title role in *Bootle's Baby*. Gladys and Lottie played the parts of two boys in *The Soudan*, with Jessie Bonstelle.

'I loved the sad scene,' Gladys remembered. 'I fairly revelled in the death of Little Willy, the part I played in *East Lynne*.' Eva in *Uncle Tom's Cabin* pleased me, and so did Dick, the waif in

*The Soudan.* At the age of seven I delighted in playing this consumptive boy. I always kept one eye open in a death scene, and at a matinée I would note and almost count the handkerchiefs.'

Her last appearance with the Valentine Stock Company was as Mabel Payne in *The Little Red Schoolhouse*, a play written by Hal Reid, whose son Wallace Reid later became a movie star. Toronto was even then a tryout town for Broadway and Mr Reid arrived in town during the summer of 1901 to supervise the production.

The three other Smiths had managed to get small parts in the play. (Lottie as Mabel's boyfriend, Jack as a child extra and Charlotte as an understudy only, and one with no prior acting experience.) Reid said he would hire all four of them for the New York production in the fall. On the strength of this promise, Charlotte sold all the furniture and stood ready to launch her family's theatrical career in New York, come September.

However, Reid sold the producing rights to *The Little Red Schoolhouse*, and forgot the Smiths. A young girl named Lillian Gish won the role of Mabel Payne and went with the play on tour. In Buffalo, Lillian's chaperone got sick and she and Lillian had to return to New York. Somebody remembered Gladys Smith and sent to Toronto for her. Charlotte wired back that her only interest was in a package deal, and the producers were desperate enough to hire the four Smiths—at $20 a week—for the play. Lottie understudied her old role as the boyfriend and appeared with Jack in a group schoolhouse scene, while Charlotte understudied the adult female roles. During the run the foursome scraped enough money together to buy a theatrical trunk. Charlotte Smith and her brood were ready to take on New York.

# Chapter Two

EW York just after 1900 was faster and bigger than any other city in North America. But the Flatiron Building at 23rd Street and Fifth Avenue was about as high as the city went then, and the trolleys and other traffic were the same as at home. The Torontonians weren't terribly impressed. However, New York was *the* theatrical center, and this was where the work was parceled out, even for the one-night-stand touring companies that traveled the North American continent at the turn of the century.

There were 314 plays running in New York in the 1901–2 season, when the Smiths arrived, and perhaps twice that many productions on tour in the United States and Canada. The city was dotted with theatrical boarding houses full of hopefuls. But with that much going on no one with any talent or previous credits stayed out of work for very long. Even the newly-arrived Smiths, after a few days of pavement-pounding, came up with something: a 1902–3 tour in *The Fatal Wedding*, 'starring (for the first time) Baby Gladys Smith'. In the small role of an Irish maid Charlotte Smith was making her actual first appearance on a stage, although she had lied and said she had lots of experience.

For nineteen weeks of eight and nine performances a week, a different day in each city, the four Smiths pressed on. Charlotte made clothing and kept her three children (who never got to sleep in the same beds two nights running) on time for the next train. They hit small towns like Pottsville, Pennsylvania and Boonton, New Jersey. There was no food on the trains except stale sandwiches, and no sleeping accommodations of any kind. For years afterward the older Smith daughter described crimson, the color of the upholstery in those milk-run trains, as her least favorite color.

Gladys played the lead role of Jessie, the little mother, in *The Fatal Wedding*, and she was unquestionably the star. The handbills spread about in every stop proclaimed 'Baby Gladys Smith is a Wonder'. Lottie was her sister's understudy, five-year-old Jack an extra and Mother Charlotte somehow managed to get through her part of the maid.

Other mothers and their offspring, some of whom were to become famous, hundreds more who weren't, were living a precarious life in New York and an itinerant theatrical life. Lillian and Dorothy Gish and their mother, like Gladys and the Smiths, during their time in New York, whether looking for work or rehearsing for a new road play, with the whole family or alone with a guardian lived in a succession of theatrical boarding houses. The Gishes and the Smiths even lived together one summer in the West 20s, simply to save on the rent. Gladys thought Lillian looked so delicate that she was going to die and was afraid to be around her.

Gladys as the oldest of the children, 'was the boss', Miss Gish remembered. 'You always did what she told you to do. She had one of those cute little Irish tempers. She'd get mad and everyone would adore her for it. And she had the most perfect natural blonde hair. My mother always said that when she smiled you could hear the angels sing.' Lillian was younger enough than Gladys that she could say seventy years later, 'I don't remember the world when Mary Pickford wasn't in it.'

In 1900 Adelaide Ella Marsh Fairbanks Ulman and her youngest son Douglas legally changed their names to Fairbanks (after her late first husband), and sold their worldly goods to raise their fares to New York. His older brothers John and Robert stayed in the West to work, but Ella had never liked Denver or Colorado and was eager to leave. When Ella and the seventeen-year-old Doug arrived in New York, Margaret Fealy, the celebrated actress and her daughter, the even more renowned Maude Fealy, were both on Broadway in *Quo Vadis*. Doug had started acting lessons at age thirteen at a school run by Margaret Fealy (who also launched Ernest Truex, one of Mary's future co-stars), and he was confidently predicting his own New York stardom.

He looked up Frederick Warde, a well-known Shakespeare player who had worked with Edwin Booth and Maurice Barrymore, and whom Doug had met in Denver the year before. Warde hired him and Doug started in a road company, as Florio, a lackey in *The Duke's Jester*, at the Richmond Academy of Music in Richmond, Virginia, 10 September 1900, and varied his entrances in the non-speaking part as much as possible. In Duluth, Minnesota later that year he was understudy for Cassio and Laertes in Shakespeare's *Julius Caesar* and *Hamlet* and went on in both parts. His first review might have discouraged anyone else: 'Mr Warde's supporting company was bad but worst of all was Douglas Fairbanks as Laertes.'

He left Warde and tried to enroll at Harvard, but lacked sufficient credits from East Denver High. For five months he took a special course to try to make up his missing qualifications but spent much of his time at the school's gym. Douglas then went to Europe for the first time by working as a steward on a cattle boat, and saw England, Belgium and France before returning to New York, not to work in the theater but as an order clerk in a stock brokerage, dressing more like a stockbroker. He also spent money on various gymnasiums and health clubs, and once, between plays, worked in a hardware store to keep himself in clothes. He made his Broadway début in *Her Lord and Master*,

24 February 1902, in a minor role. He played a larger role in *A Rose O' Plymouth Town*, starring Minnie Dupree, who said: 'I thought he had a bad case of St Vitus' dance.'

In the next few years of touring in plays, the Smiths, who were far from working on Broadway, occasionally returned to Toronto between engagements, staying in rooming houses since their house had long since been sold. Gladys' friend Gertie Clegg, Ethel's sister, in later years remembered the two of them going 'suping', looking for small parts at the stage doors of the Princess, Grand and Majestic theaters. Gladys was eleven or twelve, had outgrown the 'Baby Gladys' billing, and had to take what parts she could. On the road then she was known as Gladys Milbourne Smith—Milbourne being a totally made up name to add interest to the common 'Smith'.

As it became increasingly difficult to find work together, the family separated, Lottie and Gladys going on the road and leaving Charlotte and Jack in New York.

Late in the 1904 season, the two girls went out with *The Child Wife* (a pre-eminent theme of turn-of-the-century melodrama). As Dolly, the title part in that play, which had been written by Charles Taylor, Laurette Taylor's first husband, Gladys made $25 a week and would change her salary into one-dollar bills to make it seem like more. Charlotte Smith would have to trust to a succession of chaperones for her daughters on these road trips and, while most of them were kind, a few were negligent, and she continually tried to get work in which the whole family could be together.

In 1905 Gladys created the part of Freckles in *The Gypsy Girl*, another play by Hal Reid. Gladys was up to $40 a week then, and sent $15 of it to Charlotte, who was living with the two younger children in Brooklyn. In 1906 all the Smiths applied to Chauncey Olcott, an Irish actor-producer in New York.

Olcott was looking for two larger boys and one little girl for *Edmund Burke*, and of course the Smiths were just the reverse.

23

Charlotte was determined, however, and the dark-haired Lottie actually played two boys' parts, Pat, an Irish peasant, and Lord Archie. Gladys played Lord Bertie, and little nine-year-old Jack, to his disgust, was cast as Lady Edith.

'We had a fine season that year, when we were all together,' Mary recalled. 'Mother who had never acted till it was necessary to support herself and us, was playing a part too. This play is one of my happiest memories for not only were we together but Mr Olcott was most kind and we were playing better theaters in better towns, and therefore to better audiences. I always hated the tawdry run-down theaters, just as I detest poverty. The more harmonious colors and the whole atmosphere of the better hotels appealed to me. I wanted nice things.'

After *Edmund Burke*, Mrs Smith and the two younger children returned to Toronto and then Gladys, who was gradually emerging as the star of the family, and the most talented actor, signed to do another boy's role. It was Patsy Poore, in *In Convict's Stripes*, or *New York Life*, also by Hal Reid. Her golden curls were in temporary jeopardy but Charlotte was able to convince the director to make do with a wig rather than cut them off.

Rehearsals were in New York at a theater on West 107th Street, but it was a road tour and Gladys' chaperone was an older actress in the company. She helped the thirteen-year-old girl with assorted schoolbooks that she usually took with her on the road.

'During those years of course I had little chance to study,' Mary said. 'I had gone to school two winters in Canada and had been taught the beginnings of the sound system then used. I learned a great many words and names of places travelling: I would read billboards and signs from car windows. I would learn one word and then wait until the same poster flew by again and thus I'd get to know a whole sign. At an early age I read the letters and figures on freight cars, and once during a long wait on a station platform I learned to spell Schenectedy.'

The solo tour as Patsy Poore, in what Mary termed 'a lurid melodrama', was at least a step backwards from *Edmund Burke*, which had a classical tone and a top flight production. 'I was back in the poorer theaters giving fourteen performances a week as Patsy, a breaker boy in a coal mine who died in saving the hero. The big scene was in a sort of grotto where by chance there was a strange idol with all-powerful arms and concealed knives. The hero was easily led there, only to be saved by me. "Dear God, don't open the gates wide, it's only Patsy," I said as I died.

'These ten-twenty-thirty cent theaters had hooting, jeering, galleries. I loathed it all and I was lonely. The performances we gave seemed so futile. I was getting nowhere. I used to comfort myself with the thought that at the end of the season I would go back to New York and get an engagement at a first-class theater on Broadway.'

It was 1906, and Gladys Smith announced: 'I'm thirteen and at the crossroads of my life.' She made a firm decision to 'land on Broadway or give up the theater for good'. Lillian Gish inherited her role in *In Convict's Stripes*, and Gladys, her family still in Canada, attempted in any way she could to meet David Belasco, the playwright who had become the top producer on Broadway.

She had tried, with hordes of other actors, for open auditions Monday mornings at ten o'clock, only to be sent away week after week. Then Gladys decided to try to see Blanche Bates, who was playing in Belasco's *The Girl of the Golden West* in Brooklyn, and the younger actress waited backstage. She never saw Miss Bates, but the star's maid persuaded her to allow the little girl to use her name for an introduction to William Dean in the producer's office.

It took several more attempts to get to see Dean, but she finally did and tried to persuade him that she had to see Belasco. The producer was casting *The Warrens of Virginia*, at his theater on Broadway at 42nd Street, where his *Rose of the Rancho* was already running.

'In *The Warrens of Virginia* two children, a boy and a girl, had very important parts,' Belasco wrote in his memoirs in 1920. 'I could not find a little girl to suit me, when one day my stage manager asked me if I would see a child (who) was then a vision of girlish beauty with long golden-brown curls. She said she had been hanging about my stage door for a week, wanted the part and in fact was at that very moment ready for it.'

For her audition Gladys picked a particularly melodramatic scene as Patsy Poore in *In Convict's Stripes*, where he pleads with a policeman not to arrest him as he is the sole support of his old blind mother.

Belasco immediately offered her the role of Betty Warren in the play by William De Mille, brother of Cecil B., who was also in the cast, at $30 a week. But he said her name, Gladys Smith, would not do, and plucked Mary from her middle name, Marie, and Pickford from the family tree (her great-grandmother Hennessey's maiden name). Her cherished goal achieved, the girl wrote to her mother in Toronto that night in newspaper head-lines: 'GLADYS SMITH NOW MARY PICKFORD ENGAGED BY DAVID BELASCO TO APPEAR ON BROADWAY THIS FALL.' (Lottie and Jack were tired of the anonymous-sounding Smith, too, and quickly changed their last names to Pickford, going so far as to register the change in the Canadian capital, Ottawa.

The new Mary Pickford quickly endeared herself to Belasco and the rest of the cast by coming to rehearsal the next day with her lines completely memorized. The cast, besides De Mille, who would later direct Mary in two movies and become one of the most successful producers in Hollywood, included Frank Keenan, Emma Dunn and Charlotte Walker. There were four weeks on the road, beginning in Boston, and then on 3 December 1907 *The Warrens of Virginia* opened on Broadway at the Belasco.

'She was a hard worker,' Belasco wrote a decade later, 'the first at rehearsals and the last to go. It was remarkable how she could visualize a story, and even as I told it she would illustrate it with her ever-changing expressions and delicately subtle movements of body.

'On the first night of *The Warrens of Virginia* little Mary was the most composed of the entire company. Her features did not become strained. She was all repose—easy and graceful at all times.'

Mary Pickford's own memories of her first Broadway engagement are a typical mixture of glamor, practicality and pure little girl. 'I lived on five dollars a week and often went for days before I would break a dollar bill. I walked to and from the theater in any weather; on matinée days it meant walking four miles. In the two seasons the play ran I saved $240 which I turned into the common purse.'

She gloried in the Broadway audiences: 'What a magnificent sight it was from the stage in those days—the women wore gorgeous evening gowns and the men were always in formal attire, their white shirts and waistcoats gleaming in the dimness. And I shall never forget the wave of perfume that wafted across the footlights to us on stage, how happily we all basked in it.'

Her own costume as Betty Warren wasn't so elegant. 'My one regret was that the period required that I wear short skirts and long pantalettes. I was at an age when I was beginning to feel conscious of clothes.'

After opening night she told Belasco she would feel more comfortable in her role if she had a doll to play with. 'He said "Betty"—he always called me by the name of the character I played—"what sort of a doll do you want?" I told him that I remembered my mother saying that when she was a little girl she played with a doll that had its whole head, hair as well as face, made of china. Such a doll, the last I played with, was provided.' As a bed-ridden woman of eighty, Mary Pickford still had the doll, which Belasco had given her, in her bedroom at Pickfair.

*The Warrens of Virginia* ran through 16 May 1908 in New

27

York, then toured all over the United States with Mary as Betty Warren along. In Kansas City, she was actually reviewed; according to the *Kansas City Post* of 15 February 1909: 'Two children's parts are excellent, with Mary Pickford and Richard Storey.'

Although Mary was doing well, Douglas Fairbanks, undaunted by his early professional reception, was doing even better. William A. Brady, who both managed prize fights and produced Broadway plays and had discovered both James J. Corbett and Katherine Cornell, had put him under contract. Douglas' first play for Brady was *The Pit*, an adaptation of the Frank Norris novel. The Fairbanks name went up in lights for the first time with the short-lived *A Case of Frenzied Finance*. Douglas was then in a big hit of the 1905-6 season, *As Ye Sow*, written by a minister and starring Noah Beery, and then in *Clothes*, which starred Grace George, Mrs Brady, in late 1906. For a supporting part in *Clothes*, Fairbanks got $50 a week.

George Broadhurst's *The Man of the Hour* provided his first real starring part; Douglas played in all 479 performances and the play was still running when Mary opened in *The Warrens of Virginia* down the street.

It was in Chicago, during her tour with *The Warrens of Virginia*, that Mary saw her first movie, *Hale's Tours*, in a narrow store on State Street furnished with old streetcar and train seats. The movie camera had been mounted on a moving engine to give the illusion of actually being on a train. Mary claimed that the film made her carsick, but whatever reservations she had about the flickers as entertainment, she was quick to see their economic potential.

She applied to the Essanay studios in Chicago. They had been founded in 1907 by 'Bronco Billy' Anderson who found lasting fame as the screen's first cowboy star, and George K. Spoor. 'S 'n A' was where Chicagoan Gloria Swanson and Wallace Beery later got their starts. But Essenay wasn't interested in the theater's Mary Pickford. She applied to another company in New York, Kalem, and again she was turned down.

Technically, the movies had come a long way since early experiments. The earliest films had been only of actual events or incidents: *Troop Ships for the Philippines* and *Burial of the Maine Veterans* in 1898, *Admiral Dewey Landing at Gibraltar* and the *Sharkey–Jeffries Fight*, 1899, President McKinley taking the Oath of Office (Second Term) and McKinley's Funeral Cortège, 1901, Anna Held performing, 1902, the Princeton–Yale Football Game 1903, Opening Ceremonies of the New York Subway, 1904.

'Getting in and out of a chic automobile was story enough for a picture in 1900,' Lillian Gish recalled.

But in 1901 came the first political satire on film, *Terrible Teddy, the Grizzly King*, in which the man portraying the outdoorsy Vice-President and soon-to-be President of the United States overacts outrageously in aiming a rifle to kill a simple house-cat, while two other actors run around holding placards saying 'My Press Agent', and 'My Photographer'.

And in 1902 the movies slightly satirized themselves and their audiences with *Uncle Josh at the Picture Show*, in which the hero gets all involved with the characters on screen and attempts to help the film-within-a-film heroine. Besides being the first movie-within-a-movie *Uncle Josh* introduced the techniques of double exposure and pre-photography (filming a scene against a projected previously filmed background, later called 'process' filming). Also in 1902 the film companies began to tell stories in movies, with *Jack and the Beanstalk*. *Uncle Tom's Cabin* followed in 1903.

Edwin S. Porter, who later directed Mary in *Tess of the Storm Country*, working for Edison installed the first projector, and Kinetoscopes for individual viewing were soon eclipsed by projected movies on a screen. They were shown in converted storefronts, often in poor neighborhoods, as the five cent admission charge was within reach of all and in silent films there was no language barrier for immigrant groups. Because of the price these makeshift movie theaters were called 'nickelodeons'.

As electrical engineering and entertainment, then, movies were marvelous. But as a place for a fifteen-year-old girl to work, they were dubious.

Being an actress in the theater was, according to the polite society of the first decade of the twentieth century, bad enough. Because of the touring system actors were literally in a fly-by-night profession, particularly when they weren't making enough to pay their modest hotel and boarding house bills. Bad credit risks were the nicest names they were ever called. And the Smiths had done their share of stealing away in the night.

Even worse off in pay and status were child actors. While child labor laws were only then haphazardly applied to youngsters in the theater, and truant officers scarcely bothered, there were some do-gooding agencies with great moral force behind them condemning the exploitation of children and attempting to get them back to school. Two of the first things a child ever learned were to lie about his age and a whole lot of other things, and to hide when the Gerry Society came around. By the early 1900s, this group, founded originally as The New York Society for the Prevention of Cruelty to Children, had become active in theater 'sweatshops'—and renamed for reformer Elbridge Thomas Gerry. Lillian Gish recalled how the girls were taught to wear makeup and high heels at the age of nine or ten so as to look sixteen if they had to appear in court. Mary had long since found her own way around the rules. 'The Gerry Society insisted that there be two children for one character and they were supposed to alternate,' she said. 'My sister Lottie was often my understudy, but as a matter of fact I never allowed her to play the part.'

'Flickers' then were even a step down from the sordid life of the theater. And it was a step that in the spring of 1909 Mary Pickford was reluctant to take. Her mother, however, just back from the road with her younger children in another Chauncey Olcott tour, *Rugged Robin*, seized on the possibilities of the new medium and pushed Mary into applying for work at the Biograph company in New York. Mary was persuaded to do so partly because, although the family was reunited in a theatrical boarding house on West 17th Street, they had gone through most of their savings. The latest rounds of the theatrical producers had brought nothing. The only remote prospects would separate the family again. And they actually faced eviction from the boarding house.

Mary's objections to movies were artistic, if inflated: a Belasco actress simply didn't lower herself by going into a motion picture studio where the players actually called each other by their first names. But Charlotte's sense of artistry had never been as high as her daughter's, and the family needed the $5 a day that everyone—extras and leading players—was then paid in the movies. That would do a lot to make up for the lapse in standards. Perhaps even Lottie and Jack—who unlike Mary were avid movie fans who raced off to a converted store on West 23rd Street every time they got a nickel, to see the latest reels—could get work in pictures too.

# Chapter Three

ARY had registered at Biograph once before, with a girlfriend, as more or less a lark. 'They recorded the color of my eyes and hair and that I could swim but gave me no job.' This time it was serious. She faced either the prospect of summer stock in the outdoors or finding a new profession altogether. She drew 'quite well then' and often considered studying design. She wrote to the *Ladies Home Journal* after seeing an advertisement about women making money selling the magazine. 'I was too timid, however, and never even made an attempt to get a subscription.'

For theater, at fifteen she was getting too old to play children, and she was too young and too short for the ingenue or young leading lady. The economic motive, as always, was powerful: 'When I saw things that other girls had, I determined to have them. I'd work for them. I'd have a fur coat one day and it would be warmer because I had known what it was to have insufficient wraps. I always thought I'd be successful, if not in the theater, then at something else.'

The compromise was the wave of the future and the craze of New York—the flickers. 'I decided to condescend a little and apply for work once more in pictures. I planned carefully that if I walked down Broadway, took a cross-town trolly on 14th

Street, I could get a transfer uptown, apply for work at the Biograph company and get home, spending only one nickel.'

Biograph was housed in a typical four-storey New York brownstone of the 1850s, which had been a private home, at 11 East 14th Street, between Fifth Avenue and Union Square. Basement shops opened onto 14th Street. The entrance to the studio was half a flight of outside stairs from the sidewalk, through double doors and then up another short flight to the main floor. Mary Pickford arrived at this building one day in the spring of 1909. Dressed in a plain navy-blue serge Easter suit, a blue-and-white striped lawn shirtwaister, a rolled-brim Tuscan straw sailor hat with dark blue bow and silk-stockings and high-heeled shoes—her first—she walked into the marble-floored foyer of the old mansion. She encountered D. W. Griffith, then Biograph's only director, and as a result never visited a theatrical agency again.

The American Mutoscope and Biograph Company had been in business since 1895, when it was founded by Edison's then-disaffected assistant, William Dickson, and Henry Norton Marvin, a machinist. They were publicly launched by a presentation in October of 1896 of short movies of William McKinley in his first successful campaign for the Presidency. The candidate's brother, Abner McKinley, was one of the company's principal backers.

David Wark Griffith, then 33, had been at Biograph for about a year when Mary marched in. At first he had worked as an actor at the five dollar a day rate, occasionally selling story synopses as well. For the twelve preceding years he had been a member of several touring provincial stock companies, and also had experience as a melodramatic playwright.

Griffith was the grave, lean, hawk-nosed, gray-eyed fourth son of a Confederate-side Kentucky Colonel, 'Roaring Jake' Griffith, the only man in the army who could allegedly shout to a soldier five miles away. Had the Civil War dragged on any longer, Jake

33

Griffith was slated to become a Confederate General and he passed on to David an abiding love for the Southern cause, which showed up in many of the director's works, most notably of course in *The Birth of a Nation*.

Griffith also got his father's deep, stern bellow, but he was remembered by his co-workers as being most soft-spoken, a courtly southern gentleman of the old school. He stood about five-ten, although to the Gish sisters and Mary Pickford he seemed a great deal taller. His collar was too big, his string tie too loose, and the high-laced hook shoes with loops on the back for pulling them on, more often than not caught his trouser cuffs. He wore a huge hat, especially when directing, and his long, thinning hair shot out in spikes. He was a chain-smoker. He had secretly married Linda Arvidson, an actress he met while touring in various productions on the West Coast. (The Griffiths had agreed not to announce their marriage publicly for fear of ruining their separate careers in the theater, but she was with him at Biograph, acting under her own name and writing at least one screenplay.)

The permanent acting company at Biograph when Mary arrived also included Mack Sennett, Florence Lawrence (the 'Biograph Girl' who made 1908s *The Taming of the Shrew*, Griffith's only Shakespeare film), Harry Salter (her husband), Kate Bruce and a handsome, jovial Irishman named Owen Moore.

While Mary sat waiting to see Griffith, of whom she hadn't heard and whose industry she held in contempt, she created a stir among the other members of the company. Linda Arvidson was struck by the golden curls, 'such perfect curls as I had never seen'.

When Mary saw Griffith himself, she recited her stage experience of ten years, two of them with David Belasco, 'trying hard not to seem boastful and yet wanting to be believed'. He told her she didn't look old enough to have done all that, and pronounced

34

her 'too little and too fat'. But, he said, 'I think I'll introduce you to the camera.' He thought she might be a good Pippa for his version of Robert Browning's *Pippa Passes*. Griffith, who doubtless was more impressed by her looks and curls (and could envision what his cameraman's lights and camera would do to enhance them) than he was with her acting experience, himself did Mary's makeup for the screen test.

'It was deadly white, with eyebrows such as might be put on a bandit,' she said, 'more appropriate for Pancho Villa than Pippa.'

In a costume appropriated from the pipe rack that served as the Biograph wardrobe department, and carrying a mandolin, Mary Pickford was instructed to walk across the studio and improvise some dialogue with other actors she hadn't even been introduced to. Griffith wanted Pippa to walk around singing and strumming the instrument and this Mary tried to do.

'It was difficult for me,' she said. 'Not only was I nervous, but I did not play the mandolin. But Mr Griffith seemed to be pleased.'

Months later he decided that Gertrude Robinson was the right girl for Pippa, but at that moment he decided Mary Pickford was right for the movies. The other actors hovering around also sensed an important new presence, and Owen Moore in particular showed an interest in the new girl, but made the mistake of asking, during the test, within her hearing, 'Who's the dame?'

'I forgot all about the guitar, the scene, my grotesque makeup and Mr Griffith, and turned the full force of my indignation on this boor,' Mary recalled in *Sunshine and Shadow*. ' "How dare you, sir, insult me? I'll have you understand I'm a perfectly respectable young girl, and don't you dare call me a bad name!" In those days "dame" meant to me just one thing—a loose woman. I had just never heard a girl publicly referred to as a dame.'

Mary Pickford found out that Owen Moore had meant her no harm. She married him in 1911 and many years after they were divorced pronounced that 'whatever his faults, obscene language in the presence of a lady was not one of them'.

To D. W. Griffith it was Mary who had committed the unpardonable: 'Never, do you hear, never stop in the middle of a scene,' he shouted. 'Do you know how much film costs per foot? You've ruined it. Start from the beginning.'

She not only repeated the scene but she also did a walk-on role in a new Griffith temperance drama *What Drink Did*, along the same lines as his earlier *The Drunkard's Reformation*. *What Drink Did* starred Harry Salter and Adele deGarde, but Mary Pickford's bit was cut from the final print of the film.

Mary's first day's work in movies ended past eight p.m. After turning Griffith down for dinner, but saying she would be back the next day for work, she was given five dollars. Charlotte was back in Brooklyn with Chauncey Olcott's company, and Mary raced off to tell her about the new job. 'When I got outside it was raining very hard. Mr Griffith walked me to the subway under his umbrella. But when I arrived in her dressing room not only was my new $3.50 hat ruined but even the five dollar bill that I clutched in my hand the whole way was wet.

'My brand-new high-heeled shoes were ruined, and so were my silk-stockings. My beautiful $15 suit was one wringing mess.' (No matter how rich she became, Mary Pickford was always aware of the cost of everything she owned, and of how her money was spent and invested and in very rare cases—wasted.) Charlotte put the clothes and the bill on the radiator of her dressing room to dry, feeling vindicated in her insistence of making Mary try the movies.

Griffith was soon subjected to the first in a long line of Pickford movie money negotiations. 'For my first three days I was paid twenty-five dollars and after that a straight five dollars a day. This total was more than the others got, for only Florence Lawrence was engaged regularly. She had a contract calling for twenty-five dollars a week. I was cautioned not to tell anyone of this arrangement.'

/ * * *

In 1909 there was no accepted creative structure in the movie business; that came much later, in the 1920s and as the major studios acquired their size and power into the sound era. There were actors, of course, all of them from the stage at first. Gradually Griffith and others began employing men and women with 'faces' or some other indefinable star quality and no acting talent—much to the disgust of Mary Pickford and others who were stage-trained. There was someone who made up the story or adapted it loosely (or stole it outright) from classic works of literature (Dickens, Browning, George Eliot, Poe, Tolstoy) and contemporary melodrama, but story lines were largely verbal, and as all films were silent there was no specific dialogue.

'As far as I recall,' said Mary Pickford, 'D. W. Griffith never adhered to a script. At least in the old Biograph days I don't think such a luxury had even made its appearance in the studios. Improvisation was frequently the order of the day. Sometimes the camera registered an impromptu piece of off-stage action, and that too stayed in the film.'

The stories frequently came from the actors. Lionel Barrymore contributed *The Burglar's Dilemma*, and Mary herself did two originals for Griffith, *Lena and the Geese*, and *Madame Rex*, and many more for other directors.

'The titles of our pictures at the Biograph Company tell a good part of their stories,' Mary remembered, *All on Account of the Milk, The Englishman and the Girl, The Italian Barber, A Lucky Toothache, What the Daisies Said*. All these stories were of the simplest sort, and we were not very careful where we got them. Anyone outside could turn anything in and no questions were asked. It was not thought that there was anything dishonest in this, for the films were to be exhibited only in the five-cent shows, which were of no importance anyhow. *Thais* was submitted, bought for twenty-five dollars and filmed without considering any owner.'

Apart from the actors the other essential person in early movie-making was the cameraman, and Biograph had two of them when Mary arrived. Gottlieb Wilhelm ('Billy') Bitzer, a former electrician who had been there since the McKinley Mutoscopes, and Henry Marvin's brother, Arthur. The cameraman took care of lighting and scenery and the actors applied their own makeup as they were accustomed to doing in the theater.

Costumes were usually improvised from their personal wardrobes or bought at local department stores for the occasion. 'The company's permanent wardrobe consisted of ten dresses, all of which were too big for me,' Mary said. 'If we used our own clothing and it was damaged the company paid for it. Toward the end of the summer the men were anxious to get rid of their straws and get fall hats at the expense of the company. Combinations were gone into . . . I'll break your hat, if you'll break mine.'

Grudgingly, it was admitted that there was a need for someone called a director, who would rehearse the actors for a scene and then turn them over to the cameraman, who would then do the creative work: determining camera angle, length and shot (all were medium to long shots showing the actors' whole bodies in the early days), lighting, and covering up the director's clumsiness in staging.

The job of director had been offered to Griffith, since no one else at Biograph seemed to want it, and since the principal attributes of a director apparently were energy and a slight understanding of actors. Fortunately no technical knowledge of film was required.

Griffith went on to make at least two short films a week and had made over 110 of them when Mary Pickford started working for him. He was in charge of all production for Biograph and

Billy Bitzer had replaced Arthur Marvin as his principal camera-man. Bitzer and Griffith were already, in 1909, experimenting with camera and lighting techniques.

With Bitzer's help Griffith in subsequent years invented or developed the close-up, the dissolve, flashback, cross-cutting, pan shot, high and low angle shots, soft focus, back lighting, moving shots and the hazy photography effected by putting layers of chiffon over the camera lens to make the face and hair of his angelic young leading ladies, even more angelic. 'What Griffith's mind saw, Billy Bitzer was able to get on film,' said Lillian Gish.

*   *   *

The next morning Mary walked the whole way to the studio to save five cents, and arrived at nine. 'I remember praying that no one would see me walk up the Biograph steps.'

Griffith put her in her first feature, really as an extra playing a ten-year-old girl. The movie was *Her First Biscuits*, a seven minute split-reel farce about a newly-wed wife who tries to be a good cook like her mother. Mary played one of a group of hungry itinerant actors who eat a batch of the lady's leaden biscuits and writhe in agony. Most of the Biograph Company played in *Her First Biscuits*, which was shot at the New York studio in one day, as was usual with the short (split or half-reel) comedies. The full reel stories usually took two days.

'I was glad of this extra work,' Mary said, 'as I soon realized that I knew little about pantomime, with all my arrogance of ten years on the stage.'

As she was leaving the studio after her second day's shooting, Griffith asked Mary if she could play a love scene. Neither her stage experience nor her limited social life had prepared her for love scenes, but Charlotte Smith-Pickford's sixteen-year-old daughter assured the director she could. He then asked her to demonstate on a papier-mâché pillar.

'Hoping to escape, I said: "Please, Mr Griffith, how could I make love to a cold pillar?" I had no sooner said that than Owen Moore stepped out of the men's dressing room. "Come here, Moore!" Mr Griffith shouted to him. Moore walked over to us, a puzzled smile on his handsome Irish face. "Stand there," Mr Griffith directed him. "Miss Pickford doesn't like to make love to a lifeless pillar. See if she can do any better with you."

'I was ready to rebel and walk out on the whole business when I remembered the money I was making. I pulled myself together and tried to recall how I had seen people make love in the theater. I decided that the way to do it was to look lovingly into the man's eyes. I made up my mind right then and there that there would be no kissing. I had been taught to regard kissing in public as vulgar in the extreme and completely unnecessary in the theater, where one could pretend.'

Griffith corrected her movements and Mary remembered her nose being pressed against Moore's coat lapel in 'a most uncomfortable fashion' and her voice sounding strangely muffled as she muttered 'I love you'. Griffith said, 'After ten years more of life and rehearsal you should be able to do a love scene very well.' But he was satisfied enough to assign her the leading part of the daughter, Giannina, in *The Violin-Maker of Cremona*, her first leading role.

In this one-reel melodrama, Mary was an Italian girl whose father and two suitors were violin-makers. One suitor, Filippo, was ugly and deformed but a better craftsman (played by David Miles), the other was Owen Moore. There is a violin-making contest for her hand and the wrong man wins but realizes he would only make the girl unhappy so he smashes his winning violin and repairs to his room, crippled and 'dejected, yet contented in the thought that he has made her happy' (according to the Biograph handbill) by turning her over to her true love, played by Moore.

At the crucial scene, when Moore puts his arms around her

40

'my heart was pounding so fast from embarrassment that I was sure he could hear it'. But this being a silent film, no one else could, and the picture was completed in two days in the studio.

A few days later *The Violin-Maker of Cremona* was screened in the Biograph projection room, and the advance word-of-mouth on Mary was so good that the whole studio turned up. Griffith was so delighted with the result that he had a conference with her after the showing and offered her a contract for up to $40 a week. His superiors, the Biograph management, pronounced him mad, but after a very hot argument Griffith threatened to resign and so they agreed.

Within a week Griffith started on a more ambitious effort, *The Lonely Villa*. In terms of plot it was standard melodrama, about eleven minutes long or three quarters of a reel. The story was based on a synopsis written by Mack Sennett, who claimed to have based it on a newspaper item (although it bore a strong resemblance to a popular play of the period, *At the Telephone*, by André deLorde). Sennett was paid $15 for his synopsis and so Mary Pickford and the other players started scanning the newspapers, something most actors of any age are not noted for, unless it's to find their own reviews.

The movie was made in two days entirely on location in Fort Lee, New Jersey, and involved a mother who with her three daughters is left alone in a remote farmhouse when their husband and father is tricked into going into New York City by thieves who then attempt to break in. Marion Leonard starred as the mother, and Mary Pickford played the oldest child, aged thirteen. The father finds out about the plight of his family when he stops to call them, and he returns home with the police. The telephone drama was very popular in these early silent film days because most people did not yet have telephones and were fascinated by them, especially as instruments of rescue.

Griffith did most of his innovative work on *The Lonely Villa* in the editing rather than the shooting process. He used cross-cutting or parallel editing to show a last-minute rescue by the father and the police, cutting back and forth between scenes of the mother and children barricaded in the library of the house, the thieves breaking through the other rooms to reach them, and the rescuers. But to get the excitement of this effect in the editing, the acting and filming had to be just right, and Griffith was not happy with the robbers, whom he thought unconvincing. He decided on a complete retake, which in the following film decades and even in television was a common procedure, but which in 1909 was thought extremely wasteful.

While the retakes were in process, James Kirkwood, a noted stage actor just back from touring, arrived in Fort Lee to see his friend Harry Salter. Salter introduced Kirkwood to Griffith and the director said to the actor, 'Here, put on a board and get into this scene as one of the robbers.' Kirkwood was reluctant but Griffith prevailed and the actor made his film début—and improved Griffith's retake by helping break down a door with his shoulder.

Kirkwood stayed on at Biograph and eventually brought Henry Walthall, another refugee from the stage, to Griffith. Both became important leading men for Griffith for several years, Walthall even starring in *Birth of a Nation*, Griffith's epic and masterpiece. Kirkwood continued to hide under a beard for fear his theater fans might discover him, and he and Mary would have frequent discussions about their lowly (and hopefully temporary) occupation and wonder if it would ruin them permanently in the legitimate theater. But since she needed the money and screen players were not mentioned by name, Mary felt she could 'hide in the movies'.

The threatened family in *The Lonely Villa* was supposed to be wealthy and Marion Leonard was wearing an expensive brown silk and velvet dress. Mary had nothing suitable to wear as the eldest daughter, and Linda Arvidson persuaded Griffith to let her take $20 from the Biograph cashbox to outfit Mary from Best's, then on Fifth Avenue and 23rd Street.

She selected 'a smart pale blue linen frock, blue silk-stockings to match and nifty patent leather pumps,' Linda recalled. 'What a dainty little miss she looked, her fluffy curls a-bobbing, when she had donned the new pretties.'

With her innate, precise money sense, Mary uncovered the fact that Linda had spent precisely $10.50 of the $20 on the costume for one movie. 'If I had had any doubt before, I had absolutely none now that the picture industry was mad,' she said.

While Pickford's performance as a child in *The Lonely Villa* was not one of her most persuasive or important, the film is often—mistakenly—referred to as her first. Actually, *The Violin-Maker of Cremona* was released first, on 7 June 1909, although made second. Then came *Villa* on 10 June. *Her First Biscuits* and her first film, followed on 17 June, and in another ten days the Pickford legend was born. She had with her smile, curls and bounce, captured the hearts of nickelodeon devotees as she had captured the hearts of those who came to see her on stage all over the United States.

But the real importance of *The Lonely Villa* was what Griffith was doing with the film medium. Besides cross-cutting the three scenes during the climax, he increased the tempo of this final action by a progressive shortening of the shots. Film drama had too closely resembled its stage counterpart, but the standard arrival in time for the rescue could be delayed on film as it could not be on stage, and in *The Lonely Villa* Griffith used a rising drawbridge to delay the rescue automobile.

Mary Pickford played leading parts in twenty-six more films in 1909, and probably played bit parts or worked as an extra in many more than that, although eventually her agreement with Griffith was that she would play leading parts only.

# Chapter Four

T HE day after her juvenile lead in *The Lonely Villa*, Mary was back as an adult and in a stand-around part. She played a bewildered woman spectator in a chase film, *The Peach Basket Hat*, made in Fort Lee, New Jersey, with Owen Moore, Marion Leonard and Florence Lawrence.

Then followed such films as *The Way of Man*, *The Son's Return*, *The Mexican Sweethearts* and *The Country Doctor*, all dramas. In this early Biograph period 'I made a film in which I was the mother of several children, the eldest of whom was five years younger than I,' Mary said. 'I played scrubwomen and secretaries and women of all nationalities. I noticed rather early that Mr Griffith seemed to favor me in the roles of Mexican and Indian women— perhaps it was because I was then the only leading girl at Biograph with eyes that photographed dark, though mine are hazel. Whatever the reason, I portrayed them all—Indian maidens and squaws and Mexican senoras and senoritas. I learned to apply thick applications of a red clay mixed with water to my arms and legs with a sponge. Often at five-thirty in the cold morning I would don a black horse-hair wig and a beaded dress weighing many pounds and topped by a necklace of alligator teeth.

'I got what no one else wanted and I took anything that came my way because I decided that if I could get into as many pictures

44

as possible I'd become known, and there would be a demand for my work.'

*The Renunciation*, despite its title was a one-reel comedy, and Mary was a miner's niece who visits the mine and in minutes has every one of the mine-workers in love with her. Duels and threats ensue among the miners but Mary steps up with her choice, which, according to the Biograph handbill, was 'the most effeminate, namby-pamby dude one has ever gazed upon'. James Kirkwood co-starred as the uncle. Billy Quirk, an aging and married juvenile who was to become a Pickford leading man in a whole series of adolescent comedies, played the dude.

In *The Seventh Day*, Mary Pickford played a brief two scenes as a maid, but two weeks later she had another starring role, in *Sweet and Twenty*. It was a 'contemporary adolescent' love comedy and Billy Quirk was again her leading man. There was much spatting between the youthful sweethearts and she even hit him on the head with a rolled-up magazine, but at the end of a half-reel, shot in two days in Greenwich, Connecticut, they were kissing. (Pickford, sixteen, was still pretending in her love scenes, even though she was playing age twenty.)

*They Would Elope* was Mary Pickford's twelfth film at Biograph, and a significant one in several respects. With it she got her first movie review, her first of countless salary raises, and, even more important, power at the studio to get jobs for Lottie and Jack, and better and better parts for herself. *They Would Elope* established Mary Pickford, more than any of the other early short films, as a pre-eminent romantic young leading lady of the day— the more famous parts, in which she played juveniles, both girls and boys, would come later.

Little Falls, New Jersey, was selected as the location of *They Would Elope*, 'a contemporary comedy' about a young couple who elope in very elaborate fashion, thinking her family will be in hot pursuit, when in fact they are at home, delighted and busily preparing a big wedding celebration. Shooting took three days in

July and involved—as other Griffith location films—townspeople as well as the regular players.

New Jersey was favored by Biograph and other early film companies for its closeness to New York and the great variety in terrain, vegetation and scenery. Farms, hillsides, valleys, woods and small towns and villages like Fort Lee and Little Falls were used in a variety of pictures. The rural countryside along the Passaic River was surprisingly western in feel and was used for countless cowboy-and-Indian movies. Paper wigwams were set up along the Passaic and war canoes were improvised by covering regular river canoes with bark or paper. Local extras played Indians, but one Little Falls resident recalled that 'anybody able to stay on a horse for a few minutes got to be a cowboy'. Local cowboys and Indians, like Biograph regulars, got $5 a day.

Little Falls was a sleepy but elegant village in the first decade of the twentieth century, with great elm trees lining Main Street, almost touching in the middle. The town dated from the mid-eighteenth century, having been settled mostly by Dutch farmers who had quickly become prosperous, and it was one of those places that George Washington really rode through, even if he didn't stay over night. Pre-revolutionary houses were still standing, augmented by the large Victorian homes of the 1840s and 50s built by immigrant industrialists who also built mills along the Passaic River, near the little falls. Local quarries provided much of New York City's brownstone, as well as amethyst and topaz, and a freshwater pearl found in a local brook made its way to the Empress Eugenie's crown.

Griffith made no fewer than ten films in Little Falls in 1908–10, and probably even more in Fort Lee. *They Would Elope* made use of the estate and gardens of Robert Beattie, a local rug manufacturer, with the elopement starting in a stable with a stolen horse and carriage. As Mary Pickford and Billy Quirk (as the young couple) rode away—there were no stunt extras in those days—the wheel came off the carriage. They switched to a canoe, which was scheduled to dump Mary into the river. When Griffith gave the cue, she obediently overturned the canoe into the muddy Passaic. After the shot 'the boys fished her out and rushed her, wrapped in a warm blanket, to the waiting automobile,' recounted Linda Arvidson. 'It was the last scene of the day—we reserved the nasty ones for the finish. Mary's place in the car was between my husband and myself.

'Hardly were we comfortably settled, hardly had the chauffer time to put the car in "high", before Mary with all the evidence of her good sportsmanship so plainly visible, naively looked up into her director's face and sweetly reminded him of his promise to give her more money. She got her raise. And I got the shock of my young life. That pretty little thing with yellow curls thinking of money at a time like that!' The elopers' escape continued the next day in an automobile that blew up.

Mary's appearance as the bride in *They Would Elope* brought this comment from the New York Dramatic Mirror of 21 August 1909: 'This delicious little comedy introduced again an ingenue whose work in Biograph pictures is attracting attention.' Her name could not be mentioned by the reviewer because it was not known. All Griffith's players were anonymous at first, but Mary's incipient following was not lost on her, her mother or Griffith. She was raised quietly from $40 a week to $100 a week, an unheard of salary for a repertory actor at that time, much less a movie actress of sixteen.

Griffith was also beginning to make private deals with some of his leading players for more money. He even got Biograph to double the daily rate for regulars in leading parts, thanks to a ploy by Owen Moore and Billy Bitzer. One day, as he often did, Griffith suggested that the actors try to work out a scene in the New York studio for themselves while he took a walk. If he came back and deemed their staging successful he would work to get the raise.

With Griffith gone, Bitzer tried to arrange the actors as a crowd in a fashionable hotel toasting a wedding. It was unsuccessful until one actor suggested raising Owen Moore, the bridegroom, to their shoulders and chanting a college-type yell when Griffith came back, all the while Bitzer capturing the scene on film. As Griffith returned they hoisted Moore up, lifted their glasses to Griffith at the camera and shouted,

> 'Biograph! Hah, Hah, Hah,
> Ten dollars,
> Ten dollars,
> Rah, Rah, Rah!'

The scene worked and so did the strategy. Griffith got the raises, to $60 a week for six days, although extras and minor players continued to get $5 a day.

But Mary Pickford, as she would throughout her career, stayed well ahead of the pack. And she used her new clout to get jobs for her brother Jack and sister Lottie in the one-minute Mutoscope (a series of flipping photographs to simulate action, seen through a viewer) dramas that Biograph still made. A few months later she brought them both into feature films.

In the summer and early fall of 1909 there was more and more location shooting, in New Jersey, Connecticut and New York State. Griffith had great enthusiasm for location shooting when the weather was right and he hired a woman to work just as his location lady at $25 a week. She scouted sites for western, Mexican or simply outdoor films, subject to his approval. A prop-wagon took the props, costumes, camera and tripods to the location the night before the actors were due. Each actor would have packed his own make-up box and costume for the wagon. Then, in the morning of the days they were headed for New Jersey, in Miss Arvidson's words:

'We had no automobiles; we'd dash from wherever we lived to the nearest subway, never dreaming of spending 50 cents on a taxi. We left our subway at the 125th Street Station. Down the escalator, three steps at a bound, we flew, and took up another hike to the ferry building. And while we hiked this stretch we wondered—for so far we had come breakfastless—if we would have time for some nourishment before the 8.45 boat.

'A block this side of the ferry building was "Murphy's", a nice clean saloon with a family restaurant in the back. We stuffed ourselves until the clock told us to be getting to our little ferry boat. Who knew when or where we might eat again that day? We would rush to the ferry, seek our nook in the boat and enjoy a short laze before reaching the Jersey side. At one of the little inns along the Hudson we rented a couple of rooms where we made up and dressed. Soon would appear two two-seated buggies, and according to what scenes we were slated for, we would be told to pile in and off we would be driven to location.'

Actors arrived on location wearing make-up, self-applied, and shooting was begun with the first bright sunlight so as not to waste it. Lunch was precisely an hour, and sandwiches were brought out for the company, although Griffith usually had lunch with Bitzer at the hotel or inn. Filming at the studio, while involving a long day, was not of course tied to the weather. On location the camera was set up in the shade for the cameraman's comfort, usually under a tree, and the position of trees more than Griffith's concepts, dictated the angle of many shots. He could get the cameramen to move out of the shade by sending prop boys to the local village for beer and then holding it in front of the cameraman until he moved the camera to a new setup. It usually took two bottles, according to Billy Bitzer, to get the camera moved.

Even in the summer Griffith would wear an old straw hat, but with the top unravelled because it was his firm belief that the sun would keep him from losing his hair. He also wore a large black Chinese prayer ring and jingled coins in his pocket as he worked. His direction, whether in the studio or outside, was both intense and crisp: 'Come quicker, not quite so much support, good enough and once again, please'; 'Pickford enter, and remember not to take up too much film in doing what you rehearsed—footage costs money.'

Mary Pickford made several films with the Biograph Company at Cuddebackville, New York in the summer of 1909, The town was in New York State's Orange Mountains, a few miles from the New Jersey line, a half-day trip from the studio. These included *The Indian Runner's Romance*, and *The Mended Lute*, in which she played an Indian maiden. The two films were shot simultaneously and in preparation for them a Mrs Young Deer taught authentic Indian dances to the company after supper. Mr Young Deer was in charge of costumes, bows and arrows and other props. *The Mended Lute*'s plot was standard but the villains were white and the Indians were heroes, and triumphant in the final chase.

*1776* or *The Hessian Renegades* had Mary Pickford in her first superpatriot American girl role. In *1776* for the first time Griffith used medium close shots, cutting the actors at the knees, presumably in order to keep unperiod background from creeping into the film. (There were no telephone poles during the revolution, much less motor cars.) But the effect was to create a more compelling, less static narrative than would have been likely with long shots. (Previously actors had been shown only in full frame, the theory being that patrons of movie theaters had paid to see whole people.)

And then came *The Little Darling*, a very short comedy about some old folks who are expecting a visit from an infant, only to find she is a pretty young girl of seventeen (Mary). Lottie Pickford made a brief appearance in this location film at Cuddebackville, perhaps her first in a feature. (Although Mary insisted her sister's début was in something called *Granny*, which is either lost to history or came out under another name.)

Mary was less prominent in *In Old Kentucky*, based on the soon-to-be familiar Griffith Civil War theme of two brothers, separated by the war and fighting on different sides, and starring Owen Moore and Henry Walthall.

Back at the studio, Mary made the comedies *His Wife's Visitor*, *Oh Uncle!*, *Getting Even*, *A Midnight Adventure*, *The Trick that Failed*, and *The Woman from Mellons*. Billy Quirk was in all but *The Trick that Failed*. *Getting Even* and *The Woman from Mellons* were part of a Pickford-Quirk teaming in a second series of films known as the *Muggsy* films—all comedies. Quirk had been a female impersonator and a comedian in vaudeville and had also worked for Belasco. In *Getting Even* and *The Woman from Mellons*, the short, slight Billy Quirk played women, the title role in the latter film.

In *The Little Teacher*, made in Greenwich, Connecticut, Mary played the title role, a woman faced with unruly students, Billy Quirk chief among them. There were other dramas, like *The Restoration*, made in Little Falls, and *The Broken Locket*, based on George Eliot's *Silas Marner*, and *The Mountaineer's Honor*, with Mary Pickford and Arthur Johnson as lovers. There were even more comedies: *What's Your Hurry* (made at Fort Lee and with Lottie in a small part), *The Test*, at Coytesville, and *All on Account of the Milk*, which was Blanche Sweet's second movie.

Three things happened at Biograph toward the end of 1909 that were to affect movie-making for all time:

The first was that Griffith made a basic change in the staging of movies. Actors now came on camera, not from the right or left as they would enter a stage scene, but they came from behind the camera and exited toward it, which meant that actors could be seen in long- and medium-range (and later even in close-up) in the same camera shot.

Secondly, Griffith hired another full-time director to assist him. Frank Powell, who had been company manager and chief actor in businessman's roles, was allowed to direct a comedy, *The Day After*, in which the young Blanche Sweet made her film début as the spirit of New Year. Powell also directed *All on Account of the*

*Milk*, in which Mary Pickford, as mistress of the house, and Blanche Sweet, as the maid, exchange places and Mary falls in love with the milkman.

Another director at Biograph left Griffith free to develop film-making techniques and plan more complicated and meaningful projects. It also gave the actors more possibilities. Mary had sold a scenario to Griffith, *May and December* for $15 'to the great annoyance of the men', but he turned it over to Powell to direct. Griffith continued to supervise all Biograph productions for three and a half more years, but now there could be more variety and more simultaneous activity at the studio.

The third development, and most important for Mary Pickford, was that Florence Lawrence, the original Biograph Girl (a title Mary inherited) and her husband, Harry Salter, left Biograph and joined the Independent Motion Picture Company 'IMP'. They had been negotiating secretly with Carl Laemmle, IMP's founder. Salter would direct Florence's movies, although he had only been an assistant director at Biograph, but the most important thing about the move was that Florence Lawrence would be billed under her own name—as the star of her movies.

Gone was the anonymity that Griffith insisted upon, even for 'the Biograph Girl'. This possible new status was not lost on Mary or Mrs Charlotte Smith-Pickford, and Mary began to get restless, and think about moving on herself. And for the next twenty-four years, whenever Mary Pickford got restless, the entire movie industry was likely to feel the repercussions.

\* \* \*

Also at the end of 1909, on 9 December, Douglas Fairbanks and his new blonde wife, the former Beth Sully, had a son, Douglas Fairbanks Jr. Beth was the daughter of Daniel J. Sully, 'the Cotton King', and she had captivated Fairbanks to such a degree that her father was able to talk him into giving up acting in exchange for permission to marry her. Douglas had then gone to work for one of Sully's respectable corporations, Buchan Soap. But when Sully was ruined financially in a cotton market panic, Fairbanks went back to Brady and Broadway in the embarrassingly appropriate *All For a Girl*.

Douglas Fairbanks Jr. offered a different version of this story. 'I was always under the impression,' he said, 'that the reason my father quit was because it was a slack season on Broadway and no theater jobs were open. According to my mother's recollections, he was so depressed by the slump in his fortunes that he felt he ought to do something else for a time. It was at this point that my grandfather offered him the job with the soap company. Incidentally, one of his basic sales talks was that if potential customers didn't believe the soap was pure, he would eat it.'

# Chapter Five

IMING counts for a great deal in any career, and Mary Pickford had the good fortune to come along at a time when there were 10,000 nickelodeons in America, some changing programs daily, some even twice a day. The movies were already in mass production, but the increasing demand for good and different products and the increasing competition among companies to provide it was improving the quality of films along with the quantity. It also had the secondary effect of improving salaries and working conditions for already-proven stars.

Mary, who had looked on movie-making as a summer job, was settling in to the Biograph routine at the start of 1910. 'On Mondays we would rehearse,' she recalled. 'Mr Griffith would call the company around and assign our parts. Then and there the story would be written or built up. Tuesdays we took interior scenes and Wednesdays we took exteriors. Our hours were from nine a.m. to eight o'clock at night. If we worked after eight we were paid more. We received daily pay checks okayed by Mr Griffith himself, and we stood in line to get our money.'

Griffith made 142 films in 1909, just under three a week. Mary remembered being involved in about two a week over her two-and-a-half years at Biograph, but 'she couldn't begin to remember the names of most of them'. The names of 103 Biograph shorts are known, and Mary Pickford owns about eighty of them.

The pictures were released twice a week, on Mondays and Thursdays. Comedy-drama and straight drama were almost always one full reel, 1,000 feet of film, comedies and slapsticks were usually half a reel.

The Biograph studio had an ex-ballroom serving as the main stage, but no rest rooms. There were two dressing rooms, one large one shared by twenty-five women. 'It was divided down the middle by a shelflike dressing table,' Mary wrote in a *Ladies' Home Journal* article in 1923. 'On one side the lesser persons made up and on the other side the women who had been with the company longer and were more important. On this side were two dressing tables. From the first day it was my ambition to get on the other side to where the supposed stars dressed. I wanted one of those dressing tables. In succession I moved to "the star side" and when Florence Lawrence left the company I got that coveted dressing table.'

One of the unique things Mary Pickford brought to pictures—a legacy from her decade of stage work—was a restrained acting style, in contrast to most of the other players who used the exaggerated gestures of the French Delsartean school of pantomime. By standing still she riveted audience attention on herself. Griffith constantly tried to get her to make her movements more in keeping with the melodramatic style of the day but 'I swore, that whatever the temptation I would never overact. He always wanted me running around trees and pointing at rabbits and I wouldn't do it.' On several occasions after arguments on this subject, Mary would quit Biograph and Griffith would let her, but they always made up within a few hours. That and money were the only things about which Griffith and Pickford fought in those early Biograph years.

Their fiercest scene came during the filming of *To Save Her Soul*, in which Mary played a wronged church choir singer,

55

whose fiancé (Arthur Johnson) at one point threatens her with a gun. Most movie actors who followed them wouldn't think of having a drink at lunch, even a beer, on a day they were working, but in the early Biograph days Johnson, Owen Moore and others would gather at Luchow's or some similar neighborhood place for a few mid-day snorts. Johnson on this particular day was very wobbly, and when it came time for the gun scene he waved it at Mary, 'As if it were a piece of hose,' she said. And her long velvet dress was several sizes too big and held together by safety pins, meaning she had to keep her back constantly turned from the camera. As a result, she wrote in *Sunshine and Shadow*, 'I had a very hard time reaching the proper pitch of emotion'.

'What's the matter, can't you play it with feeling?' Griffith bellowed at her, putting his hands on her shoulders and shaking her.

'How dare you lay your hands on me?' she asked.

'I'm teaching you to act.'

'I can act. And if I can't you can't beat it in to me.'

'You can't act; you're a stick of wood.'

Mary bit him on the hand and Lottie, who was standing by, jumped on his back and began pulling his ears.

'How dare you, you horrid man, hurt my sister?' Lottie screamed.

Griffith called the two girls 'wildcats' and told them to 'Get out and stay out.'

They got out, and were on the sidewalk when Griffith ran out and apologized. Mary was upset and, pinned back into her dress, did her scene again, without rehearsal and with more tears than were called for.

\*　　\*　　\*

Liking location work as much as he did, Griffith was impatient with the long northeastern winters, and he pestered the Biograph management to let him take a small company to California, which he knew well from his days as an itinerant actor. So, in January 1910, and right in the middle of *The Newlyweds*, a contemporary comedy, Griffith got permission and quickly organized his little band, planning to finish *The Newlyweds* on the coast. Frank Powell was selected to make the trip, as company manager and second director. Mary was selected as one of the four chief actresses, and Quirk, Walthall and Sennett were among the actors slated to go. The two cameramen went, as did prop boy Bobby Harron, and thirteen-year-old Jack Pickford, who wasn't picked but who made such a scene at Mary's leave-taking that Charlotte allowed him to go, as a chaperone for his sister, if nothing else.

The company took a ferry to Jersey City, where they boarded the Lehigh Valley's Black Diamond Express to Chicago to catch the California Limited. On the ferry dock the Pickford party and Owen Moore made a scene. Owen, although interested in Mary and she in him, had refused to go West without a ten-dollar raise that Griffith had turned down. Mary, who hadn't got a legitimate acting job for the winter and seemed less disposed to look for one —although once in a while she'd threaten to go back to Belasco, was glad of the three months of work assured by the trip, and content to stay calm. But Charlotte couldn't resist making an attempt to squeeze a further raise for Mary out of Griffith. The director said he had Gertrude Robinson waiting to take Mary's place on a moment's notice if she didn't want to go, and that was the end of the discussion.

Owen stood hoping Griffith would relent, Jack was crying and Charlotte was dealing. The one compromise Griffith agreed to was to take Jack, pay his fare and $15 a week.

The company's meal allowance was $3 a day apiece for the train, which in 1910 bought the best food and most attentive service. Mary revelled in the scenery, while some of the men played cards on the four-day trip. At San Bernardino, California, the Biograph women were greeted with bouquets of carnations.

The arrival of Biograph in late January 1910 was not the first by a movie company in California. The Los Angeles Chamber of Commerce in 1907 had sent literature East, extolling the climate, the varied scenery of mountains, deserts, seashore and rivers—and the almost-certain 350 days a year of sunshine. Selig, the New York Motion Picture company, Kalem, IMP and Essanay had all preceded Biograph to Southern California.

The movie industry was clearly shifting westward, although Biograph and many other companies would also continue to film in the East for a few years.

'Hollywood was a small hick town when I arrived in 1910,' Mary Pickford recalled. 'I used to take a streetcar to work and get off to gather poppies at what is now Hollywood and Vine. The first impression southern California made on me was one of great and novel beauty. From a car window at Pasadena I saw the palm trees in the moonlight. I have come since to dislike the palm trees and it was not till I had been out here three times that I began to like California. The first winter I found it difficult to adapt myself to work under the changed conditions. I longed to go back East.'

On arrival the girls of the Biograph company were registered at the Alexandria Hotel, one of Los Angeles' recent structures, until they could find apartments or rooms which they would have to pay for. William Randolph Hearst ran into Mary in the lobby one day and remarked how pretty she was. After a brief stay in a rooming house, Mary and Jack and two younger girls in the company moved into a two-room hotel suite with bath costing the quartet $5.50 each per week.

Mary of course budgeted both her and her brother's expenses and found an inexpensive café for lunch and breakfast in an open market near the studio. Jack was allowed 50 cents a night for his dinner, and nights he would watch the older men play poker while Mary went to the movies. Between them Mary and Jack saved over $1,000 in the three months the company was in California. They turned it over to the family purse.

For his studio Griffith found a vacant lot on Grand Avenue and Washington Street, with a board fence around it, high enough to provide privacy, although young boys did sometimes climb nearby telegraph poles and shout down.

'There was a platform there with a revolving shed that used to turn so we could get the sun,' Mary remembered. 'When we were working we were "on the lot", which explains the origin of the term. Our skirts and the hangings and table cloths in the sets would flap wildly; this often showed in the pictures.'

Such dressing rooms as there were consisted of tents but costumes were usually put on at home. Muslin shades were suspended on wires to control the sunlight. Rehearsals were held in a rented loft which also served to store props. The loft was also used for developing the film, seeing rushes and processing the print for release. Late afternoons and evenings the company gathered to see dailies and organize costumes and props for the next day's shooting.

The cameramen, lead players and Griffith would be transported from the studio to the location in a rented automobile with chauffer. 'Those actors in high favor were asked to ride with him,' Mary said. 'The rest of the cast came by trolley. I usually rode on the trolleys.' Lunches at and carfares to location were paid by Biograph and Mary Pickford figured she received $14 weekly for expenses. The six-day week still prevailed and on Sunday Griffith would hire a car and scout locations for the week.

Griffith took some of his cast and crew to the San Gabriel Mission for *The Thread of Destiny*, a melodrama in which Mary played an orphan and which required Bitzer to photograph the interior of the chapel. Thanks to the rays of the sun slanting through one window, shots of an old priest blessing the congregation from the pulpit turned out properly dim and religious, supporting Griffith's notions of back-lighting.

Locations were important to most of the films made by Biograph that first season in California. *A Romance of the Western*

*Hills* was filmed in the Sierra Madre Mountains. Mary, with her high cheek bones, reddish brown grease paint and black wig, played yet another Indian maiden. 'With alligator teeth around my neck, leather clothes and beaded leggings, I'd have to tramp day after day in the hills,' she remembered. 'Small wonder that I did not like California.'

*Love Among the Roses* was shot in Hollywood proper, at the Château of Paul de Longpré, the painter also famous for his gardens, which contained every variety of rose then known.

The one ocean setting of the 1910 California season was *The Unchanging Sea*, based on the Charles Kingsley poem, *The Three Fishers*. The company went to Santa Monica beach and Port Los Angeles for the filming of the story of a husband lost at sea and then washed up on a foreign shore. His wife and small baby daughter await him, as he grows older and his beard gets longer. With parallel editing, Griffith also showed the mother (Linda Arvidson) getting older thanks to makeup, and Mary growing up from the baby girl. Shots of these solitary figures against a background of ocean and beach were held for several seconds to emphasize that while we all grow older the sea is, well, unchanging.

One day in the loft, surrounded by actors sitting on the floor, Griffith asked if anybody had a scenario for a split- (or half-)reel. Mary raced for paper and pencil and came up with *May and December*, which Griffith bought for $15. He gave the slight romantic comedy to Powell to direct, with Mary playing 'May'.

Spurred on by this success, Mary tried a full-reel story and another half-reel comedy. Griffith rejected them and she and her brother Jack rented horses to ride out to Niles, California, to see Charles Spoor of Essanay, who paid her $40 for the two stories.

Mack Sennett was jealous of her selling scenarios and tried to get her to agree to put her name on his stories, thinking it was the golden curls (which took an hour a day and three separate types of rollers at night to produce) that accounted for her sales. She agreed, for five dollars for split-reels, eight dollars for features, so long as she approved the stories before putting her name on. She didn't approve of the first he submitted to her, a story of policemen cavorting in an outrageous way. Sennett refused to change the police into private detectives as Mary suggested, and so she lost a percentage of the first Keystone Kops film.

Griffith took the company to the mission of San Juan Capistrano by chartered overnight train at the end of March 1910 for *The Two Brothers*. For three days after they arrived it rained and almost the entire company was crowded two and three to a bed into a ten-room inn and a nearby Spanish house. *The Two Brothers* was the story of a good and bad sibling, and pretty señorita (Mary) who the good one gets to marry in the mission church.

The shooting of the wedding scene fell on Good Friday, which was bad enough, but the local Spanish-American population was further incensed by the filming of an outdoor religious procession they construed as a mockery of an Indian funeral, held in the village the day before. A watching crowd rushed the actors and especially the man playing the priest and carrying a cross. The players ran into the inn, the real mission priest spoke to the crowd in Spanish and they were calmed by the promise of a riding and roping exhibition by Biograph's 'cowboys', hired by Griffith as doubles for riding shots.

Mary Pickford's last picture of her 1910 stay with Biograph in California was *Ramona*, the most lavishly mounted movie up to that time. One reason for the bigger budget was the necessity of buying the rights of the Helen Hunt Jackson 1884 best-selling romance from her publishers, Little, Brown. Biograph paid $100 for the rights, an unprecedented departure in an industry accustomed to paying an average of $25 for a stolen scenario. The location was Camulis in Ventura County, one of the five homes attributed to the real Ramona and selected by Mrs Jackson as the setting of her novel. It was the first time a movie had gone to the literal site of a story.

The story in the film version emphasized Griffith's by-now-familiar theme of white man's injustice to the Indian, but he used a great many panoramic shots in which actors were almost incidental. The scenes of sheep-shearing, a barren mountain top where Ramona buries her baby, dead from the white man's injustice, a flower-covered outdoor chapel, and Ramona's wedding on the family patio were the first real long shots in any movie. Griffith even appeared in it again as an actor. The Biograph Company put out a special brochure on the movie with pictures. It was one of Mary Pickford's most acclaimed and most successful early films.

Apart from her work, Mary was mostly unhappy on that first trip to Los Angeles. One day, passing an eastbound Sante Fe Limited, she sighed, within Linda Arvidson's hearing, 'God bless all trains going east and speed the one we go on.' She missed her mother and Lottie (who had gone on the road with *Custer's Last Stand*) but the real reason was her not-so-secret love for Owen Moore.

'There wasn't much social life in those days because there was no place to go,' she recalled one day at Pickfair. 'Perhaps once a week we'd go to the old Alexandria Hotel Grill for dinner. In the lobby was the million-dollar rug, named because so many deals had been made there. Paul Whiteman played there too, long before he became famous.'

The troop returned to New York in April 1910 to resume production at the studio, which had been dark, leaving the actors who didn't go to California out of work. Mary gave hers and Jack's savings—all in $50 bills—to Charlotte, who thought at first it was stage money. 'It was the most money we'd had at one time since my father's death.' Enough of the West-Coast pictures had been released to confirm that the trip had been a great triumph, and Griffith busied himself with editing the remainder.

Mary quickly made two more Muggsy comedies with Billy Quirk, *Muggsy's First Sweetheart* and *Muggsy Becomes a Hero*, but Griffith was more interested in casting her as a romantic leading lady than as an adolescent comedienne. She made a dozen more melodramas and romances at the New York studio and on location in New York and New Jersey in the rest of 1910, including such titles as *A Victim of Jealousy*, *A Child's Impulse*, *An Arcadian Maid*, *When We were in Our Teens*, *When a Man Loves* and *White Roses*.

The Indian maiden genre was represented by *The Song of the Wildwood Flute*, made at Fort Lee, New Jersey and Fishkill, New York and co-starring Dark Cloud, one of Griffith's Indian 'advisers', who went on to act in other Griffith shorts with his wife. Jack and Lottie Pickford supported Mary in small parts in many of these dramatic films, and in the contemporary comedies *Examination Day at School* and *A Gold Necklace*.

*The Call to Arms* was filmed at Lambert Castle on Garrett Mountain, Paterson, New Jersey, which was owned by a Mr Lambert, a wealthy silk manufacturer. The period was medieval and the story had to do with a missing jewel. Mary was required to wear tights and act the part of a page bearing a message on an armored horse. She gets tired during her ride and falls in with a band of gypsies.

It was made on a hot, muggy day in late June, and the actors had to change at a tiny frame hotel near the station of the Delaware, Lackawanna and Western railroad. Sennett and Dell Henderson were required to wear armor, and their distress was matched by Mary, who complained about her tights and despite the heat stayed huddled in a velvet cape until she was called for her scenes. Her beloved Owen Moore was there and the two of them had a secret that the rest of the company only suspected. Mary talked peculiarly and just didn't want anyone, even Owen, seeing her in tights.

Throughout the summer and fall of 1910 Mary seemed subdued and a little aloof from the rest of the company. There were two reasons: the growing seriousness of her involvement with Owen Moore, and the fact that Charlotte Pickford was busy behind the scenes negotiating with Carl Laemmle of IMP for her daughter's services. The lesson of Florence Lawrence hadn't been lost on Charlotte.

# Chapter Six

here are some things a girl doesn't tell her best friend, even when her best friend and constant companion is her mother, or maybe especially then. One of the things she might not tell is the story of her first love. Mary Pickford kept her passion for Owen Moore a secret as long as she could, though it meant hiding, months of lost sleep, disobedience and betrayal.

Mary and Owen had been taken with one another from her first day at Biograph, despite a ten-year age difference. He had dark hair, dark blue eyes and an Irish complexion. 'Moreover, he was the Beau Brummel of Biograph, always dressed with immaculate elegance,' Mary noticed. She showed all her feelings, he hid some of his.

For hard-working actors in the theater and in movies there is little opportunity for any kind of social life apart from that with other members of the project at hand. It is nearly impossible to make a dinner date with someone outside and to be sure of keeping it. As a result most actors spend even their free time with one another. That was particularly true at Biograph in 1909–12, where meals frequently were work sessions and at odd hours. One went out with or was married to someone else in the company or one didn't go out.

Despite her relatively free-wheeling profession, Mary Pickford was sheltered, by her mother, little brother and by circumstance. She was sixteen when she met Owen Moore and he was very much around and there were few if any alternate candidates. Beyond that she was very attracted to him and he had taught her how to make love on the screen. She was always an actress who lived her parts. Her first separation from him, when she had gone to California and he stayed home because he didn't get the ten dollar raise, confirmed her feelings. And suddenly the Biograph company had a serious romance on its hands.

At first Charlotte paid little attention, thinking he was too old for her and that they both would lose interest. 'Almost no man would have seemed suitable for me in Mother's eyes,' said Mary. But Owen was cursed with an Irish affliction as well as complexion—he drank too much, even while working, and the studio carpenter warned Mary that he'd caught Owen sleeping off too much beer at Luchows.

Owen was constantly at the Pickford apartment and somebody warned Mrs Pickford that things were serious. Charlotte 'now made one of the few big mistakes of her life,' according to Mary. She told Mary not to see Owen outside of work and to tell him he was not welcome in the Pickford home. 'If you don't I'll have to tell him myself,' Charlotte said.

Mary, usually obedient to a fault, started seeing Moore secretly, and their fellow actors at the studio would conspire to see that Charlotte didn't catch them together at work. The more Charlotte forbade the romance, the more they saw of one another. And on nights when they couldn't get together, Owen, a strong swimmer, would get drunk and swim from Whitestone to Claussen's Point and back, a distance of three miles.

Mary's first disobedience of her mother made her miserable, but finally Owen cut through it all by proposing to his then seventeen-year-old sweetheart. When she raised the objection that her mother would never permit it, he threatened to quit the Biograph Company and never see her again.

And so on the drizzly night of 7 January 1911 they took the ferry to Jersey City, New Jersey and were married in a dimly-lit room by a justice of the peace at the county courthouse. On the pretext that she was going to a party, Mary had borrowed a long dress with a train from the Biograph wardrobe mistress, and she covered it with Charlotte's too big sealskin coat.

They returned home after a brief ceremony and Owen said goodnight at the Pickford door, as usual. Mary went to sleep in the double bed with her sister Lottie, also as usual, before Charlotte came home. Mary went to work the next morning with her wedding ring around her neck on a string. She barely spoke to Owen that day, continued to live at home and saw Owen only at the studio and in stolen moments.

In the spring of 1911, Mary was a full-fledged Biograph leading lady, earning the top salary of $100 a week. 'She was a good sport and would come in as an extra in a scene if we needed her,' wrote Linda Arvidson. 'So occasionally in a courtroom scene or a church wedding where the camera was set up to get the congregation or spectators from the rear, Mary could attend with perfect safety as the Pickford curls, from the back of her head, would never have been recognized by the most enthusiastic fan of that day. Mr Griffith would not have his Mary a "super".'

There were acts of kindness and generosity, too. One day long after she had any reason to work as an extra or 'atmosphere player', Mary noticed a young newcomer to the extra ranks, a sad-looking girl who was called away from the studio just before a mob scene in which she was to have appeared. Mary found out from the girl herself, who was clutching a telegram, that the girl's mother was dying, and that the sole support of both of them was the $5 a day she earned at Biograph. She wouldn't get it if she didn't do the scene. When the crowd was called for the scene, no one was missing, but one of the girl extras wore a wig, and a dress that was too large for her. The five dollars went to the real owner of the dress.

Mary was popular with the other Biograph players, but very restless. Although Owen was looking for a way to return to the stage, like most of his colleagues at Biograph, he urged Mary to develop a distinctive screen personality rather than settle for being just one of Griffith's interchangeable heroines. Griffith resisted that notion. Charlotte's negotiations with IMP's Carl Laemmle had been successful, and Mary was offered $175 a week and star billing. The Pickfords and Owen Moore all accepted this record offer (Mother, Jack and Lottie came along as 'atmosphere players' and Owen was signed as a leading man).

Mary's billing consisted of 'Little Mary' at home, and 'Dorothy Nicholson' in England. (Foreign distributors had no idea of the names of players as they were not billed either on film or in the bulletins printed to sell the films, and they simply made up names.)

She and her new salary received enormous publicity, resulting in demands by actors at Biograph and other companies for raises. Some critics forecast the ruin of the whole motion picture industry as a result of the actors' greediness.

Mary later told Samuel Goldwyn her reason for leaving Biograph: 'I felt that I was getting to be a machine under Mr Griffith. I got to be like an automatic doll. If he told me to move my left foot, I moved it.'

Griffith telegraphed Blanche Sweet, who was travelling on the road with a play, to come take Mary's place at Biograph, Blanche being the same Griffith type.

The Independent Motion Picture Company, as the name implied, was apart from the Patents Company Trust in which Edison, Biograph, Essanay and others were combined to monopolize motion pictures and keep other companies from making them. When IMP was working on exteriors a guard was hired to keep Patents employees from smashing equipment.

After Mary had made only one film for IMP, *Their First Misunderstanding*, directed by Thomas H. Ince, 'the anxiety caused by this menace made it difficult for anyone to do good work, and it was decided to move the whole company to Cuba.' The party, including Owen and all the Pickfords, and Ince as director, sailed on the SS Havana.

After several months of secrecy Owen insisted that Mary tell her family about their marriage, which she did. Charlotte was apoplectic but helpless. She 'cried for three days and nights, and for the entire voyage Lottie and Jack did not speak to me at all,' Mary wrote some forty-five years later. Fourteen-year-old Jack stood at the ship's rail, 'his cap pulled over his eyes, his arm around his little dog and tears streaming down his face. I felt like the greatest sinner who ever lived. What was to have been a long-delayed honeymoon was more like a funeral.'

The trip was Mary's and her family's first outside the United States and Canada. She was miserable the whole time. The company all lived on one floor of a hotel a few miles from Havana. Among the movies made on the trip to Cuba were *The Message in the Bottle*, *Memories of Yesterday* and *The Prince's Portrait*.

Owen and Thomas Ince, the director, didn't get along, and in Havana toward the end of filming Ince's assistant insulted Mary and Moore hit him (the man said 'kicked' and called the police). Charlotte suggested hiding Owen until night when he could get a ship leaving for the United States the next day. This was done, and Mary joined him for a premature sail home.

Mary was unhappy the whole time she was at IMP and complained she was losing her art by being forced to act with carpenters. Her films, despite full-page ads featuring her picture, were not so well received as her earlier ones. Despite her higher salary she longed for the higher standards of Biograph.

None of Mary's at least thirty-three films with IMP in Cuba and New York has survived, but they also included *The Dream*, with an original scenario by Mary, and *The Sultan's Garden*, a Turkish melodrama for one scene of which she had to jump into the Hudson River, supposedly the Bosporus.

'The IMP pictures were not good,' she said. 'The photography was poor, and they did not light the pictures properly. My hair became black on their films and my light coloring became like that of an Indian. We worked from early morning until sunset without any rest. The company split up into three factions, which had nothing to do with one another. The directors not only lacked experience, they were not fair and considerate.' (The youthful Ince had only been working for a year before Mary came to him. She later became friendly with him, although she had no respect for him as a director then.)

Nine months into her one-year contract Mary fell ill, and cancelled the remaining three months. She made five pictures for the Majestic Company at $225 a week, the first of which was *The Courting of Mary*. Owen Moore probably directed the other four because Mary insisted on it: *Love Heeds Not the Showers*, *Little Red Riding Hood*, *The Caddy's Dream*, and *Honor Thy Father*. These five films, all one-reel or less in length, are also lost.

*Little Red Riding Hood*, in which Mary dreamed the fairy tale, was extremely popular with children. But Owen's direction was undistinguished and he resumed acting. Majestic was even more precariously financed and divided internally than IMP had been.

Owen's and Mary's marriage was already beginning to crack. Moore was jealous of Mary's family and they of him, and there was never to be any real reconciliation. Like any man of his day he resented the fact that his wife made more money than he. And he may have suspected, but never knew for sure, that one of Mary's many contract points in the early years of their marriage was that he be hired with her. 'It was, in many ways, an impossible position for any man. Those blonde curls hanging down my back must have been a grotesque and daily reminder that a child headed the family.'

He was a quiet man most of the time he was sober, but his temper flared when he had been drinking, which was oftener and oftener. When directing Mary in the four movies she got him at Majestic he insulted her in front of the crew and the omnipresent

Charlotte, and told her not to take liberties with her position as Mrs Owen Moore, that she was just another actress. They quarrelled frequently, though almost never in public, and almost as frequently she forgave him.

* * *

In the fall of 1911 Mary went to see *A Gentleman of Leisure*, on Broadway. It was by Wodehouse and Stapleton, and starred Douglas Fairbanks. He was by then one of Broadway's top stars, having established himself as a leading comedy actor in *A Gentleman from Mississippi*. In *The Cub* he had first demonstrated his acrobatic agility by leaping and pulling himself up to a second story to save the heroine's life. In a revival of *The Lights o'London* he had had to jump from a hiding place in the crowd and fight them all, very realistically since his fellow actors resented his show-off acrobatics and used the scene to take it out on him. Mary was impressed by the leading player in *A Gentleman of Leisure*, but not dazzled.

* * *

The start of 1912 found Mary back at Biograph, although Owen Moore went over to Victor, where Florence Lawrence now was. Mary was a bit chastened but better off for her experience. Now she made $150 a week and her name was released on posters and handbills in connection with the films, although not in the bulletins or on the film itself.

Heretofore Griffith had been so determined to keep his players anonymous that he even refused to show them mail that had come 'addressed' to them at the studio. Mary discovered this by accident one day when she said to Griffith: 'An old friend of mine sent a letter to me in care of the studio and I never got it.'

70

'The cast is not allowed to receive mail in care of the studio,' he replied.

'If there is mail for me there I have a right to get it.'

'I told you the rules; the letter'll have to go back.'

She forced him to take her to the Biograph business office where she found twenty-two letters to 'the girl with the golden curls' or 'Little Mary'. Typically she turned the situation to her advantage.

'I never got that many all the time I was with Belasco; if I get that many letters I ought to be paid more.'

Biograph was spending its third winter on the coast and the first film of the new year and Mary's return was *The Mender of Nets*, made in Santa Monica. Mary played Grace, the mender in the title, with whom a young fisherman falls in love. Then once again Mary was an Indian maid in *Iola's Promise*, in which she gives her life to protect the sweetheart of a white man who rescued Iola from a band of cut throats. Jack Pickford was also back at Biograph and he had a leading role in *A Dash through the Clouds*, made at Culver City.

There was some resentment among the other girls when Mary came back, particularly among the ingenues Blanche Sweet, Marguerite Loveridge and her sister, Mae Marsh, a brand-new-comer. But Mary felt secure enough to introduce two of her friends, Lillian and Dorothy Gish, to Griffith as potential Biograph employees.

That many girls meant almost that many stage-mothers, sewing dresses for their offspring, hanging around the studio, and pushing for parts. Charlotte's arch-rival was Blanche Sweet's grandmother, and the only time the two women could agree was during the incident of *The Sands of Dee*.

The girls all wanted the lead in the picture, based on another Charles Kingsley poem. Mary, being the one real star of the outfit, was considered to have the inside track, especially since lots of hair was important to the part. But Griffith tied the prize to a girl's willingness first to play Lilywhite in his anthropological effort, released as *Man's Genesis*, but produced as *Primitive Man*. Bobby Harron, promoted from prop boy, played the male lead. The two leads had to wear grass skirts. Mary refused to appear in bare legs and feet: 'in those days we even wore stockings and shoes in bathing'.

Blanche, Dorothy and Mabel Normand in their turns also refused, whereupon Griffith gave the part to Mae, who had merely come by one day to see her sister working and whose only job had been as a department store salesgirl. Blanche's grandmother tried to unite her fellow stage mothers in protest against the insult to their daughters, but Griffith wasn't through. With elated sarcasm he announced that since the girls had felt themselves above the role in *Man's Genesis* (a pet project of his and a serious treatment, despite the opposition of Biograph management who thought it had a chance only as comedy), he was also giving the lead in *The Sands of Dee* to Mae. 'The girl hasn't any hair,' snarled Blanche's grandmother.

There was nothing the girls and their mothers could do but wait for Mae to fall on her face in *Man's Genesis*. She didn't. Mae and Bobby were excellent, the movie was taken seriously by the public and was one of the most-talked-of pictures in 1912. Mae soon became such a star that her sister changed her name to Marguerite Marsh, which it really had been, from Margaret Loveridge.

Mary would use any angle she could think of to get more money out of Griffith, although 'I never asked for a raise except when I felt sure that I would get it'. One day she was recognized by two people on the subway and she held this up as proof of her worth. And she was livid when she thought that a shopgirl could 'give a performance as good or better than any of us who had spent years mastering our technique'. She told Griffith that she 'didn't like his bringing people in from the outside' and she was going to return to the theater 'where years of study were a safeguard against the encroachment of amateurs'. Further, she assured him it would be in a Belasco play. Griffith laughed at the nineteen-year-old's threat and said that no decent producer would have a girl tainted by three years in the movies. 'You have disgraced yourself,' he said.

Mary continued her scenario-writing and in April of 1912, when the company was still in California, she sold Griffith an outline for *Lena and the Geese*, a Dutch romance in which, naturally, she starred. The film is best known for a happy little dance step Mary did when she returned home with her geese. Griffith was so taken with it that he used it with future leading girls. During the summer of 1912 *Lena and the Geese* was seen by the Gish sisters, who were still touring in theatricals, in Baltimore. They went home to tell their mother they had seen Gladys Smith in the flickers.

'What evil days must have fallen on the Smiths,' Lillian remembered her mother saying. None the less, when they got to New York, the Gish girls and Mrs Gish went to Biograph to look up Gladys Smith. When told there was no one there by that name, they mentioned *Lena and the Geese* and the receptionist called Mary Pickford. After a giggling reunion she introduced them to Griffith, who took them on instantly as extras.

Lillian said she overcame any theater snobbery toward pictures when Mary told her she was making $175 a week and was driven to work in an automobile. 'We took off our hats and went to work for $5 a day,' said Lillian. Griffith put a red ribbon on Lillian's arm and a blue one on Dorothy's and would call them 'red' and 'blue', because they looked alike to him.

For about a month the Gish girls worked only as extras, but they were given the leading parts of two sisters in *An Unseen Enemy*, a remake of Pickford's *The Lonely Villa*, with only two sisters instead of three, but with an attempted robbery, a telephone and crosscut rescue.

Lionel Barrymore was the first of the famous theatrical Drew-

Barrymore family to descend into movies. The man who then was known as 'John Barrymore's brother' called movies 'nickelodeon performances with no sense of direction and certainly no art'. But he told Griffith 'I will do anything. I mean absolutely anything. I'm hungry, I want a job.'

Returning East from California in May of 1912, Griffith stopped in Isleta, New Mexico to make a Mary Pickford Indian film, *A Pueblo Legend*. Authentic shots of a pueblo and the New Mexican desert were used. *A Pueblo Legend* was two reels long, a length Griffith had experimented with before, but Mary's only two-reeler. The local Pueblos thought the movie company was making fun of them, particularly as they had taken some artistic license with their costumes, and the Indians' council decided the company must leave the village, refusing the $2,000 Griffith offered them. The movie was finished in Albuquerque, thirteen miles away.

Back in the East, Griffith made *Friends* with Lionel Barrymore, Henry Walthall and Bobby Harron, and Mary, who got the first closeup in a commercial movie. Barrymore and Walthall played two miners, both in love with Mary, a single girl who lives alone over the tavern (a very forward-looking circumstance for a 1912 movie). 'I wore an old dress that had belonged to my mother. It had large balloon-like sleeves and was nearer 1894 than it was 1849, but we were careless of such trifles,' Mary said.

'It was late in the afternoon when Griffith shouted to Bitzer,' Mary recalled. ' "Come on, Billy, let's have some fun. Move the camera up and get closer to Mary." Now that was a startling departure from the then accepted routine of photography. Obediently Billy moved the camera—an unwieldy contraption which weighed about one hundred pounds and in which Billy sometimes kept his lunch. Meanwhile I broke another precedent and put on a second makeup—one a day had so far sufficed for everybody in the business. Billy took the shot, which was a semicloseup, cutting me at the waist. It was a tense moment in the little drama—I have been looking at a daguerreotype of my absent lover.'

As soon as the film was developed the cast and crew crowded into the projection room, and when the results were screened Barrymore decided he was too fat and would cut out beer, and Mary was upset about an excess of eyebrow pencil and eye shadow. But she and Griffith knew they were on to something and would pursue the technique, even closer to the subject. The Biograph front office was horrified, however, since they felt audiences wanted to see a whole actor the whole time, and they were paying her a large whole salary.

These were the same men who wanted Griffith to stop fooling with the longer two-reel form, since they believed audiences would get bored (this, despite the success, in mid-1912 of a four-reel Queen Elizabeth starring Sarah Bernhardt and made by the company that was to become Famous Players). Queen Elizabeth was a static, filmed stage play, with only twelve separate shots in the four reels, and at the end the actors actually took a curtain call. But it grossed four times its investment and launched the longer story form.

In some ways Biograph's technique had improved in Mary's year away, and their cinematography was generally accepted as the best in the business at that time. But in other ways, the production values were hopeless. 'We never changed our costumes in a picture,' Mary said. 'Ten years might elapse and the leading man would be wearing the same checked shirt. On the other hand, a slight change of dress from scene to scene—the wearing of a different ribbon, hat or handbag—would be spotted by the picture patrons. In one of my pictures a man left a room just after he lighted a fresh cigar. We see him go out of the door; then we see him outside the door, and his cigar is down to the last half inch. This incident brought more than 100 letters. The answer is simple: the scenes were taken at different times, the actor remembered that he had a cigar, but not how much he had smoked it.'

One of Mary's last films for Biograph was called *The Informer*, a Civil War story in which the women of a Southern household are trapped in an old smoke-house. Mary managed to hold off a group of Yankee soldiers 'till the Confederate cavalry, summoned by the faithful Negro boy Leviticus, played by my brother Jack, dashed gallantly to the rescue and the war was somehow soon over and the lovers reunited'. Particularly with Lillian Gish and Henry Walthall, the stars of *The Birth of a Nation*, in the cast of *The Informer*, it was a kind of forerunner of Griffith's epic.

Mary was going to make good her threats to go back to the stage for Belasco, and in October 1912 she interrupted a rehearsal, something that was never done, and told a tearful Griffith goodbye. 'Well, Pickford, God bless you,' he said. 'Be good. Be a good actress.'

She made one more film for Griffith and Biograph, and the whole company worked to make it her best, which it almost was.

*The New York Hat* was from a scenario mailed in to Biograph by Anita Loos, a sixteen-year-old San Diego schoolgirl who decided, after viewing the product in her father's movie-house that she could do better. She was sent a check for $25, and of course no one knew her age or even that she was female, as she had signed the script 'A. Loos'.

The story was of an orphaned schoolgirl (Mary), whose mother left a small bequest with a minister (Barrymore), with instructions that he should use it someday to buy a nice surprise for her daughter. The girl is taken with an expensive plumed designer hat from New York in the window of a local shop, and the minister buys it for her from the inheritance. But local gossips make the secret purchase into a scandal, until the minister is forced to produce the dead mother's letter to prove his innocence. The Gishes, Mae Marsh and Bobby Harron were also in the cast. There were extensive closeups in the slickly edited film, one of Mary's best short efforts.

But the Biograph days were ending. Mack Sennett had gone

earlier in the year with Mabel Normand and three other actors, to form Keystone, and Griffith himself was to leave Biograph the fall of the next year, after his first four-reeler, *Judith of Bethulia*, had cost $36,000 to produce, twice his estimate.

Mary's formal farewell to Biograph was in the form of a party for the entire company held in her large apartment on Riverside Drive.

# *Chapter Seven*

ARY began her campaign to return to Belasco and Broadway in the summer of 1912 when she called his manager, William Dean, to urge him and his boss to go see her in *Lena and the Geese.* Fortunately she had run into William De Mille and he had written Belasco in horrified tones that 'the poor kid is actually thinking of taking motion pictures seriously . . . She's throwing her whole career in the ash can and burying herself in a cheap form of amusement . . . There will never be any real money in those galloping tintypes and certainly no one can expect them to develop into anything which could, by the wildest stretch of the imagination, be called art. I pleaded with her not to waste her professional life and the opportunity the stage gives her to be known to thousands of people, but she's a rather stubborn thing for such a youngster. So I suppose we'll have to say good-bye to little Mary Pickford. She'll never be heard of again.'

Dean and Belasco went to the screening of *Lena* at Biograph. The players, and especially Griffith, were 'impressed by the visit of this great man from the theater', said Mary. Soon after this Belasco wanted to produce *A Good Little Devil*, the fairy-tale drama by Rosamonde Gerard and her son Maurice Rostand (Edmond's wife and son). Mary had promised the producer when she left after *The Warrens of Virginia*, 'no matter where I am or what I'm doing, when you want me just let me know and I'll come'.

In the fall of 1912, four years after she had left him, Dean asked Mary to come down to his theater on 42nd Street. She did in the time it took her to dress and catch a subway from 72nd Street. When she arrived Dean had her remove her high-heeled shoes and her hairpins, letting the curls fall down her back, and stand behind a piece of scenery. When Belasco came upon the surprise Dean had set up for him, it was little Betty Warren again.

'I have a wonderful part, one that is just suited to you,' Belasco told Mary. 'It's Juliet, the blind girl in *A Good Little Devil*. You will make a great success in it and I need you in it.'

'Then I'll come back to you,' she said.

The play went into rehearsal around 1 November 1912, and Mary's salary was $200 a week. It tried out in Philadelphia in December and Griffith and a group from Biograph came down from New York for the opening night. Griffith himself followed the play to Baltimore, where it opened at Ford's theater two days before Christmas, 1912. He was more nervous about it than Mary. The cast also included Ernest Truex and Lillian Gish, who had left Biograph temporarily to go back to her first love, the theater.

*A Good Little Devil* opened at the Republic Theater in New York on 8 January 1913, to great acclaim for Mary Pickford. 'Her success in the difficult role was phenomenal,' Belasco wrote. 'Nothing like her remarkable performance of a child's part had been seen in New York or elsewhere.' But Lillian Gish termed the play a 'good little failure' and she left it in time to rejoin Biograph for winter filming in California. The play ran until 3 May 1913, but was not the box-office success that *The Warrens of Virginia* had been.

'I was never happy in the part of Juliet,' Mary recalled. 'I loved the theater, and was glad to be back again, but I did not like the character I was playing, who seemed to me stilted and anything but human.'

Mary's stand-by as the blind Juliet was Clare Booth, who later became a playwright, Congresswoman and Ambassador. She was then a nine-year-old girl (Mary was nineteen, playing twelve).

'She was very little for her age, I was very big for mine,' Mrs Luce recalled. 'I felt like a giant. We wore the same size clothes and had long blonde hair and curls in common. Her curls were longer than mine, though. She was healthy and dedicated and never missed a performance, of course, and my services weren't even required. There was my dear mother wishing Mary ill, saying things like "if only she'd get the measles". I didn't spend too much time at the theater, I didn't have to, I could just call in. I don't suppose she ever spoke to me. Why should she? I was just some not-so-little girl they'd hired in case she got sick. It was so unpromising that I left to work in another play. Of course after I left Mary did get sick and the girl who replaced me got to take the play on tour.'

Thirty-five years later, as the new wife of *Time-Life's* Henry R. Luce, Clare and her husband accompanied Mary and her new husband Buddy Rogers on a cruise to Honolulu, which was in effect a delayed double honeymoon.

After three years of silent movies, just saying lines was a terrifying experience, particularly since Mary never had got rid of her Canadian 'rs', and in rehearsals the dialogue director spent a lot of time on her diction. But even more difficult was playing a blind girl, 'unlike anything else I had done. It had to be worked out in minute detail. I would close my eyes and count the steps to the bench, to the door, wherever I had to walk. When I opened my eyes I would try not to see anything. I can't describe how nerve-wracking it was not to look into people's eyes, to stare blankly over their heads or just beyond their faces. That constant staring was the most exhausting strain of my entire career on stage and screen. When I left for home after the performance I was aching in every nerve, bone and muscle of my body.'

Mary got restless for the movies, despite the silver star on her dressing room door. And there was a good deal of evidence to suggest that much of the success of her play depended on the loyalty of Mary's movie following. Fortunately among the admirers of her Juliet and *A Good Little Devil*, was Adolph Zukor, the founder of Famous Players.

Zukor was a Hungarian immigrant who first went to Chicago, where he became a successful furrier. After marriage to a Hungarian girl and two children he lent $3,000 of his savings to a friend to invest in a nickelodeon in New York. That got him into the theater business and within ten years he owned several buildings worth a total of $250,000.

Zukor organized Famous Players with $300,000 in capital and quickly brought in ten times that amount, prompting the *New York Evening Journal* to run short editorials warning the Broadway theater against the Zukor assault. He merged with Jesse Lasky's company, and later Paramount was formed as their distributing company. Paramount Pictures became the surviving company and Zukor became Paramount's chairman of the board.

But when it came to money and swiftly rising fame, he met his match in Mary Pickford. Zukor made a deal with Belasco for the film rights to the play, including the right to use members of the New York cast, especially Truex and Mary Pickford. 'Famous Players in famous plays' was certainly a motion picture concept that appealed to her, and she had read of Zukor's company in newspapers, backstage at the Republic Theater. She qualified as a famous player, and who could object to following Bernhardt in any venture? And it would be a chance to get back into movies, for more money, without sacrificing her art.

One of Mary's goals since the days of one-night stands had been to make $500 a week before her twentieth birthday, which was imminent. She got it out of Zukor but not before Charlotte made a last-ditch attempt to get the same amount out of Griffith at Biograph once again. Griffith was still unwilling to let the star dominate the story (or director) and he had already groomed Mae

Marsh to replace Mary. He reportedly said Mary wasn't worth more than $300 a week to him, and so the deal with Famous Players was signed by Charlotte (since Mary was still a minor).

Zukor, at age ninety-seven, recalled the events in an interview at his memento-strewn office in the old Paramount building. 'She was good in the play, very very good-looking and very bright. She didn't have to be trained or rehearsed. She had a mother who took very good care of her and kept her in line.'

A Good Little Devil as a five-reel motion picture was a disaster, however. The actors read their entire speeches to the silent camera to reproduce the stage play, and Belasco himself appeared in a filmed prologue. Like Queen Elizabeth it was static, instead of, in Mary's words, 'what it should have been, a restatement of the play in terms of action and pantomime'.

Mary made two minor four-reel films released by Famous Players before a A Good Little Devil was nervously brought out. She played a thief in In the Bishop's Carriage, which was directed and shot by the pioneer technician, Edwin S. Porter, most famous as director of The Great Train Robbery of 1903 and now a vice-president of Famous Players. Mary's austere Methodist Grandmother Smith agreed for once in her life to go to the movies, to see it and Gladys, thinking this was a religious subject. 'I was told she almost had a fainting spell when I came out in a short ballet costume. She left the theater hurriedly,' wrote Mary.

The second picture, Caprice, also starred Owen Moore and Ernest Truex. Howard Hawks who directed his forty-fourth film (including many of John Wayne's best known) at the age of seventy-four in 1971, was a prop boy at Famous Players at this time. Caprice had been an early success for Minnie Fiske on stage, and was best known for the song, In the Gloaming.

'We created the star system in movies,' Zukor said of his company, and he proved it with Mary in her next picture, Hearts Adrift, made in California, with Porter as director and cameraman. It was such a success that although she had been with

82

the company less than a year she asked Zukor for a raise. To her surprise, without much negotiation he doubled her to $1,000 a week.

Then he and Mrs Zukor took her to late afternoon tea across Broadway from the theater where *Hearts Adrift* was playing. It got dark and Zukor was lingering, talking about nothing, reluctant to leave. He led her to a mezzanine overlooking Broadway and pointed. 'Suddenly I saw it,' Mary said. 'One of the most thrilling sights of my whole career, my name blazing on the marquee in electric lights. The dear sweet man had planned his surprise with such loving care and I had repaid him by asking for a raise.'

*Hearts Adrift* was even surpassed by Mary's next movie, *Tess of the Storm Country*, a five-reel film produced in California on a budget of $10,000. 'That was really the beginning of my career. Tess was a character completely different from what I'd been doing.' It was the beginning of the tackily-dressed, dirty-faced child-woman with long curls, but it worked so well that Mary, never one to tamper with success, made *Tess* again in 1921.

In production, starting in February of 1914, the picture did not bode well. Charlotte and Mary used their own personal possessions as props. Porter despite his fame and his versatility (in addition to being the producer, director, cameraman and studio executive, he was still working as head electrician) in Mary's view knew 'nothing about directing, nothing'. Negatives had to be sent back East to New York to be developed and so there were no dailies to give an indication of how the company was doing. It was edited and released in New York without the California crew having seen any of it. But its success was so phenomenal that it saved Famous Players, Zukor confessed. He had pawned Mrs Zukor's diamond necklace and borrowed on his life insurance to meet the Saturday payroll. But after *Tess* opened in May of 1914 he and his company didn't have to worry. Mary was doubled again, in November 1914, to $2,000 a week. And there was even a more spectacular billing for her than the electricity of *Hearts Adrift*.

On the marquee of a small San Francisco theater owned by David 'Pop' Grauman, whose son Sid later owned the Chinese and Egyptian theaters in Hollywood, it said

Tess of the Storm Country
MARY PICKFORD
*America's Sweetheart*

Thomas Edison had labelled her 'the sweetheart of the Americans' and soon she was to become 'the World's Sweetheart' as well. These were titles she still kept almost sixty years later. The one time she was asked to relinquish the title 'America's Sweetheart' to an upcoming starlet after her retirement, Mary replied adroitly, 'It's not mine to give.' And in 1914 they put the American movie industry in the palm of her pudgy hand.

Universal Pictures couldn't woo her away but they had all her IMP films and re-released them in the summer of 1914, with considerable profit, and to her dismay. Her next films, *The Eagle's Mate*, *Behind the Scenes*, *Cinderella*, *Mistress Nell* and *Such a Little Queen*, proved to be money-makers, and those of other 'Famous' players considerably less so. Since Mary was carrying the company there was no stopping her and her mother's demands.

This was also the beginning of Mary Pickford's fairy-tale queen theme pictures, and Owen Moore was the prince in *Cinderella* as he still was intermittently in Mary's real life. *Mistress Nell—A Tale of a Merry Time 'Twixt Fact and Fancy*, was about Nell Gwynne and based on the romantic novel and play by George C. Hazelton Jr. Owen Moore played Charles II.

Mary's clout was such that she could get acting jobs for Moore when his services might not otherwise have been in demand. Jobs for Jack and Lottie weren't forgotten either. They both played with her in *Fanchon the Cricket*, which also introduced Fred Astaire and his sister Adele to movies.

Zukor and Famous Players continued to make most of their movies in New York in 1914–15, but the rest of the industry was rapidly moving to the West Coast, and very soon Famous Players would too. The Los Angeles area had changed drastically in the four years since Griffith and his little band had first gone there.

Huge barn-like studios were built on unrestricted property near and around the large private homes. Hollywood was soon transformed from a quiet suburb of lemon groves and other semi-tropical vegetation, to a city of producers, directors, executives and stars and the houses, subdivisions, cottages and bungalow courts, hotels and apartments they occupied. Merchants moved west toward the Pacific from Los Angeles to accommodate the affluent new trade.

Within the movie industry, in less than four years, salaries soared from the three dollars a day Harold Lloyd and Hal Roach had been paid on the 'extra bench' to $3,000 a week. Want ads appeared in local newspapers every day for extras for crowd scenes and parades. Films were shot all over southern California, in private homes and public buildings on Saturdays, Sundays and holidays when they were closed.

The Los Angeles area has always had more than its share of pretty girls, but in 1914 the stage mothers of the nation were bringing or sending their beautiful or talented daughters to what had become the undisputed new film capital. Some became famous but many more became waitresses, even then. The tourists started coming to see how films were made and to look for celebrities at local restaurants. Lemon ranch acreage that sold for $700 in 1910 was going for $10,000 an acre for subdivisions by 1915, a year when the Los Angeles area movie industry payroll reached $20 million a year.

Douglas Fairbanks became part of it all when he and Beth and five-year-old Douglas Jr. were walking one day in Central Park in the fall of 1914. A movie cameraman recognized the Broadway star of *He Comes Up Smiling*, a youthful vagabond adventure story, and *The Show Shop*, a satire of theatrical life. The cameraman asked permission to take a couple of hundred feet of film of Fairbanks leaping over a park bench.

A few weeks later Harry E. Aitken, a promoter, was raiding the Broadway season of 1914–15 in the way everybody had been afraid Zukor was going to do two years before. Aitken signed up more than sixty stage actors for the movies at prices that threatened even Mary Pickford who had grown up in the newer medium.

Billie Burke, Eddie Foy, Dustin Farnum, Texas Guinan, William S. Hart and De Wolf Hopper (later Hedda's husband) were those who best survived the transition from stage to film. One of the lesser salaries in this raid, $200 a week, was offered to Douglas Fairbanks to join Triangle Films, a new company formed by the then Big Three of motion pictures, D. W. Griffith, Thomas Ince and Mack Sennett. Aitken, who had saised the $60,000 for Griffith to make *The Birth of a Nation*, said later 'we picked Douglas Fairbanks as a likely film star not on account of his stunts, but because of the splendid humanness that fairly oozed out of him'.

At first Fairbanks was reluctant to take the offer, although he also had doubts about the durability of the stage and his career in it. Frank Case, his friend and owner of the Algonquin Hotel, where Doug and Beth had lived in New York since their marriage, urged him not to sneeze at $10,400 yearly. 'I know . . . but the movies,' sighed Douglas.

He signed with Aitken although he still had several months to run in *The Show Shop*. In April of 1915 he attended the New York première of *The Birth of a Nation*, as one of the Triangle Company's new stars. Whatever reservations he had had about movies were dispelled by the Griffith epic, which Doug went back to see several more times. The next month, near his thirty-second birthday, *The Show Shop* closed, and Douglas Fairbanks and family moved to Hollywood.

As might be expected from their vastly different temperaments, the overwhelmingly serious Griffith and the manic jumping-jack Fairbanks did not get along. The Triangle crew resented all intruders from the Broadway stage, and deliberately conspired to give him the wrong make-up for his first film. Douglas, by laughing along with them, won the crew over. He fared less well with Griffith, who first tried to palm Doug off on Sennett to work in two-reel comedies.

Fortunately he was put instead with director John Emerson and writer Anita Loos, then still a teenager. Doug's first film was *The Lamb*, adapted from his role of Bertie 'the lamb', which he had played in *The New Henrietta* on Broadway. Griffith supervised the production but Christy Gabanne directed.

Nobody at Triangle thought much of the picture or of Fairbanks in it, but it was the only feature ready for release in the fall of 1915 when the company wanted to experiment with releasing non-spectacular movies at legitimate theater prices, fresh on the heels of the triumph of *The Birth of a Nation*. *The Lamb* opened in New York at the elegant Knickerbocker theater, whose management wanted to start off with a Griffith picture.

Paderewski was guest of honor at the première, which was also attended by many leading lights of the New York theater, but Doug missed it because he had stopped to see his brother Robert and his family in Utah en route. 'The three-dollar movie is a reality,' screamed The *New York Herald* the next morning, and reserved-seat programs not involving spectacles had indeed arrived. So, after the reviews and public acclaim were in, had Douglas Fairbanks.

In late 1915, at a Sunday afternoon party at the Tarrytown, New York home of Elsie Janis, the stage star who had given Mary encouragement in Toronto, Mary and Owen had met Douglas and Beth Fairbanks. It was a meeting that changed all four of their lives, although both marriages by then were rocky.

Mary had recently left Owen when he had called her mother

names and then refused to apologize, but they were temporarily back together. Never one to miss the competition, Mary had seen Douglas in *A Gentleman of Leisure* on stage, and in *The Lamb* on screen. His movie stardom had been instantaneous and Mary noted that, although she had the highest salary in the industry, his was the highest *per picture*, as a result. On a walk with Elsie and Owen, Douglas picked Mary up and carried her across a brook, but otherwise the meeting was unromantic and might have been one of those days you could easily forget.

Mary and Doug met for the second time at a dinner dance given by Frank Case at his Algonquin Hotel. They had impressed each other that Sunday afternoon at Elsie Janis's with Beth and Owen nearby, but she had thought him a bit of a showoff, while he had been captivated by her completely. This time at the Algonquin she was smitten too, and the romance really began.

As actors usually do on first meeting, meaning it or not, they complimented one another on their work. 'Beginner's luck,' he replied to her praise of his first film, and when he told her she was Chaplin's equal in restrained pantomime she gloried in this compliment as she had in none before, even though she got them from everyone except perhaps her husband. 'Owen was more likely to belittle my work than to praise it,' she recalled.

In 1915 Mary was doubled again to $4,000 weekly against fifty per cent of the total profits of Famous Players. She was written about in the press as the highest paid woman in the world, and she undoubtedly was.

Still it was not enough, and she and Charlotte would stand outside movie theaters, which along with her celebrity and pictures themselves, had become larger and grander in some cases than even 'legit' theaters, and actually count the number of people going into both Pickford and non-Pickford films, and use the comparisons—always in Mary's favor as negotiating points with Zukor.

'She was never extravagant, and she always appeared as she was,

88

not as a big glamorous movie star,' Zukor remembered of Mary at this point. 'And she didn't have to go out of her way to maintain her popularity. She never cavorted with any boisterous society and she was not a spendthrift or a wastrel. No matter how much money she made, to her a dollar was still a dollar.'

'I am almost a fanatic on the subject of saving,' Mary agreed some years later. 'I could not waste a dollar knowingly. I do not mean that I believe in being stingy or in going without things that will add to comfort and contentment, but I do believe that everyone, regardless of income, should save.'

Mary did indulge herself slightly on two counts in 1915. She set up her mother and brother and sister, who no longer had to go on the road in melodramas, in a spacious apartment in New York, which she furnished for them. And she bought herself a cream-colored Cadillac. All those years of trams and subways, walking and coach cars of trains had made her long for her own limousine, and she was never to tire of owning big, expensive chauffer-driven cars like Rolls Royces and Lincolns.

Driving up Broadway one day on her way home, Mary noticed long lines at the Strand theater where her film *Rags*, in which she played another tattered heroine, was playing. A week later at the same time she passed the Strand when another Famous Players film—not hers—was on. There were no lines and Mary had the chauffer drop her at the box-office. 'I bought a ticket, went inside and began a statistical survey. The orchestra was less than half-filled. As for the balcony, a cannon could have been fired into it without harming anyone.' The next day Charlotte and Mary visited Zukor who admitted that her films brought more in rentals than his others.

As her salary soared he had to raise the guarantee he got from exhibitors, from $35,000 a Pickford picture, to $165,000. Charlotte had heard another Famous Players executive say one day at the studio of some dogs the company had produced: 'Don't worry, we'll hang them around Mary's neck.' At contract-

89

negotiating time, all this made Charlotte and Mary determined that her pictures be sold separately, and not packaged with other Famous Players products. She thus got to pick what other movies would play on the bill with hers. Since she was successful at the box-office and other studios were bidding for her services, Zukor had to give in. Her vanity demanded it as much as anything else.

Shortly after their second encounter, at the Algonquin, Douglas Fairbanks invited Mary and her mother to tea at his mother Ella's apartment around the corner from the Algonquin. The tea was catered by Sherry's and Doug and Mary chatted like adolescent lovebirds in an alcove, while the two mothers got acquainted. Both Charlotte and Ella realized what was going on with their children and even met for tea several more times to provide the opportunity for Doug and Mary to meet in semi-privacy and above suspicion. Mary's mother had never liked Owen and did like Douglas, and Mrs Fairbanks, although friendly with Beth, was temporarily at odds with her as the new romance gained steam.

Douglas's career was moving rapidly, and he made a total of eleven films in 1916, several of them with Emerson and Miss Loos. He even directed one himself, *Arizona*, an unsuccessful effort. At the end of the year he formed his own production company in Hollywood.

Doug fought a redwood forest fire in *The Half Breed*, written by Miss Loos, and dived from an ocean liner, leapt from a train twice and fought a professional boxer in *His Picture in the Papers*. In *The Mystery of the Leaping Fish*, he became a human submarine and fought opium smugglers and Japanese thieves. He was completely a contemporary hero at this point, however, although he slightly satirized modern mid-nineteen-teens American society in the highly popular films *American Aristocracy*, *Reggie Mixes In*, and *Manhattan Madness*.

Most of these early Fairbanks films were either simple comedy or melodrama set apart only by the Fairbanks acrobatics. The distinctive Fairbanks screen character was forming slowly, but he was already so popular that movie fans referred to him simply as 'Doug', just as they called her 'Mary'.

For the whole of 1916, both in Hollywood, Doug and Mary separately fought their feelings for one another, and Doug moved his family into a larger house in West Hollywood when Doug Jr. started school. But at the end of 1916 Ella Fairbanks died in New York of pneumonia, and after Doug's trip East for the funeral there was no turning back from his love for Mary.

He called Mary, who was back in New York, after the funeral, and the two went for a drive in Central Park, talking about Ella the whole time. He began to cry as he hadn't been able to before, and it was then that Mary noticed that the dashboard clock had stopped. Further, it had stopped at the hour of Ella's death. Ella had been superstitious about clocks and heard from mammies at home in the South that clocks stopped when someone in the family died. Doug and Mary were superstitious as well, and began to make promises to one another 'by the clock'.

Both stars tried to lose themselves in work but realized, in Mary's words, 'that we were falling in love (and) it was too late to save the loneliness and heartache and to escape the cruel spotlight of publicity. We fought it, we ran away from it . . . The roles we portrayed on the screen had built up a special picture of Douglas and me in the world's eyes. Both of us, I perhaps more acutely than Douglas, felt this obligation to the public.'

When Mary was working in Hollywood, the as yet unsuspecting Beth would have her to dinner often at the Fairbanks' home. Doug and Mary met secretly around Hollywood, frequently disguised in dusters and goggles in an open car. Their friends and associates knew about the affair but it wasn't as yet common knowledge.

\* \* \*

Charlie Chaplin, who started in pictures in 1912, three years after Mary, and was her only possible rival in stardom, left

Essanay in 1916, to work for the Mutual Film Company at a salary of $650,000 a year. A few weeks later her contract at Famous Players was up for negotiation and she demanded more money than Chaplin, because, among other reasons, 'I'm making full-length pictures and he's only making two-reelers.'

She was courted by, and nearly signed with the American Tobacco Company, which was attempting to get into film production and offered her $7,000 a week. Vitagraph bid even higher. Mutual, with Chaplin in their stable already, offered a deal that meant a million dollars a year to her. She kept Zukor informed of all these offers. He told her, 'Mary, sweetheart, I don't have to diet. Every time I talk over a new contract with you and your mother I lose ten pounds.' And Samuel Goldfish, later Goldwyn, who had recently joined Zukor in Famous Players, added: 'It took longer to make Mary's contracts than it did to make her pictures.'

But Zukor offered her half the profits of her films, with a $10,000 weekly guarantee. 'Mary, that's my limit,' he said. 'Others may offer you more, but it's as much as I can afford.' Mary took it, along with a $300,000 bonus for signing—and to put her ahead of Chaplin. She also got her name on films and marquees, a studio named for her and parlor car transportation to the West Coast for her mother, who also got $150,000 a year for standing by and 'good will'.

'I like to work with him,' she explained to a friend about Zukor, 'we have the same ideas. We've been down in the world and up in the world together, and I'm sure of him. And $10,000 a week is enough, Lord knows. Besides, he's established. I don't have to worry about getting my money.'

She was made president of the Mary Pickford Famous Players film company, and Artcraft, a new division of Famous Players, was set up to handle the distribution of her pictures. She of course had final approval of casts, scripts, and directors—and the assurance that her name would be billed above the title in the largest type.

In *A Girl of Yesterday*, Mary was the first actress to fly in a picture.

The script called for the girl of the title to fly (with a pilot) and it had been assumed that Mary would stay on the ground in a one-propeller biplane and let a double take her place on the plane. She insisted on doing the brief scene herself, however, and there was nothing director Alan Dwan could do but stew and fret down below.

*A Girl of Yesterday* also had in the cast her brother Jack, Donald Crisp and a young San Francisco newspaperwoman, Frances Marion.

Jack also worked in *Poor Little Peppina*, in which Mary played an Italian girl. With that and *Hulda of Holland*, *Little Pal* (in which she played a Maskan Indian), *Less than the Dust* (a Hindustani) and *Pride of the Clan*, Mary was doing another series of her teenage ethnic heroines.

*Pride of the Clan*, which is one of her few pre-1918 features to have survived, was an interesting failure. At seven reels it was longer than most films had been, and its bleak Scottish setting, courtesy of the Massachusetts coast, makes it at times seem even longer. Critics termed it too arty and audiences of 1917 avoided it. But Maurice Tourneur, the director, used extensive night photography, and shots of the coastal rock employing shadows, silhouettes and mirror reflections far in advance of their day. Ben Carré designed the small Scottish village, which Mary as Marget MacTavish, takes over as a toughie clan leader on the death of her father. 'Those who will not be led, must be driven,' she says, cracking a whip.

The character lived on a small houseboat, which was constructed to sink on cue during a storm. The boat didn't wait for the cue and began to sink with Mary and two dozen crew members on board. She started to dash to her dressing room for her make-up kit and missed all the rescue boats. At the door to the dressing room she stopped—'a voice inside me said don't you go there, the same voice I have heard time and again in my life'. She dived into the near-freezing sea and was rescued by a crew member from one of the small boats, who had to pull her about ten feet under water before pulling her out to avoid a speedboat also attempting a rescue. This near-death experience permanently colored her recollections of *Pride of the Clan*.

But even the biggest star in the industry in the mid-teens could afford a few failures. 'Making movies in the early days was fun,' Mary said, looking back fifty years or so. 'There is not much fun today when one mistake can be fatal. In the old days a star was loved through good, bad and indifferent pictures. Today three bad pictures and a star is finished.'

At age twenty-three, Mary Pickford achieved the financial pinnacle of her profession and was the best-paid and most in-control movie star in history. She behaved as if she thought it couldn't last, that she must make the money and run, or at least salt it away to insure her family's security, even as she had as a child in the theater. But incredibly, the real golden days of the little girl were still ahead of Mary Pickford.

# Chapter Eight

URING her first eight years in movies, Mary had portrayed such a wide variety of heroines, many ethnic, most of them teen-aged or a little older, that it is surprising that she emerged with such a consistent little-girl image. Equally surprising was that the public was so constant in preferring her as an innocent, albeit scrappy, sub-teen 'little mother' of even younger children, or beginning in 1917 with *The Poor Little Rich Girl*, the fantasy children who provided her most phenomenal successes, helped a generation bear World War I and the turmoils of the late 19-teens and early 1920s.

Apart from countless real married mothers, Mary in the movies had already been a girl who faked pregnancy to save someone else in *Tess of the Storm Country*, had an illegitimate baby on a desert island in *Heart's Adrift*, lived with a man out of wedlock in *Fate's Interception*, and showed a vital if not aggressive sexuality in *Rags*.

There was strong social comment, too. In *The Eternal Grind* in 1916 she played a factory worker to protest sweatshop labor. For Griffith she had even played criminals and prostitutes, despite his predilection for wispy romantic heroines traceable to his love for Tennyson, Browning and other Victorian poets. Critics extolled her virtuosity and audiences doubtless appreciated her acting ability. But they responded more to 'little Mary' of the long, backlighted blonde curls (that photographed darker in the early days), the radiant smile of eternal goodness, in Tattered-Tom clothes, a sometimes smudged face, and with no visible breasts.

Zukor and Pickford couldn't fail to notice that the further away she got from that, as in the exotic Hindu characterization in *Less than the Dust* or the stepping-in-for-the-dead-man toughie Scottish girl of *Pride of the Clan*, the more the box-office returns dropped. Accordingly, she became more and more American, her curls got even longer and her clothes more outlandish. She also got younger.

America was drifting toward World War I and the movies in general were getting more and more into escapist fantasy, helped along by the movies of Douglas Fairbanks. And whereas in the first years of films the patrons were more often than not working-class poor, who accepted Mary as their smiling inspiration and champion, whose struggles they could understand and whose scrapes and situations they could laugh at, after 1915 the audience cut more across economic lines. Pictures had achieved respectability, and were shown in elegant theaters rather than slum store-fronts. People had lined up to pay the then enormous sum of $1 for *The Birth of a Nation*, and it had been an enormous hit. So now there was a new movie audience, containing more women and children, for one thing. Perhaps because of the war, perhaps for other reasons, humor and optimism for a time replaced realism and romance as the most sought-after qualities in films.

Mary Pickford would continue to make films of social comment, period costume drama and she would even play a coquette again. But from 1917 to 1926, as a woman of from twenty-four to thirty-three and involved in an affair, a divorce and one of the two most famous marriages of the twentieth century, on screen Mary Pickford was the little girl that Gladys Smith had never had time to be. In this period she also achieved her greatest fame, and made the most money. She and her films were also to satisfy a nostalgia and yearning for a rural small-town America of the late nineteenth century, already missed by an America growing up and moving too fast.

In 1916 Mary did *The Foundling*, an otherwise forgettable film in which she played one scene as a flash-back to the childhood of her grown-up character. Lillian Gish advised her always to play 'the adorable little girl' of that movie throughout a whole picture. Mary thought 'the public wouldn't be interested in a story without a love theme'. But Lillian insisted it was the best thing Mary had ever done. And so later that year, after *Pride of the Clan*, Mary undertook *The Poor Little Rich Girl*, with Tourneur directing again. She personally hired Frances Marion to work on the script, from a story by Elinor Gates.

It was Mary's twenty-fourth feature film, and in it she played Gwendolyn, a wistful ten-year-old girl with money who was none the less unhappy, a victim of circumstances, neglected by her socially-involved parents. The rich were satirized and seen as lacking in responsibility or virtue in *The Poor Little Rich Girl*. More than any of her other long films it was aimed specifically at children, but its special technical effects, superimpositions, double exposures and dissolves, particularly in an impressionistic dream sequence, brought on by an overdose of sleeping powder, were sophisticated beyond any other work being done in 1917.

Although the girl of the title was quiet and thoughtful, she was capable of a show of temper. In the most memorable scene she throws her entire expensive wardrobe out of the window, including the dress she had on, leaving her standing in her underpants.

More importantly, 'I had found my place,' said Mary. 'I became the little girl I had never been.'

Mary and Tourneur fought most of the time during filming. He wanted a quiet film, she wanted more comedy and would conspire spontaneously with Frances Marion on the set to insert new bits of business, such as a mad fight in a greenhouse.

97

'Where, exactly, ladies, do you see that in the script?' he would ask. 'I am a dignified director and my pictures should be dignified.'

Mary prevailed, of course, and most of her improvisations stayed in the script. She also had discovered during the course of filming the effectiveness of using artificial light from below. Mary was putting powder on her nose one morning at 6.30 or so at home in front of the large mirror on her dresser. A small makeup mirror on the dresser at an angle caught the early morning sun and flattered her twenty-four-year-old face. Since she was playing a girl aged ten she tried to convince Tourneur to try placing one spotlight on the floor and direct it at her face. He told her it wouldn't work but she convinced him to try once with and once without the light. Her experiment was so successful that lighting from below, called 'baby spots', became standard practice in the industry.

But when the finished film was screened for Zukor and other Paramount officials, the lighting was about the only thing that did work. The Pickford–Marion comedy induced no laughter. Frances hid under her bed and refused to come out, Mary cried herself to sleep. Zukor insisted that Mary send a telegram to Cecil B. De Mille in Hollywood saying she would not interfere in casting, story or editing when she did her next two pictures for him. She did, and there was no reply.

But when *The Poor Little Rich Girl* opened early in 1917 it got the most exuberant reaction from exhibitors of any Pickford picture to date. And the response at the box-office was overwhelming. The public wanted more of the little girl, and Mary, after making two features for De Mille under humiliatingly submissive conditions—for her—was going to give the little girl to the public. She was eternally indebted to Lillian Gish for her suggestion. Significantly, a portrait of Mary as Gwendolyn, *The Poor Little Rich Girl*, has hung in the reception room at Pickfair since it was painted (from photographs) in 1943.

Between the completion of *The Poor Little Rich Girl* and its release and success, Mary was on the verge of a nervous breakdown. Owen was back with her in New York, after a series of temporary separations. Despite her stature in the industry Mary did think she had ruined it all by acting up in the making of the picture. One solution offered by her doctor was for Mary to leave Owen, and get out of town. Accordingly, Zukor sent her, Charlotte, Jack, Lottie and Lottie's daughter, Gwynne, to California in early 1917. It was to have been a temporary move, to make the two committed pictures with De Mille. But Mary Pickford found she was in Hollywood to stay. Zukor closed up Famous Players studios in New York, and moved the production group completely to the Coast.

*　　*　　*

But after Mary and Charlotte had moved into a bungalow in Los Angeles, their first house together since University Avenue in Toronto, Owen besieged her with presents and letters. He arrived at the studio and asked to come back. She let him and, although Charlotte offered to move out, the three of them lived in the house in uneasy coexistence. His drinking got worse and Mary threw him out for the last time in 1917, although she didn't get a divorce for three years after that. 'Perhaps an older woman would have shown greater tolerance. Being a girl, I don't know how I survived the whole dismal experience.'

The robust adventure, *A Romance in the Redwoods*, made in the California outdoors, took Mary right back to the tarnished teenager she had just overcome so successfully, but since she had relinquished control to De Mille there was nothing else she could do about it. In this film she fakes another pregnancy to get her lover to marry her.

Vachel Lindsay, reviewing *Romance of the Redwoods* in *The New Republic* of 7 July 1917, said, 'When the nickelodeon was a black and stinking conspiracy, with a sagging sheet for a screen . . . the

99

films were scratched till they looked like a rainstorm of pitchforks and haywagons . . . Someone dashed past the pitchforks to our hearts. There she stayed . . . (But) Mae Marsh is a finer actress and artist than Mary Pickford. She has had better directing. Mary Pickford has the advantage of a unique and lonely start. Naturally the first-born of films has been given the crown. It is also a great deal in a time of sorrow to be the incarnation of the Happy Ending.' The notice was headlined 'Queen of My People'.

In her second film for De Mille, however, she had a little more to say. It was *The Little American*, an unabashedly patriotic saga based on the sinking of the Lusitania, an American protest of German atrocities against France. The sinking scenes were done in the Los Angeles harbor at San Pedro. Some of the film's extras, who included Ramon Navarro, got splinters when they slid down the side of the boat.

\* \* \*

Miss Pickford's patriotism wasn't confined to the screen, however, and when the United States entered World War I in 1917 she adopted the second battalion of the First California Field Artillery. As 'war mother' to 600 'Sammies', she made frequent visits to Camp Kearney near San Diego, where they were stationed, and presented each of them with a gold locket containing her picture. These were worn by the men in action in France. She was made an honorary colonel, and the battalion was actually known as 'Mary Pickford's Fighting 600'. At Paramount's studio in Hollywood she kept a permanent tobacco fund for the armed forces and collected money and cigarettes personally from co-workers. She also adopted a regiment at the Arcadia, California Balloon School, which sent observation balloons up in the morning and wound them down at night.

She bought thousands of dollars' worth of Liberty bonds, and spent thousands more in subscriptions to the Canadian War Loan.

Charlotte personally took the money to Toronto. As one of the most active volunteer Liberty bond salesmen on the government's list, Mary was asked to tour the United States to promote and sell bonds. This she did, together with Douglas Fairbanks, Charlie Chaplin and Marie Dressler. The group went to Washington for the opening of the drive, met with President Woodrow Wilson and the Assistant Secretary of the Navy, Franklin D. Roosevelt. And they were in frequent contact with the Secretary of the Treasury, William Gibbs McAdoo. The stars made anti-German speeches and Mary herself raised millions of dollars in war bonds.

The bond tour gave her a legitimate excuse to be with Douglas and, as Charlotte Pickford was along as usual, ostensibly nothing was amiss. Bennie Zeidman, Doug's friend and the publicity man for his company, was advance man for the bond-selling trip, which was also a personal publicity triumph for its three stars. Charlie Chaplin did his distinctive walk, Mary appeared in her curls (though usually grown-up dresses) and Doug responded to the crowds' adulation (the first time for him) by jumping and climbing every chance he got.

'I am only five feet tall and I weigh 100 pounds, but every inch of me and every ounce of me is fighting American,' Mary would shout to the crowd.

Mary was fighting and winning in her personal life, too, and when the tour landed in New York Doug didn't join Beth who was waiting for him at the Algonquin, but went instead to the Sherry-Netherland. It was Beth's first indication of the break Douglas had been fighting, and was being urged to fight by his brothers, friends and business associates. She filed for divorce in late 1918 and it was granted in March of the following year. Doug settled half his assets of $1 million on his wife and nine-year-old son. Mary still resisted the finality of divorce, then very much more of a stigma than even in the 1930s.

*   *   *

Her commitment to De Mille fulfilled, Mary could go back to movie-making on her own terms, and the project she turned to next was a total triumph, *Rebecca of Sunnybrook Farm*. It was her best-known and maybe her best picture, certainly a classic, and is as funny and evocative today as when it was made.

She hired Frances Marion to write the screenplay and Marshall Neilan, her co-star in earlier Famous Players films, to make his début as director. Neilan had impressed Mary particularly in *Madame Butterfly*, when he made many suggestions to the director to enliven the pace of that film. The director had ignored him, fought with her, and produced the leaden opus Mary termed 'Madame Snail'. Neilan's début in *Rebecca* was so stunning that he went on to make six more movies with Mary.

Rebecca *is* the Mary Pickford little girl, more than any of the other characters she played. Rebecca lives in a small town in a rural America where roses bloomed on every front gate all year long, where the horse and buggy hadn't been replaced by the motorcar, and where church, home and schoolroom were all the social centers one needed. It had never really been quite like that, of course, except in children's books. But Pickford's adult fans were nostalgic for something they thought they remembered from twenty years before, and her child fans thought that this was just the way to spend a childhood.

There are wonderful scenes in *Rebecca*, as fresh and funny fifty-six years after the picture was completed as they were in 1917. Anyone who ever went to school can take delight in Rebecca's confrontations with her arch-rival, Minnie Smellie, the preacher's daughter and town snip, whether it's Rebecca's turning around and tweaking the poor girl's nose when the teacher isn't looking, or getting up at class-day exercises and reading a poem on the disagreeable things about Minnie Smellie, to a horrified collection of parents.

Rebecca holds a circus in the barn where she does her own stunts, riding bareback on a horse and suspended from a wire so she could be pulled up and down. Mary had to wear a harness for this and the scene took several days.

'The harness made me so sore on the first night that I couldn't sleep, move or breathe,' she recalled.

Among the spectators in the small California country town where *Rebecca* was filmed was Zasu Pitts, whom Mary hired as an extra for the circus sequence. She gave Zasu a larger role in a subsequent feature, *A Little Princess*, and launched her toward stardom.

Perhaps the most memorable scene in *Rebecca of Sunnybrook Farm*, is the one in which her aunt has forbidden her blackberry pie for dessert because Rebecca has complained about the size of the piece. The girl takes the pie plate still containing her piece of pie, back to the kitchen, and starts to steal it. She looks up on the wall and sees a sampler motto saying 'Thou shalt not steal'. She puts the pie back, then spots another sampler saying 'The Lord helps those who help themselves'. Rebecca helps herself.

Rebecca may grow into a formidable woman, but we don't see it, only sense it, in this picture. She grows up in some ways but at the end of the movie she is still all girl. She has raised hell and been punished for it and got away with it, in just the right proportions. She might have lived in a fantasy world that never was. There were no villains in *Rebecca* only over-protective guardian aunts who melt under just enough affection, and nuisances like Minnie Smellie, but the girl is real, earthbound, charming—and just plain pretty.

And yet Mary even here didn't give up her character as champion of the deprived and oppressed. Rebecca pleads with her small townsmen—in an era much less tolerant than any since—to accept a local common law marriage.

*Rebecca* was an even bigger success than *The Poor Little Rich Girl* had been, and Mary was stuck with the little girl, like it or not. Most movie-goers knew Mary was a woman, but they accepted her as a child. She was just a fraction over five feet tall, and her gingham or organdy costumes, intelligent lighting, and sheer acting ability almost completed the illusion. Just to make sure, all furniture and props were scaled one-third larger than life-size for the Pickford little-girl pictures beginning with *A Little Princess*, so she would have to climb into an easy chair instead of just sitting down in it. Doors and windows were bigger than normal, doorknobs higher. Frequently even extra-tall supporting players were used to heighten the effect.

Off-camera the illusion was maintained as well. 'In Mary's public appearances her mother was always in evidence,' said Zukor, 'but her husband, Owen Moore, hardly ever. If the public did not recollect that Mary was a wife, no harm was done. While Mary was not asked to appear in curls and pinafore off the screen, we did, frankly, want her to seem a teenager. It was understandable that Mary wished to dress her age and in the height of fashion, but neither of us could afford it.'

'In the old days stars were glamorous—and they worked at maintaining the illusion they presented on screen,' said Mary. 'If fans came to see me on the set and I wasn't dressed for a role, I'd run into my dressing room, let down my curls and put on the little-girl dresses they expected me to be wearing. An actress is only important to the public as an actress, not as an individual. I wouldn't dance in public. Perhaps that was old-fashioned but I had a strong feeling about staying in character.'

In *A Little Princess*, Mary reverted to the more fairy-tale quality of *The Poor Little Rich Girl*. Neilan directed again, and Charles Rosher, who was to become Pickford's favorite cameraman, assisted with the photography. Mary played Sarah Crewe, another girl of about ten. The extra-proportion sets and props, including dishes and glassware, were used for the first time on screen, a technique that persists in movies whenever adult actors play themselves as children for example.

Neilan, with the help of Jack Pickford and Charlie Chaplin, tricked Mary into a precise reaction he wanted on screen. Miss

Pitts as the maid was pretending to be an elegant lady, and a closeup of Mary would show her reaction of surprised laughter in full sequence, from the initial shock to uproarious outbursts. Jack, wearing a hemp wig backwards, pieces of lace and ribbon and artificial flowers, did a dance with Charlie behind the camera as the director whistled Mendelssohn's 'Spring Song', to get the effect.

But Mary Pickford was still adventurous, and when Zukor was away from Paramount for several weeks in late 1917, she decided to sneak in the most uncompromising and challenging movie of her career. She was at the absolute pinnacle of her popularity and could have done one commercial little girl film after another, but perhaps now was the time for integrity, when she could do no wrong.

Zukor would certainly never have approved of *Stella Maris*, and when he returned to the studio in the midst of production, he was horrified to see his Mary immersed in the role of the poor ugly Cockney girl, Unity Blake. Mary was also shrewd enough to play the title role, that of a wealthy crippled girl, totally confined to her bedroom in a tower overlooking the ocean and immune to all the unpleasant things of life that Unity is so familiar with.

It was Mary's first dual role, and the first time she played an ugly girl. As Unity, she is totally unrecognizable as herself. Her curls were slicked down with vaseline, her face and mouth deformed and with one shoulder drooping from having carried younger children on her hip (that last was a Pickford suggestion).

Unity is also an example of the cruelty of placing orphans in workhouses, and a plea to stop it. Zukor was scarcely reassured when he came upon this creature (bandaged and bed-ridden after a drunken foster mother beat her with a hot poker) on the set and Mary told him it was okay because she died before the picture was over.

'I could end one of the characters unhappily,' she explained several years later, 'and not sacrifice the desired happy ending.'

Unity comes into the service of Stella Maris, and their scenes together are triumphs of staging and photography for director Neilan and cameraman Walter Stradling, surpassed only in *Little Lord Fauntleroy* five years later. The film parallels the lives of the two girls, and after they meet it becomes a psychological study contrasting the miserable orphan and the protected cripple. It was a straight tragedy, not a melodrama, and in that sense a departure also.

Unity is quite possibly Mary Pickford's finest silent performance, made all the more spectacular by her simultaneous portrayal of Stella. In one shot, thanks to Stradling's camera, Unity moves from one side of the frame to the other while Stella stays in the frame, then leaves behind Stella opposite the side from which she came in.

*Stella Maris* was, amazingly, accepted by audiences, and while not the hit *Rebecca* had been, made money, to Zukor's shock and Mary's satisfaction.

Mary made five more films for Zukor, in 1918, beginning with *Amarilly of Clothesline Alley*, and *M'Liss*, two more Neilan–Stradling collaborations, albeit lesser ones. Then came *How Could You, Jean?*, *Johanna Enlists*, and *Captain Kidd, Jr* in which Wallace Berry appeared. In all five of these films she is back to playing a somewhat scruffy late-teenager with romantic possibilities. In *Amarilly* she actually has a fiancé who is tempted to visit a brothel. *M'Liss*, in which she befriends forest animals and has to act with a snake and a bear, is the best remembered of the five. But surprisingly, these were less well received than their predecessors and have faded into obscurity compared with other films just before and just after them.

# *Chapter Nine*

**F**OR five and a half years under Zukor at Famous Players Mary had most of the power that is normally reserved for the producer, the choice of directors and co-stars, for example. But she was a producer in fact only, not in name, and the last contract with Zukor hadn't delivered all that was promised. She felt particularly constrained since the studio maintained final approval of scripts. And, there was always the lure of more money.

Accordingly, on Armistice Day, 11 November 1918, Mary Pickford established herself as an independent producer, and signed a contract for the distribution of her films with First National. Her basic salary jumped to $675,000 a year, or $350,000 per picture—eclipsing Douglas Fairbanks's record price—against fifty per cent of the gross receipts of her films. Charlotte was given $50,000 for her 'good offices' and it was clear she was even more eager to make the move than Mary was.

Mary still felt kindly toward Zukor as a person, while regretting the growing impersonality of his company, and they remained close friends throughout their long lives.

'I always liked his ideas,' she said.

'She taught me a great deal,' he remembered. 'I was only an apprentice when we started, she was an expert workman.'

He had Jewish-fathered her: if her dress had too-short sleeves he'd worry that she'd catch cold and seem immodest. They were a match in shrewdness and it was that which broke them apart, even as it had brought them together. She and Charlotte tried to get Zukor to match the First National terms. When he wouldn't she called him and said, somewhat coldly, 'I'm about to sign with First National, have you anything to say to me?'

'Only God bless you, Mary, and I wish you well,' came the reply. 'Better to let her make her own way for a while, and go on our own,' he told his associates at Paramount. For all her value to the company she had been reducing them 'to the position of the tail to the kite'.

Mary set immediately to work on her next picture, *Daddy Longlegs*. She helped write the script—it was Charlotte who had gone to New York to buy this story and *Pollyanna*—and made a smashing début as producer. Marshall Neilan was hired as director, naturally, and he also played a small part. Charles Rosher did the camera work.

In the film Mary plays Judy Abbott, an orphan wrapped in newspaper and left in a garbage can. In the film she grows to maturity and becomes a well-known writer, but she is raised in a gruesome orphanage and there is as much social comment throughout the picture as there is hilarity. It is an exposé of shoddy orphanages and impersonal management, and yet another slap at the rich who run them and other institutions that oppress the poor. One title says: 'John Grierson made his millions in convict labor. He ran his orphanage on the same principles.' Another title precedes a scene of the children lined up like prisoners: 'All orphans look alike from any angle: exhibit A, rear view.'

Judy Abbott, being a typical optimistic but rugged Pickford heroine, is a rebel leader who organizes a strike in the orphanage dining hall against prunes three meals a day. She leads an occupation of the kitchen and tells her fellow conspirators to eat all they want. In pigtails this time rather than curls, the girl (real-life age twenty-six) gets herself and another orphan kid drunk on hard cider, swings on the playground trapeze, tries to draw water from a well but sees buildings swaying back and forth, and sobers up only when she sees a dog, also high, trying to walk a straight line on its hind legs.

*The Hoodlum*, a satire of the upper class, saw Mary as a more mature girl, Amy Burke, who gets blackened by a coal-chute in one scene of the Frances Marion screenplay. Rosher was again the cameraman. Mary was firmly convinced that the best way to make pictures was to hire the very best people, like Marion, Neilan and Rosher, pay them very well and make sure they were available every time you wanted to work. Rosher, for example, was allowed to work for other directors, so long as he came back to Mary when she needed him. Rosher and Pickford stayed together through *Coquette*, in 1929.

Rosher said of Mary: 'She knew everything there was to know about making a movie; she could do everything, she was a walking motion picture company. She was one of the finest characters I ever knew, and a clever businesswoman too. She did a lot of her own directing. The director would often just direct the crowd.'

Mary denied this contention: 'I have always taken an active interest in my films from beginning to end, from the script down to the editing and titling. I tried to learn everything I could about making motion pictures. But I always felt the need of a good director and I relied upon my directors. They were hired for what they could contribute—new ideas and intelligent ways to make my pictures better. They weren't expected to "yes" me, and I insisted they use their initiative and authority. Being my own producer I could have directed my own pictures, but I never wanted to. I've had some of Hollywood's best directors and they didn't need anyone's help.'

When *The Hoodlum* was released in 1919 the reviews were enthusiastic. *Variety* said, 'Mary Pickford gives First National the real goods . . . the very best photography, direction, scenarios, lighting effects and attention to detail. In these technical respects, Paramount, most consistent of performers in the production field, never did anything better than *The Hoodlum*.'

The paper went on to praise 'that elusive, amazing charm which is Mary Pickford, which persists and does not end. After six years she is still queen of the screen and she has a mastery of pantomime that is unique, a charm of manner and personality that cannot be escaped and is past defining.'

Mary's third and last picture for First National was *The Heart of the Hills*, a Kentucky hills melodrama-romance reminiscent of some of her Biograph films. Again she is an adolescent rather than a child. She gets into Ku Klux Klan robes to mete out justice, and does a jazzy barn dance, makes obvious eyes at John Gilbert, and sets out to 'raise h—l generally', in the words of the title frame.

Despite the praise her three First National releases were given and the near-ideal working conditions, Mary at the most could still only collect fifty per cent of her movies' profits. There was also talk around Hollywood in late 1919, mostly emanating from Louis B. Mayer, that stars' salaries had got way out of hand, and the studio heads should get together and get them back in line and keep tight control over them. The only defense against that, and the only way to keep all the profits, was for Mary to go into business for herself, really for herself this time. Chaplin, and Fairbanks who had saved his first million in 1918, faced the same situation. They were the only stars with comparable salaries and comparable clout. The three were also close friends, and with D. W. Griffith, they met at the Santa Barbara, California bungalow of William Gibbs McAdoo, the Treasury Secretary they had met on the Liberty Bond Drive, in January of 1919. They discussed the idea of forming their own distributing corporation, keeping their individual producing units. And on 17 April 1919, Mary Pickford, Douglas Fairbanks, Charles Chaplin, and David Wark Griffith formed one of the most aptly named corporations in history: United Artists. As the company evolved, McAdoo was eased out along with Oscar Price, the first president. Other actors came and went, Griffith failed and faded, but the 'Big Three' remained the nucleus of the successful combine for almost two decades, until Douglas Fairbanks' death in 1939. Mary and Charlie keeping their share of ownership into the 1950s.

The formation of United Artists prompted one studio head to say: 'The asylum is now in the hands of maniacs.'

'But we maniacs had fun,' Mary Pickford said fifty years later, 'and made good pictures and a lot of money. In the early days United Artists was a private golf club for the four of us. Then we let too many other stars in and it began to change. But we produced and financed our own pictures, and if they had lost money —which they never did—we were prepared to accept the losses as well as the profits.'

Griffith was definitely the odd man out, but in 1919 he still was the only director of sufficient stature to warrant inclusion in the company of Pickford, Fairbanks and Chaplin.

Charlie Chaplin found Griffith aloof, cold and too hung up on his frail women and his epics, with no understanding of comedy whatsoever. The director just didn't understand Chaplin or his subtle kind of comedy, and as for Douglas, Griffith said: 'Fairbanks thinks acting is leaping from one place to another.'

Mary who had certainly had her differences with Griffith had to act as the go-between, the peacemaker. Despite his success with *The Birth of a Nation*, his three partners were bigger box-office names and Griffith felt he had to compete with blockbusting hits. Fortunately his first three films for United Artists were just that: *Broken Blossoms, Way Down East*—which had the first motion picture budget of $1 million, of which only $175 went for the story, nevertheless breaking the record set by *Ramona*, and $3,000 for the screenplay, Griffith's first to be all written down—and *Orphans of the Storm*. All three starred Griffith's beloved Lillian Gish, and her sister Dorothy joined her in *Orphans*.

Mrs Morgan Belmont of New York's 400 played a society matron in *Way Down East*, giving the movies a new kind of social cachet. *Way Down East* was the hugest success of the three and Griffith was temporarily back on top.

In 1919, from the Griffith studio came yet another innovation, and one that kept Pickford and her sister stars, now solidly in their twenties, still able to play heroines of even twelve. The technique was first tried with Lillian Gish in *Broken Blossoms*. Miss Gish was then twenty-two but Billy Bitzer had made her look ten years younger by filming her through black maline, a fine silk net that covered the regular camera lens and acted as a retouching lens. The results were extraordinary and cameramen began to experiment with netting of a variety of colors and coarseness, eventually developing the diffusion lens, with the softening factor built into the glass.

However Griffith's later pictures failed and he quickly became an anachronism and even his previous masterpieces seemed dated and mediocre. He broke up with Lillian Gish, and tried to replace her on screen with his new love, Carol Dempster. After his failures at Paramount and Universal, he came back to United Artists for a few pictures but effectively retired in 1932, broken and mis-understood, and died in 1948, drunken and ignored.

*Pollyanna* was Mary Pickford's first picture for United Artists and proved the only possible rival to *Rebecca of Sunnybrook Farm* in popularity and artistry. When *Pollyanna*, adapted by Frances Marion from the novel by Eleanor Porter, appeared early in 1920, Mary hadn't been seen as the little girl throughout a picture since *A Little Princess* three years earlier, and it was time for her to come back in the classic portrayal of 'the glad girl', the eternal optimist.

Her fans had been clamoring for years for Mary to do *Polly-anna*, and they weren't disappointed by her intelligent, sensitive and unsticky interpretation of the ten-year-old orphan who comes to live with her aunt in a small town. The girl, hit by a car when she tries to save a younger child, is paralyzed. The scene in which she finally takes a few halting steps after months of confinement and determination is one to cry at.

Pollyanna herself cries in one scene, and Mary, already tired of the little girl, injected a fly-killing scene on the spur of the moment one day to make her character more real. 'Little fly do you want to go to heaven?' she asks (on the titles). She squashes the creature between her two hands and says, 'Well, you have.' The kid is smart, fun but real. She sticks flypaper squares on the bottom of her boots to keep from muddying the carpets in her aunt's house. She then marches upstairs to her room, a strand of wool attached to one foot, unravelling the aunt's entire knitting-in-progress.

In *Motion Picture Classics* for March of 1920, instead of writing a regular review of *Pollyanna*, critic Frederick James Smith wrote a personal letter to Mary Pickford, reflecting the prevailing sentiment:

'Way back in the minds of all of us are dreams—the dreams we started with, the dreams that came to grief when we encountered life as it really is. You have the ability—indeed we should say genius—to stir those latent memories, to sweep back the years, to give us faith again. If we ever reach the point where you fail to touch us, Mary Pickford, we will know that our ideals have gone . . .

'We know—our critical self keeps repeating it—that you never did a finer, better sustained, or an infinitely more subtle bit of playing of childhood than your Pollyanna, but it is the soul beneath this histrionic dexterity that we feel. You are eternal youth, with its dream cities' high hopes.'

Smith ended the letter by calling for more *Pollyannas*. And *Pollyanna* was a great favorite in the Soviet Union, where Pickford's and other silent films were beginning to be shown.

At about this time, Mary had a serious bout of flu. *The Chicago Tribune* welcomed her back to good health with a sweet photograph and this caption: "The most beloved face in the world.

Mary Pickford's thousands of ardent admirers followed the news of her illness as devotedly and sympathetically as if it were a personal sorrow.'

Subject as she was to this kind of idolatry, there was probably only one man Mary could have married, her second time around, Douglas Fairbanks.

Even as she was the image of girlhood, he was the athletic hero of small boys throughout the world, and the ideal symbol of respectable young manhood to their parents. His mere presence on the screen served to assure the American middle class, with its lingering misgivings—that the lower and upper classes had already overcome—that the movies were really all right. In such pictures as *The Americano*, *Say, Young Fellow*, *A Modern Musketeer*, *He Comes Up Smiling* and *Reaching for the Moon*, Douglas had become a star, more a personality than an actor, pure ingenuous enthusiasm and gymnastic grace. He was the only man Mary couldn't overwhelm.

Success was Douglas Fairbanks's constant goal and the thing he most admired in others, whatever their field or work. Success was one of the things he admired about Mary Pickford. His zest and gaiety were what first appealed to her; she used to the alternating solemnity and rage of Owen Moore. Their mutual admiration now ripened into the greatest love story of the twentieth century until a King gave up his crown.

Even after their affair had got underway and Mary had left Owen for good to move in with Charlotte, Lottie and Jack, she still fought divorce from Owen.

She disapproved of the finality of it, and the admission of failure. She was ironically in her most active, creative and productive period, making most of her memorable films. Fairbanks had divorced Beth in 1918. Finally in 1919, Mary asked Owen for a divorce and he responded by threatening to shoot Fairbanks, 'that climbing monkey'.

Then he told Mary through his lawyers that he would divorce

her if she would give him a settlement. Charlotte went to their bank in Los Angeles with a bundle of bonds to cash in to pay Owen off. 'I was haunted by having had to pay for my freedom in hard-earned money; by the growing danger that the newspapers might get wind of the unsavory transaction; by the certainty that people would say I had bought off one husband to acquire another' said Mary.

Like many of her successors, the movie queen went to Nevada for a divorce. In those days the residency requirement was six months, and Mary claimed that she was a Nevada resident because Charlotte had bought a house on the Nevada side of Lake Tahoe and Mary had announced an intention to vacation there every year. Early in 1920 Mary and her mother and attorney Dennis F. O'Brien went to stay on a Nevada farm, to avoid the press. Even the chauffer who drove her around in a beat-up car rather than a limousine wasn't told who his passenger was and didn't recognize her. Neither did the judge who granted the decree on 1 March 1920, until she took the witness stand, removed her dark glasses, turned down the large collar of her fur coat and began pouring out the story of Owen's drinking and abuse, and her personal unhappiness. 'I was a wife and yet not a wife,' she said.

Once the reporters did catch up with her she told them she would wait a full year before marrying anyone else.

Mary may or may not have been pregnant by Owen Moore. There is a strong suspicion that she was, and it might have been during *A Call to Arms*, in 1910. In any case she fell off a horse in a movie during that period and could not bear children after the accident, and did not want them—at least this soon. Her career came first, family second, until after her retirement.

For a short time before her divorce Douglas had rented the thirty-six-room house belonging to Syl Spaulding of the sports equipment company, on Summit Drive in Beverly Hills. Doug was the first movie star to live in the community, which then was still given over mostly to beanfields but later became synonymous with motion picture glamor. There was only one house between the Spaulding place and the ocean seven miles distant, and Doug was fond of riding on horseback to the sea. He and Mary lived in the Spaulding house, which was later owned by George Hamilton in his Lynda Bird Johnson period (and the President's daughter visited him there), and Doug even talked of trying to buy it, but Mary objected, finding it 'too big and too brown'. Mary still kept up the appearance of living with her mother, but the potential for scandal had grown daily more dangerous.

Both Doug and Mary were afraid that their actions would finish their careers, even after they were married, but decided they would rather be together and comparatively poor than separate, rich and miserable. Still the industry was rocked by the gossip. Could the Queen really marry a prince (having divorced and bought off a previous husband) and still rule?

Doug bought a hunting lodge and the surrounding acreage across from the Spaulding house and had it converted into the first house he had ever owned. Rooms were added, and a swimming pool and well (for fresh water that the fledgling city of Beverly Hills couldn't supply) were dug, a wall went up around it, and soon the palace that was to take its name from the first syllables of its occupants' last names was ready. Would the world come to pay homage or throw stones? Douglas moved in alone.

On 28 March 1920 Doug held a formal dinner party at Pickfair for Mary, who arrived with Charlotte and was dressed in a formal white tulle dress edged in apple green with a green spray at the waist. The other guests included Robert Fairbanks and his wife, Doug's press agent Benny Zeidman, Carlyle Robinson, Marjorie Daw, one of Doug's leading ladies, and the Rev. Dr J. Whitcomb Brougher of Temple Baptist Church in Los Angeles.

Also in the house that evening was Los Angeles county marriage license clerk R. S. ('Cupid') Sparks, who had been summoned to do his job at home at night rather than at the courthouse to keep secrecy. He issued a marriage license to Gladys Mary

Smith Moore, twenty-six, and Douglas Elton Thomas Fairbanks, thirty-six, and stayed for dinner. Mary sat at the head of the table and Doug at her left, an arrangement he thereafter insisted upon at home. Even when they went out to dinner Mary would have to call the hostess in advance and request that she and Doug be together. At about ten-thirty the party adjourned to Brougher's house in Glendale and the Baptist minister married Mary and Doug in a double ring ceremony. Robert was best man, and Marjorie Daw the bridesmaid. Doug passed out seven-inch Havana cigars to the men, each in a souvenir box. Autographing one, Mary signed 'Mrs Douglas Fairbanks' for the first time. Lottie Pickford had called during the dinner, crying because she had heard a rumor of the ceremony and wasn't invited. Mary remembered that they hadn't told Charlie Chaplin, and Jack Pickford found out with the rest of the world three days later by reading it in the newspapers. Doug took his new bride home to Pickfair and gave her the house as a wedding present.

Mary at the time was making *Suds*, a complete turnabout, and as another Cockney, Amanda Afflick. *Suds* was a film version of the play *'Op o' me Thumb*, in which her co-star was a horse, Lavender. The girl and the horse work in a laundry, he spills a wagon-load of clothes during an uphill delivery and the laundry owner sells him for glue. The girl takes him to her room in a boarding-house and he breaks through the floor. Horse and girl are evicted and a high-born lady arrives in a Rolls, pays Amanda's fine to the policeman who has arrested her, and takes the horse to her country estate, where it grows so healthy it forgets the girl and bucks her off in a brook when she comes for a week-end visit.

The decrepit horse was procured for the part and put in Douglas Fairbanks's stable near United Artists. In the two weeks Lavender waited to go before the camera he gained sixty pounds and looked like a racehorse. Mary and a prop boy painted gray streaks on his sides to look like ribs sticking out, and painted bags under his eyes.

Mary went to the studio to resume *Suds* the day after her secret wedding, with her wedding ring covered by tape.

Another dinner party was held at Pickfair two days later, on 30 March, with the same guest list and a few selected members of the press. Mary and Doug greeted these newsmen at the door, with their rings and radiant smiles exposed. There was only one telephone at Pickfair at the time and it took a while, but the world read the news in the next morning's papers under banner headlines. And the world was delighted. The All-American boy had married the All-American girl, and the rest was so much celluloid on the studio floor. Logically, the clean-living symbol of health had won the world's sweetheart. And their fans in Europe were ready to share the honeymoon, whipped into a frenzy, to be sure, by Benny Zeidman and an advance band of press agents.

After the wedding Owen Moore challenged his divorce on the grounds of her insufficient Nevada residency and 'fraud and collusion' but on 31 May 1920 the Nevada Supreme Court upheld the decree. 'I am very, very happy, more happy than I can express,' said Mary from San Francisco on hearing the decision.

Doug mock-protested Mary's part of the public outpouring once they were married. 'This "America's Sweetheart" business must stop,' he said. 'She's *my* sweetheart. And if the world doesn't like it, they know the way to Beverly Hills. Hereafter, this loving business has got to be just screen stuff.'

# Chapter Ten

HEN *Suds* was finished in June of 1920, the Douglas Fairbankses sailed to Europe on the Lapland for a six-week delayed honeymoon, perhaps the most hectic, certainly one of the most public, in history. The crowds were so thick outside their suite at the Ritz-Carlton in New York before they sailed that they couldn't leave the hotel. Word was cabled ahead to England, France, Holland, Switzerland and Italy that Doug and Mary were coming. Radio-grams arrived on shipboard inviting the couple everywhere, and the royal welcome at Southampton featured roses being dropped from airplanes, also provided free especially to deliver Doug and Mary's mail.

They first stopped at the Ritz in London and crowds thousands deep waited all night to catch sight of their idols. Doug delighted in carrying Mary through the pressing throngs in London and later in Paris. They were besieged for autographs and to accept presents, mostly homemade. They ate little and slept less, saw almost nothing of Frances Marion and her husband Fred Thompson who were supposed to be their travelling companions. Doug and Mary escaped to the cottage of Lord Northcliffe on the Isle of Wight only to be discovered surrounded by hundreds of fans at dawn one morning.

These scenes were repeated on the Continent, and not really

discouraged by Mary and Doug. In Amsterdam the crowds were thinner than they had been in Piccadilly but every bit as enthusiastic. In Lugano, Switzerland and Venice, Florence and Rome the fans hailed 'Maria e Lampo' (for 'lightning', which is what Douglas was called in Italian). In Paris one afternoon they were afraid to leave their suite at the Hotel Crillon, the crowds were so thick, but they announced their intention of visiting Les Halles one morning and took satisfaction in stopping all traffic. In Venice, a separate gondola of photographers went along on the couple's moonlight ride, and Douglas scaled the side of an American warship in the Venice harbor.

Only in Germany, the so recent enemy, were they ignored, and neither Doug nor Mary could stand it. When no one recognized the famous foreigners in Wiesbaden and Cologne, they raced to France and Italy. 'No matter how demanding and exhausting the crowds were,' said Mary, 'they were infinitely preferable to being completely unknown, or if known, completely ignored.'

Word of the triumphal tour came back to New York through the newspapers, and America wasn't to be outdone in honoring the pair of cinema artists. When Doug and Mary returned to New York on the *Olympic* they were met by a crowd of fans headed by Jack Dempsey and two bus-loads from the Friars Club organized by Doug's former producer Brady, and J. J. Corbett. A motorcycle police escort kept the crowds from the Fairbankses' limousine, which was bedecked with American flags.

Back in Hollywood, Mary's first movie after the honeymoon was *The Love Light*, in which she played an Italian lighthouse keeper betrayed by a German spy. Frances Marion made her début as director in *The Love Light*, the only time Mary was directed by a woman.

An even unlikelier director was hired for Mary's next movie, *Through the Back Door*. Her brother Jack, without any observable inclination on his part, and certainly without experience, co-directed, with Alfred E. Green, this high-budget satire of the idle rich from a kitchen setting and viewpoint, with a script by Mary Pickford. The most memorable scene in *Through the Back Door* occurs when Mary, as the Belgian refugee maid, ties scrub brushes on her feet and skates over soapy water to clean the kitchen floor.

Jack Pickford, whose playboy life-style had always taken precedence over his career, was not in great demand as an actor at this time, and he had just come through a great personal sorrow. Jack had married the violet-eyed Olive Thomas, whom artist Harrison Fisher called 'the most beautiful woman in the world', in New York in late 1917 when Jack was twenty-one and Olive a year older. In a couple of years they separated but reconciled in 1920 and went to Paris on a second honeymoon. Returning to their hotel after a night partying in Montmartre, Olive swallowed a bottle of mercury bichloride, and died five days later—at the American Hospital. There was widespread suspicion of suicide but a police investigation found the death accidental and that she had intended to take a sleeping drug.

Mary's hiring Jack to be her director soon after Olive's death was an attempt to get him out of his depression and give his career a new direction. Charlotte, however, needed no such encouragement. She had long since given up her peripheral career as an actress and dedicated her life to making Mary, and hence the family, rich. She was in constant attendance on her daughter. 'If I'm not here at the studio,' Charlotte told a visitor to the set of *Through the Back Door*, 'I soon get a ring from Mary asking what's the trouble and I put on my hat and coat and come over to the studio.'

She was insistent on Mary's drinking several glasses of milk each day, preferably hot but not boiled, and she would stand over the maid in Mary's dressing room to make sure that this was done. Mary was twenty-eight at the time.

Charlotte installed herself in a director's chair next to her son

Jack on *Through the Back Door* (or next to whomever was direct-ing Mary's films) and made frequent suggestions on the actual production. Charlotte also attended United Artists meetings and her grand-daughter Gwynne, Mary's niece, maintained that for a time Charlotte ran the company. She certainly ran Mary. And Mary let her, partly to gain privacy and even more to let Charlotte do all the hard-nosed business negotiating while Mary smiled sweetly, feigned ignorance of details, and stayed in screen character. Frances Marion also held an important role in the female triumvirate surrounding the star (agent Cora Carrington Wilkenning was the third), and always on the prowl for better scripts, new talent and more money.

Doug was less prone than Mary to tamper with a successful formula, and the All-American boy he had been doing for five years in twenty-nine films was a character he genuinely liked and one that was close to his image of himself. Best of all he liked the stunts, and he liked the aura of success that surrounded him in his screen character and private life.

But soon after he and Mary returned from the European honeymoon, in the summer of 1920, Doug embarked on a picture that was to change his image somewhat and give him even greater success. *The Mark of Zorro*, a story of a dueling vigilante in the 1850s in California who cuts a 'Z' on the cheek or shoulder of his opponents, was taken from a story in a year-old popular pulp magazine, at the urging of Mary, and Robert Fairbanks (who with his older brother John had gone to work for Doug's own production company). That same year for the first time in polls, Doug turned up as the favorite male film star. Mary of course had long reigned as the female favorite. And Roscoe, 'Fatty' Arbuckle made a 1920 hit comedy movie in which he fantasized that he could be Douglas Fairbanks, too.

The little girl was absent from *Little Lord Fauntleroy*, which Mary made next, in 1921, from the Frances Hodgson Burnett story. But she was replaced by the irresistible combination of

Mary playing both the darling boy of 1885, complete with curls, and his doting mother, Dearest. The film had everything, the fantasy of a New York boy transported to late Victorian England to claim his unexpected title and estate, sets of Dorincourt castle as sumptuous and detailed as any ever constructed on a back lot, two virtuoso performances by Mary Pickford (just as effective as the mother as in the title role), and technical achievements surpassing even those of *Stella Maris*.

It was a ten-reel spectacular, Mary's first, and Rosher's camerawork was never finer. He built a special camera weighing a ton for the occasion, and even in viewing *Little Lord Fauntleroy* fifty years later it is impossible to find a line in the double exposures in which the boy and mother walk together, talk to each other or embrace. At one point he runs and jumps into her arms. There is one closeup in which the boy kisses Dearest on the cheek. 'It took us fifteen hours to prepare that shot lasting exactly three seconds on the screen,' Mary remembered.

Dearest appeared to be nine inches taller than her son, and six of those inches were achieved by specially-constructed platform shoes Mary could wear under a long dress, the remaining three by walking on a ramp whenever she was to shoot a scene of herself with her son.

Jack Pickford and Alfred Green again combined to direct *Little Lord Fauntleroy*, but Mary's hand was evident everywhere in the conception and painstaking execution. There are unforgettable long shots of the castle and shadowy interiors perfectly framing the scenes between the nervous, obedient boy and his crusty uncle, the old earl who gradually warms to his new heir. The unpolemical social protest is in the form of scenes showing the shabby conditions of serfs living on the castle grounds, and in the boy's efforts to better their lot.

The phenomenal popularity of *Zorro* led Doug to produce and star in another costume drama, his own favorite childhood story, *The Three Musketeers*. He played his fictional ideal, D'Artagnan.

Turning thirty-eight, he grew a mustache for the D'Artagnan part and kept it the rest of his life. No expense was spared in the production, now that *Zorro* had overcome the stigma previously attached to costume epics. An original music score was commissioned—to be given to the piano player in each individual movie house—and the picture's principals, who included Adolph Menjou, were taught fencing by the foremost teacher in the world. On its release in 1921, *The Three Musketeers* was acclaimed by the critics (as *Zorro* had not been) as well as by the public, and it made Douglas almost as wealthy as his wife, temporarily, until he spent his earnings on lavish presents, travel and clothes.

Mary and Doug maintained their own separate production companies within the United Artists framework. He paid himself $10,000 weekly and she paid herself the same, both adding a percentage of the profits to this sum. In 1922 they built the Pickford-Fairbanks studio on Santa Monica Boulevard in Hollywood. Mary ordered a six-room bungalow, which she furnished with three cages full of canaries.

Douglas had a dressing room, pool, gymnasium and steam bath added onto his offices. A permanent masseur was in residence and Doug's eclectic group of friends were frequently entertained in this set-up at the end of a day's shooting. The athletes of the world, whatever their particular sport, also congregated in the movie hero's gym. He enjoyed their success and learning from them. They enjoyed his success and having their pictures taken with him. 'Fairbanks was a dynamic person who lived for good health,' said Lillian Gish. 'He drank about two glasses of champagne a year. He and Chaplin trained themselves to stay fit. In those days we were really all health-minded.'

Apart from United Artists meetings, Mary and Doug did not actually work *together*, but not for the lack of opportunity. The Victor Talking Machine Company, for one, offered them $20,000 to make a spoken word recording together. He was for it, but Mary argued against it and the idea was dropped.

'I know what a phonograph record can be like, once you get sick of it,' she said. 'People follow us in the street now, and mob us at theaters, but if they have that phonograph record at home, and children, maybe, who like to play it over and over, they might get sick of the whole thing and us, too.'

United Artists had really been Mary's idea, albeit one that Doug promoted with his usual vigor and talked others into. She had dominated the meetings from prior to its formation and would for the next thirty years. Her mother was a vice-president of the corporation at first, although she was ousted later, at Doug's intervention, because she had allegedly tried to prevent the payment of $150,000 to Owen Moore. This would have prevented the divorce which left Mary free to marry Doug.

Doug was sometimes prone to go for long walks during the United Artists meetings and often couldn't resist antics like climbing back in through a window, and he seldom spoke. The prevailing impression was that Mary was the business brain of the outfit, an impression furthered by Doug's extravagance and indifference to a picture's budget and her parsimony, and cash register mentality. However, he did invest such earnings as he didn't spend in fast-rising real estate and bank stocks and became director of the Federal Trust and Savings Bank of Hollywood.

Joseph Schenk, whom Doug got into the chairmanship of United Artists, said of Doug 'this fellow knows more about making pictures than all the rest of us put together', and most of his contemporaries valued and acted upon his infrequent suggestions, often made after returning from the mid-meeting walk.

Doug also travelled a great deal on behalf of the company (and it was more than just an excuse for a trip), setting up United Artists offices in major foreign capitals. He slowed his own production pace considerably in the 1920s and tried to take a European trip after every film, bearing news of the film world to king and movie exhibitor alike. ('How's Fatty Arbuckle?' the

Spanish King asked Doug in Madrid at a court presentation Doug had worried over.)

'Douglas always gave Mary credit for his success,' said Lillian Gish. ' "Mary made me go out and get bigger stories, better cameramen and directors," he said. I think he was right. She had greater vision for him than she did for herself.'

In 1922, Mary returned to her favorite *Tess of the Storm Country*, with social protest again evident. As before, Mary organizes poor squatters against wealthy landlords who would dispossess them. In every way the 1922 version was a superior film. '*Tess* was the only picture I ever wanted to do over,' Mary said. 'I always liked the character.'

\* \* \*

Doug went on to make *Robin Hood* an even bigger production than *The Three Musketeers*, and the most expensive and exacting of all his films, budgeted at $1 million and going way over that, with its ninety-foot high castle set, the largest constructed for any movie up to that time. Douglas became an expert archer for the part, and spared no expense on cast and costumes. Fortunately on release it broke records at the box-office as well. And it is still accounted by critics as Douglas Fairbanks's best film, with only 1927's *The Thief of Bagdad* a close second.

\* \* \*

Mary attempted two more spectaculars, both with rather disastrous results. But she was determined to reassert herself as an actress rather than coast by on a character. She even thought of cutting off the golden curls, but Charlotte wouldn't hear of that. The next best thing to do was get a first-rate adult—and preferably modern—story to do and make it as successful as her child pictures, a task made even more difficult by the wide enthusiasm for *Little Lord Fauntleroy*.

In 1922's story of *Dorothy Vernon of Haddon Hall*, Mary thought she had the key to her freedom. Although the setting of the historical drama was Elizabethan England, Mary saw Dorothy as a contemporary woman. 'It wedded together yesterday and today,' she said later of the movie. 'Against the feudal background of Elizabeth's court, it offered the portrayal of a modern-minded girl.'

Mary engaged Ernst Lubitsch, the celebrated German director, to come to Hollywood for the first time and direct her in *Dorothy*, which he had read in German and agreed to. Mary described the events following his arrival to Kevin Brownlow in a London interview in 1965, and he published them in *The Parade's Gone By*.

After Lubitsch arrived in Hollywood, he declined to do *Dorothy Vernon*. At a conference in her newly-painted bungalow on the lot, which Lubitsch soiled with fingers greasy from the German-fried potatoes that were his staple food, he explained in his halting English what was wrong: 'Der iss too many qveens and not enough qveens.' What he meant was that the story of Queen Elizabeth and Mary, Queen of Scots would overwhelm that of Dorothy, and that the script couldn't be refocused on just the queens because there wasn't enough dialogue for them to do. Lubitsch turned out to be right, and when *Dorothy* was finally made two years later, with Neilan directing, Estelle Taylor as Mary, Queen of Scots stole the picture, the first and only time in a Pickford feature that a supporting player had outshone the star.

But meantime there was Lubitsch in Hollywood, his and Mrs Lubitsch's expenses paid by Mary, an 'idle genius', she called him. She quickly came up with another story, *Rosita*, for him to direct. The filming and the result were a total disaster. Mary called it her 'worst picture, bar none, that I ever made', and said it was the one she would never allow to be shown. Mary played a grown-up

127

guitar-strumming Spanish streetsinger in what was supposed to be a love story. Mary and Lubitsch fought throughout and the atmosphere on the set wasn't improved by the cast and crew's constant laughter at the expense of the director's limited English vocabulary and unlimited accent. Most remembered of his gaffes was when he announced 'Dis is de scene vere Miss Pickford goes mit de *backside* to the altar', meaning 'back'.

'Lubitsch was a frustrated actor, he had to act out everything . . . He was a very uninspired director. He was a director of doors,' she said. 'He was a good man's director, good for Emil Jannings and people like that. But for me he was terrible.' She pulled rank as producer and forced him into a temper tantrum leading to his resignation from Pickford after *Rosita*, although he stayed on in Hollywood and achieved great acclaim.

*Rosita* and *Dorothy Vernon* had both been expensive to produce and were consequently given high-priced reserved seat showings, which didn't help their popularity. *Dorothy* was offered at $2 a ticket at the Criterion Theater in New York, where it premièred 6 May 1924.

In March of that year Mary had returned to Toronto, and visited her birthplace. In the summer of 1924, after *Dorothy* had opened, she and Douglas went back to Europe and were presented to the Kings and Queens of Spain and Norway. The adulatory public turned out again, as they would on subsequent trips. Douglas had always been an inveterate traveller and was to become even more so. Mary, who had been working all her life, hadn't been anywhere compared to Doug and looked forward to these trips as a way of learning, and expanding her limited horizons.

Mary considered the critical indifference to and disastrous returns of *Rosita* and *Dorothy Vernon* her 'costly and embarrassing' punishment for having tried to grow up on the screen, and in 1925 she was ready again to listen to her mother and her public. *Photoplay* magazine ran a piece in 1925, when Mary was over thirty-two, in which she asked her public to name the parts they would like to see her play in future movies. Twenty thousand replies came back and the clear favorite was *Cinderella*, even though she had already done it for IMP. The other answers were hardly encouraging to a woman wanting to be allowed to be an adult: *Anne of Green Gables* (which Mary Miles Minter had already done), *Alice in Wonderland*, *Heidi*. A prize was awarded to the woman who wrote pleading Mary not to abandon 'an illusion that there are such little girls and that we have one before us: an illusion that you are a little girl in spite of the fact we know you are a grown-up woman'.

You couldn't argue with an outpouring like that, even though most of the rest of the world was embroiled in 'the Roaring Twenties', bobbed hair, crazy dances, knee-length skirts, rolled stockings and other forms of post-war and pre-crash hysteria. So obediently, Mary plunged into one last little girl role: *Little Annie Rooney*, taken from the song of the same name. She was twelve, a motherless slum child devoted to her policeman father who is killed on duty on his birthday.

Gwynne, who was living with Mary and Douglas at Pickfair at the time, remembers her aunt coming home and telling about the trouble she had getting the other slum kids to fight with her until she started sticking them with pins. 'They were real little kids, and she was the head of the studio, they just wouldn't fight her,' said Gwynne. Because the story was somewhat more tragic than the previous little-girl roles ('Get out the rubber boots, Mary has got to cry,' shouted the director, William Beaudine, one day) and because she was older and felt trapped *Annie* was more difficult for Mary to stay into. Her pains were worth it, however, and the picture was another smash success, restoring her to top popularity and recouping the losses of 1923 and '24.

In the spring of 1925 a plot to kidnap Mary Pickford was uncovered, thanks to one of the four conspirators telling the police in advance. The plan called for sand-bagging the chauffer of the small two-seated custom-built 1924 Rolls-Royce roadster in which Mary rode to and from the studio, blindfolding and gagging the actress and taking her to a hideout in the Santa Monica Mountains, and then demanding $100,000, as ransom. The four men also hoped to capture child star Jackie Coogan, E. L. Doheny III of the socially prominent oil and banking family, and movie star Pola Negri.

The police, even knowing these plans, had to catch the kidnappers in the act, and so followed them for weeks before they made a move. Mary was asked to keep her regular schedule of going to and from work, and her stand-in, serving as decoy, took frequent rides in the Rolls, whose design Douglas had borrowed from the Prince of Wales, later King Edward VIII. A bodyguard was added to the set of *Little Annie Rooney* and Mary and Douglas armed themselves with a Colt .45 each. Finally apprehended without kidnapping anybody, the three men, a butcher, a car salesman and a delivery man for Wells Fargo, were sentenced to from ten to fifty years at San Quentin. But from then on, Pickfair was guarded by round-the-clock watchmen and watchdogs.

In April 1926 Mary and Douglas, accompanied by Charlotte, sailed to Europe on the *Conte Biancamano*. They were presented onstage at the Capitol Theater in Berlin on 4 May, during an engagement of *Little Annie Rooney*, and a German audience sang 'The Star-Spangled Banner' for the first time since World War I. A week later they were received by *Il Duce*, Benito Mussolini at the Chigi Palace in Rome. Mary gave the dictator her autograph book to sign (she had started the practice with royalty, which in particular fascinated her and Douglas both) and he also presented them with signed photographs and a rose for Mary. The autograph book, the photographs and even the rose are carefully preserved at Pickfair today.

In July they went to Russia and 25,000 Soviet fans met them at the Moscow railway station. Mobs also greeted them at Warsaw, Mary 'Marushka', especially. They planned to continue on around the world, but Charlotte took sick and so in August they returned to America.

\*     \*     \*

Mary's next part was as an older adolescent of fifteen, Mama Mollie in *Sparrows*, promoted as 'Mary Pickford's Christmas gift to everyone whose heart is young'. The Christmas was 1926, Mary was nearing thirty-four and this was to be her last silent spectacular, with scenic design rivalling *Little Lord Fauntleroy* and *Dorothy Vernon of Haddon Hall*. The setting was a baby farm in a southern alligator-infested swamp, and it was constructed complete with alligators, house, barn and quick-sand on the Pickford lot in Hollywood. Mary is the only buffer between the younger orphans and the hateful farmer who runs the evil place.

*Sparrows* is both melodrama and thriller, a combination more acceptable in its day than forty-years later, when it is outstanding for its visual effects alone. Rosher and his camera, with the necessary help of two assistants, were at work, most notably in a scene where Mary as Mama Mollie holds a dying infant as the apparition of Jesus standing in an orchard walks through a wall of the barn, where the children are huddled, to take the dead child away, and in the sequence in which Mollie leads the children in an escape across the swamp, carrying a baby on her back within inches of snapping alligator jaws.

Director William Beaudine and Rosher shot the scene straight out, with real alligators in a pool and a real baby on Mary's back. Both Gwynne and Mary remember Douglas Fairbanks being livid when he discovered this on a visit to the set one day. Mary as producer could have stopped it, and used a double exposure as Douglas suggested, but she was as interested in realism as her director and cameraman. And after six rehearsals, completed before Douglas arrived, she decided to shoot the scene live. But she never forgave Beaudine for endangering her and especially the baby and she never employed him again.

*Sparrows* made money but didn't gain the wide acceptance of the more positive juvenile films, and Mary thought in retrospect that it had been too dramatic, with no comic relief. At any rate it was the end of an era, a golden one. Next time out Mary Pickford was all grown up, a girl-friend and future wife.

Mary had been gradually slowing down the pace of her acting in films, as United Artists administration, her marriage and increasingly active social life took more of her time. From making eight feature films in 1915 and a total of thirty-nine between 1913–20, she dropped down to two each year in 1921 and 1922, to one a year from 1923–6 inclusive.

As soon as she had achieved total control of production, she had insisted on perfection in acting, stories and technology, and that took time. Since 1919 she had set standards for the entire film industry, and made at least a million dollars a year as actor-producer doing it.

There were times, from 1916 to 1926 when she so successfully lived the character of the little girl she couldn't give it up, and Zukor recalled the time when she was refused admission to one of her own films because she looked too little and too young. 'They told her to get an adult to go in with her,' he said. And there were times when she gave herself away. During the making of *Pollyanna*, a girl told her mother that Mary wasn't a real little girl because she had long fingernails. They were instantly snipped down to child-length.

'I hadn't any "methods" of acting,' she said. 'It was easy for me to act the part of a child because I adored children. I forgot I was grown up. I would transform myself into a child for the time being and act as she would act under similar circumstances. That was the way I did *The Poor Little Rich Girl*. While I was playing that part I *was* the poor little rich girl, suffering all of her unsatisfied yearnings for the things that money couldn't buy. During a picture I didn't leave the character at the studio, I took it home with me. I lived my parts.'

On 'the kerosene circuit' of one-night stands, 1900–1.

(*top*) As *Mistress Nell*, 1915. (*bottom*) Mary was the first actress to fly in a moin 1915's *A Girl of Yesterday*, with co-stars Glenn L. Martin and the single plane.

n America entered World War I, Mary, Douglas Fairbanks, Charlie Chaplin
others toured the country on behalf of War Bonds. Here she exhorts a crowd
its patriotic duty: 'I'm only five feet tall, but every inch of me is fighting
rican!' 1917.

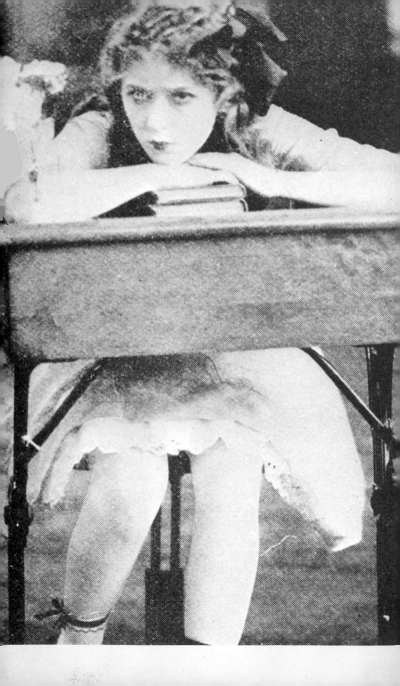

The end of Rebecca's circus career.

# MARY PICKFORD
in
# REBECCA OF
# SUNNYBROOK FARM
FROM THE PLAY BY KATE DOUGLAS WIGGIN AND CHARLOTTE THOMPSON
SCENARIO BY FRANCES MARION · DIRECTED BY MARSHALL NEILAN
PRESENTED BY
ARTCRAFT PICTURES CORPORATION

(*left*) The incorrigible schoolgirl scamp of perhaps her best-known film of all, *Rebecca of Sunnybrook Farm*, 1917.

(*above*) A billboard for 'America's Sweetheart's' biggest success to date, 1917.

(*top*) Douglas and Mary in the ill-fated talkie (his and Shakespeare's first), *The Taming of the Shrew*, 1929; (*bottom*) The Best Actress Oscar for *Coquette*, 1929, the first for a talking picture.

A screen queen retires at the top, 1933.

At sixty-three she was still Queen of Hollywood and Pickfair, and its leaf-strewn lawn. *Loomis Dean for LIFE*, 1956.

Mary's days at the studio were long and arduous. She was usually up at five, at the studio by six. She took a French teacher in the back of her limousine with her on trips to the studio and at odd moments on the set and learned to speak a stilted literary French with a flawless accent. It took three hours to wash her hair, set it and make up her face.

Colleen Moore recalled Mary's telling her about the problem of upkeeping her famous curls on location in high humidity. Mary's straight hair 'would start to droop after a while,' Miss Moore wrote in her autobiography, 'so shooting would stop, Mary would put her hair up in curlers and rags, and then the whole company would just sit there for an hour while it dried, so she could go before the camera once again.'

Filming began at nine and might finish by five-thirty, but Mary had to sign checks and give orders for the next day, view dailies from the day before, which didn't allow her to get home before between eight and nine p.m. The fabled parties at Pickfair were on week-ends and between films. On work nights there was dinner and perhaps a viewing of somebody else's movie on projection equipment like Woodrow Wilson had installed in the White House. Doug and Mary had Hollywood's first private screening room, and the second in the nation. Some nights both Doug and Mary worked so hard and long at the studio that they had to eat dinner in costume before falling into bed exhausted. Gwynne remembered more than one occasion on which she dined with Little Lord Fauntleroy and D'Artagnan.

Between shots on the set she would greet fans, distinguished visitors like President and Mrs Coolidge and overseas heads of state, see reporters and attend to correspondence. It was understandable she should want to ease off.

During this period Mary bought up as many of her old negatives as she could, including eighty Biograph short films, to protect herself from reissues. In later years she forbade screenings of her work on the grounds that people of later generations would laugh at her and her friends and for a long time planned that the negatives be destroyed on her death. Happily, she was talked out of it by Lillian Gish and others.

In 1926 she said, 'We of the pictures are of the moment only. I am content to bring enjoyment to the great multitude of picture-goers of today. I would rather live in their memories than in films which, when resurrected after many years, would seem crude and old-fashioned in comparison with pictures of a later period of technical development.'

# Chapter Eleven

IN private life Doug and Mary were always together for the first eight years of their marriage. And their public appearances, which they both took with great seriousness, were uncountable. The Hollywood première of any picture didn't start until Doug and Mary were in their seats. Together and separately they laid cornerstones, opened fairs, reviewed parades, and presided at long dinners, 'Mary conducting herself with the self-abnegation of Queen Mary of Britain,' wrote Allene Talmey in 1927.

'Mary Pickford and Douglas Fairbanks were our undisputed leaders,' said Colleen Moore.

Along with Louis B. Mayer, an active member and supporter of the Republican party, and Harold Lloyd, a Shriner and member of the Los Angeles Chamber of Commerce, Mary was one of the few in the movie colony who participated in the organizations and activities of the outside world. Even before their marriage, Mary had started on her well-known charity work by being patron of the Los Angeles Orphans' Asylum, a Catholic institution she visited regularly, and gave benefits for and her own money to.

At home at Pickfair, while Mary and Douglas had fourteen live-in servants, life could be simple if there were no guests in residence. A duke and duchess and retinue of seventeen accepted a casual invitation to spend a few days at Pickfair and stayed for months, displacing Charlie Chaplin from his house next door and causing future invitations to be a bit more specific. With no one but Douglas and Gwynne and the servants around, Mary would go without makeup and with her famous hair up or pulled back. The curls still took an hour's ironmongery every night before bed and a vegetable rinse every third or fourth daily shampoo at the studio to keep their blonde highlights.

Gwynne had come to Pickfair after a bitter courtroom battle involving her mother Lottie and Charlotte, Doug and Mary. Mary, the most vocal of the four, pleaded, in front of the child, that Lottie was an unfit mother, so successfully that Gwynne was made a ward of both Charlotte—' "Mama Pickford," she hated to be called "grandma", ' said Gwynne—and Douglas.

Lottie, four times married, was called by her friends 'madcap', but her detractors came right out and said she was wild. She had four bad marriages and Gwynne was the product of the first, to a man named Rupp. Gwynne spent more time at Pickfair than at her grandmother's, adored her Uncle Douglas and grew very close to her Aunt Mary, after she overcame Mary's treatment of Lottie, and particularly after Lottie's death.

'I could have changed my name to Fairbanks legally, but decided to keep Pickford,' Gwynne recalled. However she did live with her grandmother part of the time and remembers sitting on the front porch of Charlotte's house in Beverly Hills on the lookout for Mary. Gwynne was to warn Charlotte, a heavy drinker, of Aunt Mary's approach, so Charlotte could hide all evidence of her weakness.

In those days Mary didn't drink much and her and Doug's indifference to alcohol led to rather poorer brands of alcohol being served at the otherwise elegant Pickfair. The drinks at Doug and Mary's for everyday use were something of a local joke, although Doug installed an authentic mahogany California Gold-rush period saloon bar from Placer County, California for informal entertaining, and the best imported wines and whiskies were provided by the host and hostess for important special guests. But on at-home nights, cups of Ovaltine or a dish of fruit were passed around by the butler to signal the end of another Pickfair dinner for family and close friends like Lillian Gish, Frances Marion, Jack Pickford, and, rarely, Douglas Fairbanks Jr.

Charlie Chaplin, who lived nearby, often joined Mary and Doug at the Pickfair dining room table, mostly because he loved their company and they his. Charlie's beginnings in London's East End had been even poorer than Mary's in Toronto and his climb to the top even tougher. But if Mary and Charlie were in some ways frugal, Douglas made up for both of them with his expensive hospitality and generosity.

Although Chaplin was widely known for his thriftiness, he was also known for his loyalty to his employees, even keeping his studio staff on his payroll all year round, not just when they were actually making a film. But seeing his inactive studio carpenters sitting around, Chaplin decided to put them to work building his home next door to Pickfair. However, set-builders used to making scenery to be torn down were not a good choice to construct a permanent dwelling and Chaplin's friends secretly called his house Breakway House, because it kept falling apart.

Once Mary, Douglas and Charlie were seated around the Pickfair swimming pool when Chaplin, fully clothed, jumped into the pool shouting 'I am an atheist. If there is a God, let Him save me.' Chaplin was gasping and bubbling and going down for the third time when Fairbanks, also completely dressed, jumped in and rescued him. Mary, however, was racing around the pool screaming 'Let the heathen drown.'

*     *     *

Mary and the other girls already successful in the movies—including Loretta Young, Ann Harding, Billie Dove, Ruby Keeler

—formed a club for the express purpose of helping newer actresses get jobs. Mary was named honorary president of the group, called Our Club, which turned out to be more of an excuse for meeting at each other's houses for hot chocolate hen parties than for fostering new talent. But, just in case, Mary set down her 'Ten Film Commandments for would-be movie actresses:

1 Know some other vocation to fall back on.
2 Have money enough to last a year.
3 See if you have talent.
4 Gain some stage experience.
5 Get professional experience if possible.
6 Bring as many photographs as possible.
7 Bring a large and diversified wardrobe.
8 Try to get a screen test.
9 Be sincere and ambitious.
10 Success in the motion pictures can only be gained in the same manner as other businesses.'

\* \* \*

Douglas took the movies seriously in some ways, enough so that L. B. Mayer and others backed him to be president of the Motion Picture Academy on its founding in 1927 and, once elected, he worked hard to establish standards that are still followed today. Mary Astor, who starred with him in 1925's *Don Q, Son of Zorro*, recalled that working with him 'was kind of a pleasant social event'. She wrote in *A Life on Film*:

'There was always somebody visiting the sets, and work was interrupted to show people around and make them feel like an audience while we did a scene for them. I was introduced to Sir This and Lady That and important people of all kinds. Everybody visited Doug's set. And they were always photographed with

Doug, given tea or lunch. It was very pleasant. It was nice to get paid for—and had little to do with acting.'

Douglas Fairbanks fed the film myth even in private life. Once when Gilbert Miller, the theater magnate, invited him to a skeet shoot Doug refused to fire a gun 'with all these people here; the legend is I never miss'.

Since infancy Doug had had a deeply tannable complexion. In the 1920s his dark coloring almost singlehandedly started America's men on the fad of suntanning as an outward symbol of vitality and good health.

There was one physical characteristic that Doug couldn't do anything about—his height. He stood five-foot-eight, although on screen he seemed larger. But every other aspect of his body was subject to the most rigorous discipline. Doug worried about becoming fat and was obsessed with keeping his youth. He would diet assiduously but then occasionally go on food orgies, usually on week-ends.

On Sunday mornings he sometimes took his week-end guests horseback riding in the hills and then provided a lumberjack breakfast served up by the cook and butler from Pickfair, who had been dispatched earlier by station wagon. The guests were allowed to ride back to the house in cars, leaving their horses to the Fairbanks studio grooms.

Fairbanks's personal vanity was well known. From his forty suits in four closets each morning he would select—with Mary's help—the right outfit, complete to shirt, tie and socks, only to go straight to the studio and change into old white flannels and an open shirt. He had two more closets in his studio dressing room, full of more suits and accessories. Mary had to shut his closet doors, which he left hanging open, when visitors came in.

Despite the best efforts of the Fairbanks publicity machine to prove the opposite, Douglas was not even vaguely paternal, and for most of his life he was indifferent to his young son and namesake, who was nine when his father divorced his mother to marry the famous Mary Pickford. Beth Sully Fairbanks did all she could to keep Doug Jr from any knowledge of the possible scandal involved, and to keep his (albeit distant) admiration of Doug Sr intact.

The money Beth had received from Doug in the divorce settlement was lost in careless investments by 1923, and even her father, the former cotton king, was broke and living off this settlement, along with his former dependents. Beth and Doug Jr lived in a Paris pension where it was possible to remain genteel on less money than in America. He was then thirteen, six feet-one, his full adult height, and looked and acted older.

An opportunist producer offered Doug Jr a starring movie role, which Beth accepted in his behalf. When Doug heard about it (in a brutal face-to-face confrontation in Paris) he suspected first that the reason was money (which Doug Jr denied), and second that his son wanted an easy shot at fame by trading on his father's name. The boy in the discussion brought up his father's neglect, and the man was angry and hurt enough to disinherit and disown his son. Doug even threatened to fight Doug Jr's attempts to crack the movie industry. 'There's only one Fairbanks,' he snapped at one producer who cast Doug Jr.

*Stephen Steps Out* was the first Douglas Fairbanks Jr film, produced in Hollywood and released in 1923, the same year as his father's *The Thief of Bagdad*. *Stephen* flopped badly, Doug felt vindicated and Doug Jr returned to Paris.

In 1924 Doug Jr came back to California with a new contract, which with the sale of his mother's jewelry kept his side of the family going for a little longer. He and his father effected a partial rapprochement, and even worked out together at the Pickford–Fairbanks studio gym. But he was seldom invited to Pickfair, although he and Mary liked each other and became close friends. Doug Sr just didn't want a living reminder in his own home that he was middle aged, old enough to have an offspring working for a living.

Doug Jr also had to contend both with exploitation and belittlement in his professional career. He avoided roles similar to his father's romantic adventurers and developed his private personality and interests in different directions from the senior Fairbanks. He published short stories and articles together with his own drawings, of which his father was extremely proud.

Junior got his first real break in late 1925, with a part in Samuel Goldwyn's *Stella Dallas*, starring Ronald Coleman, Belle Bennett, Lois Moran and Jean Hersholt. Charlie Chaplin enthusiastically praised the 'sixteen-year-old's success as a young screen lover (looking a few years older).

After this he turned to the stage, did two amateur productions at the writers' club, and the title part in *Young Woodley* in downtown Los Angeles for six weeks and then in San Francisco. Mary and Doug sat in the opening night audience at the Majestic Theater in Los Angeles. One critic called Doug Jr 'a youngster who promises to go farther on stage than his sire ever did', and his toughest and most important critic whispered to his wife Mary Pickford during the performance, 'He really can act'.

Another member of that first-night audience was Joan Crawford, who pronounced Douglas Fairbanks Jr 'sensitive, colorful, a great talent'. She wrote him a fan letter and they soon were a gossip column item, despite the difference in their ages and backgrounds (she was a poor girl from San Antonio and Kansas City, who had waitressed and washed dishes to stay alive, and started in show business in a New York night club chorus).

Very tentatively and with noticeable formality Doug and his son re-established some rapport, always with the encouragement of Mary, who'd make a point of leaving the room whenever the two Douglases seemed to be starting a conversation. But the younger Doug Fairbanks would very rarely be invited to swim in the Pickfair pool with Gwynne and the four Fairbanks girl cousins, all of whom spent more time at the house than he.

Even more rarely he would be invited to dinner, and about once a year he had the supreme privilege of being asked to stay for a screening and then overnight. Doug Jr would enlist his Uncle Robert to intercede with Douglas to get himself invited to Pickfair for Sunday afternoons and then when he went he would try to wangle a suggestion that he stay to supper, which was rarely taken up. Junior recalled that 'an invitation to Pickfair was an event, issued some days ahead, worked up to, involving special combing of the hair and very careful selection of what I was to wear, like a child going off to a party'.

Mary, who was still making Doug Jr welcome at Pickfair when he was in California forty years after his father had left home, described the relationship between the two men thus: 'Senior was so much of a little boy himself I don't think he felt like a father. He was a very shy person, he didn't like to show affection or emotion. That's not unique in men, even in women. But towards the end they were very, very close, probably closer than he was to any man, including Robert. There was this sense of misunderstanding between them, augmented undoubtedly by the greed of certain people that forced his son into a position that he didn't think was right. He felt at the time that the boy was being exploited, to his injury and hurt and the detriment of his father. When that was over, I know positively he was very proud of him.'

Just by being his father's son—whatever the status of their relations at any given moment—Doug Jr was introduced to the world's accomplished, and royal and noble, and many persons attempted to get to Mary and Doug through his son, assuming he was much closer to them than was the case. A few in Hollywood knew the sad truth. Gloria Swanson was one of them, and she conspired to have him at one of her parties dressed and working as a footman, complete with wig and breeches.

As Doug Jr's romance with Joan Crawford got serious Doug Sr pleaded with his ex-wife Beth to intercede to break it up.

Doug Jr and Joan would visit Jesse Lasky at his beach house only 200 yards or so from Doug and Mary's but they almost never walked down the beach in their direction.

Joan had already become an authentic star with *Our Dancing Daughters* in which she played a flapper with bobbed hair and a propensity for gin. He was nineteen and struggling to find an identity. Despite parental opposition, Doug Jr announced his intention to marry her.

The wedding was deliberately held 3,000 miles from his chilly father and step-mother at Pickfair, at St Malachy's, the actors' Catholic Church in the Broadway theater district of New York, in June 1929. Doug at the last minute wired his good wishes.

Joan's studio, MGM, got Doug Jr on loan out to do a sequel with her of *Our Dancing Daughters* called *Our Modern Maidens*. It was their only picture together and an obvious attempt to exploit the marriage.

'It was always Mary who tried to patch up any estrangement between myself and my father,' Douglas Fairbanks Jr recalled. 'And my Uncle Robert always successfully pled my cause at Pickfair. If my father forgot a birthday or Christmas, which he often did, I'd get invited up to dinner, and maybe to see a film. I was even asked often to bring a girl friend. I was terribly precocious and always very upset if I heard of a good party at Pickfair I hadn't been asked to.

'I don't recall any opposition from Mary to my marrying Joan Crawford. I do recall my father being very opposed. I think he thought she was on the toughie side. But more than that I was only nineteen and he would rather I had been in a university. It was also partly that it was a highly publicized romance and partly that with our youthful exuberance we were overly affectionate in public. This sort of behavior embarrassed him. Despite his recent divorce and all that, he had a curiously Victorian morality, and his behavior in polite company was quite formal. There was very little opposition to her per se, it was mostly against the idea of my being married to anyone, and to my having been heavily, publicly and spectacularly engaged to a movie star.'

In the 1920s there was a good deal of competition among the woman stars in party-giving and other at-home entertainment, even as there was in business.

'There was only one group then and we all belonged to it,' said Mary. 'Later there were lots of little groups feuding with each other.'

So even Gloria Swanson and Mary were in the same set when it came to entertaining, despite their antipathy for one another. But nobody could compete with Mary and her regal appointments and royal-flush guest lists. And the only one who had the money at her disposal to even attempt to equal the Pickfair parties was Marion Davies, who with her lover, William Randolph Hearst, could send a train from San Simeon for the week-end guests from Los Angeles 175 miles away, or hire the whole Ambassador Hotel for her do's if she chose to.

Mary had a solid gold dinner service, a footman behind every chair and crystal placecard holders and, while Pickfair didn't look remotely like a medieval palace, it was run like one in those days, and the dinners there were lavish. Gwynne remembered that the dining room table was always set for twelve even if just three of them were at home or if twenty were expected, in which case additional chairs and place settings would be provided just before dinner was served.

Other stars like Gloria, 'never more than two bucks a head in her best days', according to Adela Rogers St John, the writer, gave slightly less elegant parties but they tended to be a lot more fun than the splashily elegant ones at the Fairbanks place. Gloria was a close friend of Marion's but not of Mary's, her partner at United Artists, and she did much more entertaining when she returned to Hollywood as the Marquise de La Falaise de Coudray, than she had before.

Mary in fact had few friends, almost no girl friends, except her mother and Frances Marion. As Mrs St John, a contemporary, recalled it: 'Mary was always the queen up there on the hill; she was still the phantom, the legend. I don't know whether it's true Douglas Fairbanks wanted to put a wall around Beverly Hills to keep the mortals out. But I do know that the fence he did put around Pickfair should have satisfied him. Anyway you never quite felt that Mary Pickford was human. There was a psychological wall around her and her circle, if not a concrete one.'

A typical formal dinner for a dozen at Pickfair might include the King and Queen of Siam, Babe Ruth, a well-known publisher, opera singer, feminist, the Duke and Duchess of Alba, an inventor or a violinist. Any celebrity, particularly royalty or athletes, was fair game for Douglas, whether he knew them previously or not. And celebrities visiting Los Angeles always wheedled invitations to Pickfair, and a dinner or a whole week-end soon became an important part of any distinguished visitor's stay in the Hollywood area.

'In the 1920s whenever any foreign notables came to the United States, the first place they wanted to go was Hollywood, and the three people in America they most wanted to see were Mary Pickford, Douglas Fairbanks and Charlie Chaplin,' Colleen Moore recalled. 'The guest list at Pickfair reads like a Who's Who of the World. The Crown Prince of Japan, Alfonso XIII, ex-King of Spain, Marconi, Lindbergh, Einstein, Amelia Earhart, Sir Austen Chamberlain, Crown Princess Frederica of Prussia, the glamorous Lord and Lady Mountbatten, who spent part of their honeymoon visiting Pickfair. The great authors, painters, politicians, all found their way to the hill.'

'I go to Europe to sit on the veranda of the world,' Fairbanks once said.

'Doug goes to Europe each year to book his royal visitors for the coming year,' said a contemporary, closer to the truth. Those peripheral types in the industry who were never invited to Pickfair sneeringly referred to it as 'Buckingham Palace'.

On informal nights the guest list was likelier to include any of Douglas's assorted friends and business associates, from his two brothers to his trainer, and of course Chaplin and Tom Geraghty, a well-known newspaper and magazine writer Douglas hired ostensibly to doctor scripts. But it was really Geraghty's sense of humor and ingenious imagination for practical jokes that endeared him to Douglas. Geraghty travelled with Fairbanks all over for years, at the expense of his wife and four children. Mary, who merely endured the unending practical jokes of Doug, Geraghty, Chaplin and her brother Jack, rather than enjoying them, was more often than not the only woman at the table.

A San Francisco secretary reputedly once succeeded in passing herself off as 'Princess Vera Romanoff' and the Fairbankses were so attuned to titles that they invited her to spend the week-end at Pickfair when they received a message that she was in town, at the Los Angeles Biltmore. They even sent a car to the hotel to pick her up, and held a round of parties in her honor before she returned to her nine-to-five job Monday morning. But no one who cared about his status in the movie industry in the 1920s dared refuse an invitation to any Pickfair do, and so the parties for the likes of 'Princess Vera' were as well attended as any.

Douglas Fairbanks Jr regards the Princess Vera story as apocryphal. 'I think it was Frank Case who was telling a story with affection at my father's expense,' said Doug Jr, 'and said in effect that "if someone with a name like, say, Princess Vera Romanoff were ever to announce herself to Doug etc. etc. . . ." The story then took off and was expanded until it was quoted as having actually happened.'

Gloria Swanson remembered most of the Pickfair parties as 'deadly', one in particular for Prince George, the Duke of Kent, youngest son of George V, who was later killed in World War II.

'The Prince was sailing with the British Navy and had jumped ship in Santa Barbara. He let it be known that he wanted to see Hollywood and on one day's notice Mary arranged a party for him at Pickfair. There were twelve to fifteen at dinner, the usual sort of group, Chaplin and the top echelon. A multitude was invited for after dinner. But the Prince wanted to see more of Hollywood than just Pickfair and asked particularly about Fatty Arbuckle's club at the beach.

'It was during prohibition and I called home to get some champagne sent over from my private supply. I danced with the Duke and told him to pinch my shoulder every time we passed someone he wanted to take with us when he stole away. He chose eight, naturally including Chaplin, and I think Aileen Pringle. I thought to myself, "How the heck do I leave without Mary getting into a tizzy about it?" And I knew that according to protocol none of us could leave until Prince George himself did.

'Finally I told Mary that the Marquis de la Falaise de Coudray was calling me from Paris at a specific hour like ten—it was quite early—and I had to go home to take the call. In those days long-distance calls from Europe were pretty exotic, even for Pickfair, and it wasn't possible to have them transferred to another number. I told Mary I'd already asked the Prince and he'd said it was all right if I left. So I went and then he made his excuses and one by one those we had selected began to sneak out the back door. I got my champagne and off we went down to the beach to Fatty Arbuckle's. He wasn't there but they had an orchestra and we danced and sang until three a.m. when we went back to my house in a whole string of cars.

'We brought the orchestra back to my house with us. We woke up my butler and cook but they were English and delighted to see the Prince. We served breakfast and for three solid hours Chaplin entertained us with all the acts he ever did, every impersonation, every character, before we took the Duke to the airport to go back to Santa Barbara. If Mary ever found out about it she never let on,' said Gloria.

In spite of the lavish level of entertaining at his house, Doug kept his promise to his mother not to drink until after he was forty. This promise had been extracted, when Douglas was twelve, because his father, in many ways an accomplished man, had been an alcoholic who deserted his family. 'Occasionally he'd take a sip of wine to be polite,' recalled Gwynne. 'He smoked a lot, though, out of nervousness,' despite his otherwise strict physical regimen. He had turned forty in 1923, and quickly began to feel his age. His sparring matches with Jack Dempsey and Gene Tunney (and the two boxers on his payroll), his occasional wrestling with the likes of Prince George, and fencing with the Duke of Alba and daily workouts at his gym in a sense left Fairbanks over-exercised, stiff and tight. In the late 1920s it began to affect his disposition, particularly in private with Mary, although not his surface ebullience. His muscle-bound condition also led to the circulatory problems that caused his premature death.

For all her regal role, Mary never quite forgot who she was or where she came from: Mary once gave a dinner party for the young King and Queen of Siam, both avid tennis players. Doug invited them to come up to Pickfair early on the day of the party to play a few games of tennis. The Queen slipped in some mud and Mary took her upstairs to her bathroom and ran a tub. While the royal lady was cleaning herself up Mary stood outside the door to her bedroom and said to herself: 'Imagine you, Gladys Smith, of Toronto, Canada, with the Queen of Siam in your bathtub.'

# Chapter Twelve

BY 1926 the movies had become a $2 billion industry in the United States, one of the six largest industries in the whole country. There were 20,000,000 movie-goers every day in the U.S. Ninety per cent of the industry was now centered in Hollywood.

In 1927 the Academy of Motion Picture Arts and Sciences was organized to give the industry some cohesion. Douglas Fairbanks was elected president, and 102 actors, seventy-eight directors, thirty-four producers, sixty-two technicians and sixty-eight writers were made members. The first Oscars were given for 1927-8 and the Best Picture award went to *Wings*, the silent film about fliers in World War I that made the first and very spectacular use of action in airplanes. The stars were Clara Bow, Richard Arlen and Charles 'Buddy' Rogers, and one of the supporting parts was played by newcomer Gary Cooper. The Oscars that first year for individual achievement in acting went to Janet Gaynor and Emil Jannings for their work in all the pictures they appeared in during that period. But the principal players in *Wings* all got Academy certificates thereby sharing in the Best Picture award. Buddy's still hangs in his study at Pickfair.

The coming of sound meant that the studios suddenly had to soundproof their walls, that directors who had always shouted at everyone throughout filming had to learn to be silent while the camera was running. And noisy tourists were no longer welcome on 'sound' stages. Because actors and actresses now had to talk, schools of voice and diction sprang up. Conversely, pantomime schools went out of business.

Legitimate stage actors who had held out against films now came to Hollywood, and the best musicians and most acclaimed authors came out because now their notes and words could be heard. The 'pen people' as they were called began to rank with the artists and technicians in stature instead of being some inferior breed. Mary, Douglas and Charlie were all members of the various writers' organizations founded, from 1920 with The Writers Club, on through the Screen Writers Guild of the Authors League of America, and to The Writers Inc., chartered as a separate non-profit organization in 1933 for the benevolent relief of out-of-work and older writers, and the encouragement of literature on stage and screen. Others active in these organizations included George Ade, Cecil B. De Mille, Elmer Rice, Irving Thalberg, Hedda Hopper, William Gibbs McAdoo, Frances Marion and Jesse L. Lasky.

With this second big influx of new movie talent in the late 1920s Beverly Hills, which had been so empty when Mary and Doug moved there in 1920, quickly developed into the finest residential section of any large city in the world. A thriving business developed in taxiing tourists to the increasingly grand stars' homes.

In 1926 and through early 1927 Mary Pickford was still very much in control of herself and her craft. Douglas, who'd turned forty in 1923, was showing signs of restlessness but it was nothing Mary couldn't deal with. United Artists was going from strength to strength with Joseph Schenk in charge, bringing in new stars at astronomical salaries his fellow studio heads were aghast at (including his own brother Nicholas at MGM), but making the money at the box-office to justify it.

Gloria Swanson's producing unit, Gloria Swanson Inc., was

added to the UA stable in 1926 and, while this caused some personal friction with Mary, the only other lady star-producer in the industry, it was certainly healthy for business. Gloria had proved her box-office allure as the glamorous femme fatale, and with her crowd-pulling successes and several million dollars in insurance policies as collateral she was able to get Wall Street financiers to invest a total of $1,200,000 to back her producing unit. One of her backers was Joseph P. Kennedy Sr, later U.S. Ambassador to Great Britain, and father of President John F. Kennedy.

But despite this support from Kennedy, who put up the money for *Queen Kelly*, Gloria had to keep her movie business going on her own, unlike Mary who had Douglas, her mother Charlotte and the whole United Artists organizational structure to keep her going. Gloria preferred to live in the East and kept a $100,000 penthouse at the Park Chambers Hotel in New York, a $75,000 home in Croton-on-Hudson NY, as well as her Beverly Hills house. Her monthly upkeep and payroll were $10,000, and her staff included a vice-president, a production manager, a scenario manager, four secretaries, a press agent, butler plus gardeners and maids. Gloria ran it all, down to the tiniest detail, sometimes addressing and stamping replies to her own fan mail, and at the same time she lived the wild, extravagant life her screen image demanded and her millions of fans expected.

'I will only tell you something about my involvement with Mr Kennedy,' Gloria told me in an interview in 1971. 'He never lost a penny on *Queen Kelly*, his first production; he came away from it better than I did.

'I joined UA in 1926,' Gloria told me, 'and paid them rent for the space for my production company. Sam Goldwyn was there by then, and Doug and Mary, and Joe Schenk who had brought in Norma and Constance Talmadge on salaries; Griffith was inactive, and Chaplin had his own studio. Mary'd come over to my bungalow with her little bee-stung lips and pout "I want to do

Sadie Thompson." I'm exactly the same height as she is, maybe just a half inch taller, but she affected being a child, with her little Mary Janes and those damned curls, and I'd wear these enormous high heels and act like I towered over her. I'd say very imperiously, "Get out of here, you little shrimp, I'm Sadie Thompson. You can be Sadie Thompson if you let me play Little Annie Rooney—give me your wig!" She'd get furious and say, "These are my own curls." '

Joseph Schenk had become chairman of the board of UA in October of 1924, and in rapid succession brought in John Barrymore, Swanson, Buster Keaton, Corrine Griffith, Gilda Gray, Dolores Del Rio, and his wife Norma Talmadge and her sister Constance to the company's star roster. The stars, both those with their own producing units and those under contract, pooled distribution expenses and headaches while maintaining their individual production concepts. Goldwyn then joined and brought in Ronald Colman and Vilma Banky. But Schenk had day-to-day charge of the asylum, and he ran it mostly over a gold telephone and with the aid of a violent temper. He was a large man who like his brother Nicholas spoke in a heavy Russian-Jewish accent. The brothers had come from Russia, grown up in New York's Bowery. Joseph worked in a drugstore near 'Nigger Mike Salter's' where Irving Berlin served as a singing waiter. By saving enough money from a succession of odd jobs the brothers bought Palisades Amusement Park in New Jersey on the Hudson, then went into the Marcus Loew theater organization. Joseph went into independent movie production and then to UA.

1927 began with a request from United States Vice President Dawes to show *Sparrows* at his home in Evanston, Illinois, and the screening on 2 January was the first by a government official on command and served to further elevate Mary and her medium.

The year ended with the release of *My Best Girl* at the Rialto Theater in New York—and in Rome at a benefit sponsored by Queen Elena, at a command performance in Spain for King

Alfonso and Queen Victoria, in Prague, before Czech president Jan Masaryk, and in Brussels at a charity benefit under the patronage of Queen Elisabeth. It was the first widespread use of a motion picture for charity performances by heads of state.

But, in between, the worlds of Mary Pickford and motion pictures were irreversibly changed. The onslaught of sound films changed the industry and a succession of personal tragedies changed her private world. Mary was never to regain control of either again.

Mary's last silent film was easily one of her best, and she met the changing times and tastes half-way by putting her curls up on top of her head and playing a twenty-year-old million-dollar baby working as a clerk in a five and ten cent store. *My Best Girl* for the very first time gave her the straight-ahead boy-meets-girl kind of love story that the vast movie-going public thought was ideal and wanted to see on the screen, particularly if they couldn't have it themselves.

And even more than *Wings*, *My Best Girl* made Buddy Rogers a star, and for a time he was called 'America's Boyfriend' as a result of his incredible good looks and excellent work in the film. The director was Sam Taylor who had done some of Harold Lloyd's best films, and Rosher was the cameraman—for the last time on an entire Pickford picture. The stylish picture didn't call for special effects but it did call for fast-moving camera work and long tracking shots which Rosher brilliantly provided. The film had warmth, tenderness and was a deadly accurate but amiable satire of both lower-middle and upper-middle class contemporary American life.

Buddy Rogers' happiest memory of *My Best Girl* was that 'we kissed. She had never kissed her leading man in a feature film up to that point.'

He recalled the audition he underwent for the part of Joe, opposite Mary's Maggie. He was twenty-two, a product of the Paramount Pictures School, and had made only one film. He was to have played Ronald Colman's younger brother in *Beau Geste*, and he went home to Olathe Kansas with this knowledge, a local hero and a movie star. 'They called from California and said, "Hello, Buddy, you're not in Beau Geste anymore", and I almost gave up the movies.' Instead he was sent on an audition to another studio. A friend set it up.

'She drove me to a new studio, past this big bungalow I'd never seen before, and asked me to go ring the doorbell while she parked the car. Of course it was Mary who answered—with all her curls. There were three men up for the part and we all had to hide in little cubicles. I pulled a boo-boo; Mary said "Mr Rogers, do you consider me a great actress?" and I said "My favorite is Norma Shearer". Still, to this day, she kids me about that. I was sure I wouldn't get the part and had wasted ten dollars on a new suit of clothes. But three days later I won it, and I won the girl. And she's still My Best Girl,' he said.

Mary, to gain experience for her role as a clerk in a five-and-ten, worked for an hour or so at a Los Angeles store—with horn-rimmed glasses and her hair pulled back. She made several sales before she was recognized.

'She didn't pay me much,' said Buddy, '$165 a week. I had to go out and do something else to make money.'

Douglas visited the set of *My Best Girl* one day, and saw Mary and Buddy in a love scene. 'It's more than jealousy,' he told his brother Robert. 'I suddenly felt afraid.' He left abruptly.

The girl, Maggie Johnson, was, albeit in romantic circumstances, a real-life character as opposed to a story-book heroine, and Mary was never more convincing or captivating. The screenplay was from a story by Kathleen Norris and the comedy in it was at the same time subtle, charming and hilarious. The dime-store clerk from the seedy side of town meets and instantly falls in love with the young scion of the family who own the whole chain of stores. But he works in the stockroom and at first she doesn't know exactly who he is. Eventually they each go home to the other's parents' house for dinner—no possible comic mishap in the two confrontations is either missed or overdone. Everybody ends up in night court and in a courtroom brawl. Mary is sure she will ruin Buddy's future if she marries him as he has asked her to, and to get him to go away for his own good she attempts to be a heavily painted roaring twenties gold-digger, smoking cigarettes and dancing to jazz records. There's a moment of heartbreak but the ending is happy, and so was the movie's record at the box-office and in reviews. It is generally regarded as one of the finest Pickford films, and, thanks to it masses of male movie-goers, rediscovered the latent charms of the girl next door. Following the release of *My Best Girl* Mary took a year off from filming, her first such hiatus since the start of her career.

On 21 June 1928, shortly after returning to New York from another European trip with Douglas, Mary took a fatal step. While she said later she regretted it, at the time she looked on it as an act of personal liberation. It was one she doubtless would never have undertaken had her mother still been alive, for purely commercial reasons if nothing else. But she decided she had to have cut the most famous head of hair since Medusa's, and off she went with a girl friend to the hairdressing salon of Charles Bock, at 2 East 57th St, leaving an unbelieving husband behind at the Sherry Netherland.

Mr Bock, aware of his place in history, asked if Mary was sure she wanted to do this. She assured him she did, and said that the curls had become a barrier to the progress of her career.

Of course the press had been informed in advance of the action, and photographers were on hand for the momentous first snip, to make the most publicity value of this end to an era. Six curls survived this first haircut ever in the life of Mary Pickford, and two are in a museum case at Pickfair, and two each at museums in San Diego and Los Angeles. Douglas was unhappy about it, she recalled, and many of her fans criticized her.

'You would have thought I had murdered someone, and perhaps I had,' she wrote, 'but only to give her successor a chance to live. It was a very sad business indeed to be made to feel that my success depended solely, or at least in large part, on a head of hair.

'I naturally missed my curls after they were gone. I had always taken care of my own hair, washed it and curled the ringlets over my fingers. But I thought that getting rid of them would free me, and I suppose in a way it did. I began to feel a change, a sense of ease and liberation I hadn't known before. It was my final revolt against the type of role I had been playing.'

The picture of her in the hairdresser's chair was published round the world with captions proclaiming the end of innocence. But the public—even her public—knew that it was a little late for that, the innocence was outgrown already and jazz-age sophistication was in.

And of course now there was no turning back. With adult short hair and an industry and audiences now firmly committed to sound, Mary began looking for a solid property with which to launch this new phase of her career. Her voice had been tested at the Paramount Studios in Hollywood for soundtrack effectiveness, and, while it had always been a bit high and reedy, she passed.

After all, she was stage-trained. And it was to the stage she turned for her first sound vehicle, in late 1928. Mary, at the urging of Lillian Gish, bought the film rights to *Coquette*, a successful Broadway play by George Abbott and Anne Bridgers, that starred Helen Hayes. Under the direction of Sam Taylor for the second time, Mary became the first major film star to do a stage play as an all-talking picture.

As Norma Bessant, the coquette of the title, Mary wore her bobbed hair proudly, her dresses above the knee, silk stockings and a passable but not very good Southern accent. She played a mature Southern girl, a vamp torn between an illicit lover and her father, who because of her coquetry is led to kill the boy and then himself.

The part was the radical break Mary had been seeking with her image. In London, during the year off after *My Best Girl* and her mother's death, Mary had told an interviewer: 'I am sick of Cinderella parts, of wearing rags and tatters. I want to wear smart clothes and play the lover. I created a certain type of character and now I think it is practically finished.'

Then too, of course, she sensed that the flapper style of sex found in the films of the late 1920s was what was wanted. Audiences had gone a bit beyond the naïveté that accepted Mary's melodramatic superheroines. But in going modern with *Coquette*, albeit still in a melodrama, Mary Pickford lost her uniqueness and became just another leading lady in her thirties.

Sam Taylor, who had established his solid reputation as the director of six of Harold Lloyd's silent slapstick classics (*Hot Water, For Heaven's Sake, The Freshman, Safety Last, Girl Shy* and *Why Worry?*), was anxious to prove himself with a serious drama. He also wanted to write for movies (and had written *Lady of the Pavements* for Griffith), and Mary let him collaborate on the screenplay. Like most other Hollywood directors at the time, Taylor had never done a talkie, so the *Coquette* company was all learning the new medium together. Constance Collier, the famous stage actress, was hired as a dialogue coach.

During filming Mary was under great personal strain, apart from the big gamble she was taking with her career, with the growing break with Fairbanks. She was so determined to be credible as a dramatic actress that she fought with Charles Rosher, her long-time cameraman, just because he stopped filming when a shadow fell across her face, and she fired him after the picture.

Taylor seemed to have her full confidence at the time, however, both as a scenarist and director, and he went on to direct her next two movies. Years later, though, she demeaned his contribution to the success of *Coquette* and said he did not understand the part she was playing. 'It was left up to me to make my role come alive, to get through to the audience's emotions. Mr Taylor seemed to think the important thing was just to show me off in a sound movie,' she recalled, 'as if to say "Look, everyone, Mary Pickford *can* talk." '

So intensely did Mary involve herself in the part of Norma Bessant, that in the scene where she is told of her boyfriend Michael's death, Gwynne recalled, 'She collapses down the bed-post, crying. Auntie couldn't stop crying and she cried steadily for twenty-four hours; they had to shut down production. I told her, "You don't really know him, Michael doesn't exist." She'd say, "I can't help it, it's so sad." When she toured with *Coquette* on stage in the '30s, she still had problems with that scene. On at least one occasion the curtain had to be rung down, she had broken down completely.'

She was vindicated in her obsession to perfect the character and production of her first talking picture. While the old-fashioned melodramatic story of *Coquette* all but buried the new screen image and realistic acting style she was after, Mary's serious performance was greeted with great critical acclaim, when the film opened in April of 1929. The fledgling Academy of Motion Picture Arts and Sciences awarded her the Best Actress Oscar in 1929, the first such award for a sound film, doubtless as much for past performances and for her service to, and eminence in, the industry as for *Coquette*.

In 1928, for the third and last time, Douglas turned to a screen portrayal of his adored D'Artagnan. *The Iron Mask*, based on Dumas's *The Man in the Iron Mask*, was released in the spring of 1929 and was a silent film. He 'could not visualize this role in anything but pantomime,' said his niece Letitia in her book *The Fourth Musketeer*. While Mary was looking forward, by pioneering in talkies, her husband was looking backward and indulging in a last sentimental gesture.

This rendering of D'Artagnan 'was more like the star's own life than the public ever realized,' said Letitia. 'It was one of the few times on the screen that he played the part of an older man, which he was. It was the only film in which he met death and it marked the end of the screen character the public had loved.'

Mary's enthusiasm for sound seemed genuine and unbounded: 'Screen players who have been familiar figures to the public for a number of years,' she said, 'have added something to themselves that their fans have never known before—their voices. It is astonishing how the new medium rounds out personality. It causes us to become almost different persons. I am sure that those of us who had adhered to a certain personality through many films wanted to change, but not at the cost of offending the public who had been loyal to us. For years I've been seeking a departure in my work, but in every picture up to *Coquette*, I've had to compromise because people would plead: "Don't destroy that little girl with the golden curls and the innocent heart." '

For *The Iron Mask*, Maurice Leloir, an illustrator of Dumas's books, was brought from France to Hollywood for $40,000 to do the costumes and Laurence Irving, Sir Henry's nephew, was imported from England to do the sets. 'Doug seemed to be under some sort of compulsion to make this picture one of his best,' said Allan Dwan, who directed it, 'in this one he eclipsed himself; it was as if he knew this was his swan song.' In his four later films, all talkies, he didn't half try.

It was during the filming of *The Iron Mask* that Prince George, the Duke of Kent, visited his first Hollywood set. Doug had arranged a royal reception at the main gate of the Pickford–Fairbanks studio, but when the entourage arrived they entered the casting office instead and were mistaken for out-of-work extras. Doug made up for the error by staging a 'filming' of scenes that had already been shot and were in the can, by having the actors, director, cameraman and others on the set go through their motions for a camera without film.

\*  \*  \*

Mary's second sound film was also the first talkie based on a play of William Shakespeare, *The Taming of the Shrew*. (A silent version was also released simultaneously, for foreign markets and domestic theaters that hadn't yet converted to sound, and because the UA leadership and others in Hollywood weren't quite convinced that sound was here to stay.) *The Taming of the Shrew* had, for the only time in their careers, what audiences had been demanding, Mary and Doug, the Queen and King, together in the same movie—and little else to recommend it.

It was Doug's first sound effort and a further attempt to create new film personalities for both of them in the newly uncertain movie medium. He later said it was her idea to do the play, Taylor was sure it was Doug's and Mary blamed Taylor, but said Fairbanks was enthusiastic. One thing she was sure of, 'I was talked into it against my better judgment.'

Once committed, Doug and Mary were both determined that the demand for sound on film wouldn't detract from the other aspects of their artistry. Like the Burtons almost forty years after them, the Fairbankses co-financed, co-produced and co-starred in *The Taming of the Shrew*, a vehicle in Doug's and Mary's case clearly designed to draw on their separate stage experience and capitalize on their separate movie successes and their marriage. The play was safely classical and yet sufficiently light, comedic and adaptable.

The screenplay, by Sam Taylor, was a loose adaptation, and on paper at least, reasonably faithful to Shakespeare. Unfortunately almost the most memorable aspect of the finished movie was the line in the credits: 'By William Shakespeare/Additional Dialogue by Sam Taylor.' Mary opposed the credit (which was specious anyway as there was almost no additional dialogue), calling it 'positively silly' but said she was outvoted by Doug and Taylor. Taylor's career went quickly downhill after *Taming* and Mary blames the ridicule occasioned by this screen credit (a contemporary cartoon showed a bust of Shakespeare at the Library of

Congress being replaced by one of Taylor), which she has since ordered excised from all releases of the film.

Mary blamed Taylor for much of what went wrong with the movie. She said he entered the project determined on a broad comedy fashioned to the existing screen personalities of herself and Douglas, rather than asking them to grow into something more serious. Taylor encouraged Fairbanks to play Petruchio as he had D'Artagnan, the Black Pirate and Robin Hood, and 'I was furious when he remarked that the important thing was to keep the "Pickford bag of tricks" in the film.'

Taylor did supply a lot of visual low-comedy slapstick of a sort usually not employed in doing *The Taming of the Shrew*, but he defended it later as necessary to broaden the public acceptance of the picture, and indeed for many audiences this is what saved the picture. Taylor also said he never intended to be faithful to Shakespeare in the first place. And Mary obviously had (together with Doug, at least) total creative control and must have tacitly acquiesced in what Taylor was doing at the time.

Doug's attitude as an actor was another major problem during production, and Mary said 'I was jumpy and nervous from morning to night while we made the film.' The sets, costumes, camera work, lighting and other production values were up to the high standards Mary and Doug had set and held to in all their separate film work, but he clearly wasn't.

Even though it was their own money they were spending Doug would dawdle doing his daily calisthenics and morning sunbath until eleven-thirty a.m. or so, while Mary and the crew waited and fumed from the nine a.m. makeup call (even that was late for a shooting start, in deference to the superstar-producers). The delays, which Mary calculated at $30 a minute, did nothing to further her good humor.

Doug, even when he did show up, wouldn't know his lines and they would have to be written on large blackboards, the forerunners of TV cue cards, for him to read from. That necessitated adjustments in blocking and camera work and frequent retakes. But if Mary wanted a retake, because she was unsatisfied with her performance, Doug would snap at her in front of the working company that idolized them and refuse to do it.

The final result was a fast-moving fluid version of the play, with plenty of Fairbanks runs and jumps and plenty of Pickford silent fury, deviltry and latent sensuality. The sound was incredibly good for so early in the form, and did not clutter the track as was so often the case with the first talkies, in a desperate effort to prove they were *sound* films. Mary in particular was able to play whole scenes almost without words (the wedding of Kate and Petruchio, for example, when she wilts him with one look on his adolescent behavior). Fairbanks, for his part, came across well in speaking dialogue and seemed right for the boisterous role.

The whole of *Taming* didn't add up, however, and Mary's portrayal of the heroine by her own admission, lacked the usual sparkle, and wasn't shrewish enough. 'I have no qualms about admitting that Katharina was one of my worst performances,' she said.

On release, most audiences didn't like the movie: it satisfied neither the fans of Pickford and Fairbanks nor those of Shakespeare, and word-of-mouth destroyed it at the box-office in its early weeks. Mary was better than she thought but not as good as usual. Incredibly, the supporting players, who in Pickford–Fairbanks pictures were usually first-rate, were poor in *The Taming of the Shrew*. The silent version particularly was an unsuccessful pastiche and looked like just what it was: a sound film with the track removed, a clear demonstration that silent and sound films were two distinctly different forms.

Many critics of 1929 loved the picture, however. *The New York Times* named it one of the Ten Best films of the year, and said: 'While it sticks closely to the immortal bard's lines, its doings smack frequently most heartily of Hollywood. Petruchio is oft Doug, and Katharina is not seldom mindful of the purse-lipped

Mary of years gone by on the screen . . . if it be entertainment one seeks, here it is.'

And at a retrospective in Paris in 1965 attended by Mary, the audience gave the film a standing ovation. That prompted her to give it a brief commercial re-release in 1966 (the first Pickford picture to have one)—coincidentally at the time of the Burton–Taylor remake—and again some critics acclaimed it and felt it held up. I find it a very dated big-star vehicle, and festival audiences in recent years seem mostly negative, particularly with some of her truly great pictures shown side by side with it. It was never a box-office success—as the Burton version wasn't and filmed Shakespeare seldom is.

'The making of that film was my finish,' Mary wrote. 'My confidence was completely shattered, and I was never again at ease before the camera or microphone. All the assurance of *Coquette* was gone.'

Whether it was the ghost of the little girl haunting this lately grown-up woman, the advent of sound and a different kind of movie audience, or her personal sorrows—or all of that—the first and greatest lady movie star was just about to pack it in at age thirty-seven, an amazing thought, given her non-stop ambition and dedication hitherto. The past was a heavy weight and so was the present, the future too uncertain. And yet she tried twice more.

In 1930 Mary went into production on *Secrets*, the story of western pioneer homesteaders Norma Talmadge had already done as a successful silent picture. Her old friend and collaborator, Micky Neilan was director, and Kenneth MacKenna was signed as her leading man. But the script was weak, MacKenna photographed way too young for the lady star, Neilan had lost his touch, and Mary was beset by her personal tragedies.

Less than a third of the way into the filming, Mary was so unhappy she ordered production shut down on *Secrets* and the negative burned. She wrote off a $300,000 loss. No public explanation was ever offered, but within the industry Neilan was considered most at fault, and his and Mary's friendship was strained thereafter.

Just at this time Joseph Schenck needed a fast flow of United Artists product and he offered the battered star the lead in *Kiki*, another Norma Talmadge silent hit. Schenck would finance and produce the film and Mary would work as an actress only, on a straight salary for the first time since she had left Adolph Zukor.

This casting was the most bizarre yet for the ex-World's Sweetheart. Kiki was a French chorus girl, a singing-dancing gamin desperately trying to snag a husband away from his adulterous wife. No effort was spared by Mary or the production in trying to make her a credible singing, dancing tart since sex was a prime commodity of early-depression cinema and 'all-talking, all-singing, all-dancing' films were the craze.

Whatever her displeasure with Sam Taylor on *The Taming of the Shrew* had been, he was hired again in 1931 for *Kiki*, as director and scenarist for the story, which was based on an old Belasco play. Busby Berkeley was choreographer. But this time the miscasting was unmistakable, the film was, in her words, 'a misadventure'. Mary finally 'decided not to use Taylor again'.

When *Kiki* was released, the reviewer for *Photoplay*, the picture industry's house organ, asked, 'Why has Mary been hiding all this fire?' Other critics gave her points for energy but nothing else, and the film, which also starred Reginald Denny, was an embarrassment to the Pickford body of work and, even more importantly, at the box-office, where it failed quickly and totally. Some movie magazines even asked their readers, 'Is Pickford through?'

Miss Pickford dismissed *Kiki* as her worst film ever except *Rosita* and wanted no one ever to see it again. The production is at least note-worthy in that it provided the first Hollywood work for a young dancer-actress, Betty Grable, who was Mary's leggy stand-in in the *Kiki* chorus line.

The resumption of *Secrets* came next, in 1932, this time with

Britain's popular Leslie Howard improbably cast as Mary's rugged California frontier husband. She had thought long and hard about coming back to the project, and finally decided it was worth remaking from the ground up. She hired Frank Borzage, winner of two Oscars (for Janet Gaynor's silent *Seventh Heaven* in 1927, and Sally Ellers' talkie *Bad Girl* in 1931), at a premium salary. She selected Borzage for his success with sentimental drama and particularly with women stars.

Borzage was ill during most of the filming, but did get a performance from Pickford on a par with *Coquette*. The admittedly sentimental film held up very well forty years after its initial release and provided Mary a solid dramatic role, and a sublime end to a unique glittering career (although she never planned it to be her last movie).

But *Secrets* opened in twenty-five U.S. cities on what turned out to be the 1933 Bank Holiday, and went unnoticed by critics and audiences alike. Speculating years later, Mary felt that a successful formula comedy might have kept her career going a while longer.

Never one to misread public opinion, and with her ever-increasing burden of personal tragedy, Mary firmly decided that this time it was time to quit. After only four sound pictures, Pickford *was* through.

'I knew it was time to retire,' she said in Paris during the 1965 retrospective. 'I wanted to stop before I was asked to stop.' She told Kevin Brownlow (in *The Parade's Gone By*) in London on that same trip, just after the Paris showings: 'I left the screen because I didn't want what happened to Chaplin to happen to me. When he discarded the little tramp, the little tramp turned around and killed him. The little girl made me. I wasn't waiting for the little girl to kill me. I'd already been pigeonholed. I know I'm an artist and that's not being arrogant, because talent comes from God. I could have done more dramatic performances than the ones I gave in *Coquette* and *Secrets* but I was already typed.'

At the time of retirement from films in 1933 Mary didn't actually announce that she was leaving the screen for good, but somewhat bitterly she made it clear she had no intention of letting that little girl be laughed at, ever. She had bought eighty original negatives of her Biograph films, all she could find, in 1922, and kept them in safe storage. She began buying up other of her works and said all her films would be destroyed at her death. 'I would rather be a beautiful memory in the minds of people, than a horrible example on celluloid,' she said. In much later years she was talked out of that attitude by Lillian Gish and others, and the negatives had been so beautifully preserved that they were readily convertible to more permanent film and, because she owned the rights to almost all of them, she and her company controlled distribution, in perpetuity.

Never really having got over the insecurity of her youth, Mary saved money and treated her fame as if both might end tomorrow, which stood her in good stead for the end when it did come:

'I've always been scared to death,' she said. 'I've always felt that everything was luck, and that every year is my last and so I'd better make good. Chance plays an important part in an actor's life. He needs that lucky break more than a writer does, or a producer or a director.'

Her luck had run out in 1933, and she knew it, almost before anyone else did.

# Chapter Thirteen

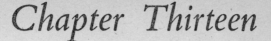

NE day during the filming of *Little Annie Rooney*, Mama Charlotte Pickford was foraging in a theatrical trunk looking for black material for a mourning dress for Mary in the title part. The trunk lid fell on Charlotte's breast and slowly a painful growth developed. Surgery was recommended but she refused, having had three other serious operations and not wanting that part of her body mutilated. Other sorts of treatment failed and the condition worsened and became fatal. Mary quit work and she and Douglas moved into Charlotte's beach house with her and stayed for more than four months, until she died on 21 March 1928. At her death Mary remembered becoming hysterical, hitting her husband in the face and lashing out verbally at her brother and sister. 'For perhaps three or four hours nobody could come near me. I was like a wild animal in the jungle. I am ashamed to say that during those hours I even hated God and said so . . . I was completely out of my mind.'

Charlotte Pickford left two houses, the other in Beverly Hills, which Mary never drove past again after the day of the funeral, although it is on a direct line from downtown to Pickfair and it means going several blocks out of the way. Both were full of expensive furnishings, silver and paintings, mostly gifts from

Mary and Lottie and Jack. Her estate was worth a total of $3 million, and she bequeathed $200,000 each to Lottie, Jack and Gwynne, the remainder to Mary.

'After her mother died I don't think she was much interested in continuing to work,' Adolph Zukor told me, but Gwynne disputes this view, stating that the real tragedy was Douglas and the deterioration of their marriage, which began simultaneously. It is a fact that Mary acknowledges her mother to be the most important person in her life, and still hangs a large portrait of Charlotte prominently on the wall of her bedroom at Pickfair, which with her *Coquette* Oscar is an unchanging feature of the room's décor. At the time of Mrs Pickford's death, Mary began experiments with spiritualism and ESP, although she was sure her mother would disapprove, and she still claims to communicate with Charlotte almost nightly.

Less than five years later Jack Pickford died in the American Hospital in Neuilly near Paris, on 3 January 1932, at age thirty-six. Officially his death was caused by 'progressive multiple neuritis which attacked all the nerve centers'. He had been in the hospital three months, having collapsed on a world cruise. Unofficially, according to his niece Gwynne, 'he died of too much of all the right things; women, drink and riotous living!' Jack, whose career had always taken second place to his lifestyle, had been married three times, all to beautiful Ziegfeld girls, had countless affairs, was a confirmed alcoholic and a rumored dope addict. Gwynne denies the last, pointing out that alcohol and narcotics aren't a likely combination.

Jack's death, attended by his secretary and some friends, was an unfortunately fitting end to an essentially tragic life. Two years after Olive's untimely death, Jack had married Marilyn Miller, the star of the stage and screen versions of *Sunny* and *Sally*. They were married very grandly at Pickfair in a highly publicized and impressively attended ceremony. That marriage ended in divorce in Paris, in 1927. 'For Marilyn a career came first,' explained Mary, 'she was probably the most ambitious human being I have ever met.' Jack then married Mary Mulhern, who went from the Follies to movies, but that lasted just over a year.

Scandal seemed to attach itself to Jack Pickford, and apart from the charges of drug addiction, which were never proved, he became notorious for his Navy record, which ended in a discharge after a court martial in which he testified for the prosecution against an officer who had accepted money from rich youths in exchange for safe positions in the Naval Reserve during World War I. Navy records showed that Jack, an enlisted man, had served as a go-between. Mary also suspected that Jack was procuring pretty girls for the older man, who had succeeded in moving into Jack's New York apartment and appropriating his mother Charlotte's limousine and chauffer.

Always overshadowed by his more successful sister, Jack's acting and directing career never even made it to the end of the silent film era. His last acting role was in 1926 as the romantic hero in *Exit Smiling*, the MGM classic movie début of Beatrice Lillie, one of his romantic interests. The comedy had Sam Taylor directing and co-writing the screenplay, and was a Lillie turn, despite Jack Pickford's star billing.

His health in adult life had never been good and this last cruise to Europe was an attempt to overcome emaciation and nightclub pallor. For several weeks after coming to the hospital, his condition improved, as Douglas found on a visit during one trip to Paris, but a blood transfusion a week before he died didn't take, and Mary, at Pickfair, was notified of her brother's critical condition just the day before he died. She cabled from Los Angeles that she was chartering a plane to New York to rush to his bed-side—she would have to cross the Atlantic by ship still, in 1932. Mary also suggested last-minute recourse to Christian Science healing techniques, although Jack had remained a nominal Catholic. She never got on the plane and her only public comment on hearing of his death was 'There is little that I can say now that he is gone.'

Lottie Pickford, the 'madcap' unpredictable younger sister of Mary and older sister of Jack, whose constantly saving grace was that she was the mother of Charlotte's only grandchild, suffered even more at the hands of Mary than Jack, whose death left Lottie apparently literally heartbroken. 'She was never the same after Jack's going,' Mary wrote in her memoirs, 'they were so very close in temperament and even in looks. It was as though with my brother's passing the better part of her had died too.'

Lottie developed a serious heart condition and spent much of her time hospitalized. Lottie had married four times—'At least I married them all,' she told her daughter Gwynne shortly before her death, 'I didn't have round heels.'

She lost Gwynne to Mary, Doug and Charlotte in a custody fight, and after securing a children's radio program was as much as ordered off the air by Mary during the time of her own twenty-six-week series. 'One Pickford on the radio at a time is enough,' Mary shouted at her sister. 'Auntie broke my mother's heart,' recalls Gwynne. Lottie died 9 December 1936 at age forty and Mary was left, in her words, 'the sole survivor of a fond and vivacious family that had triumphed so long and so bravely over the uncertainties of life'. Mary was finding it increasingly hard to cope, never mind triumph, and she turned to the waiting Buddy, eleven years her junior.

Throughout the making of her last five movies, the period encompassing the deaths of her mother and brother Jack, Mary's relationship with Douglas grew daily more desperate. He was increasingly restless and took to travel, even lessening his production standards to the extent that he produced a shoddy movie —*Around the World in 80 Minutes*—just to have an excuse to keep moving.

Separations had been unheard of in the first several years of the married life of Mary and Doug. If he was making a movie on location three hours from their studio, she would go there in a trailer after work and stay the night with him, get up at dawn, lie down in the trailer and sleep while the chauffer drove her back to Hollywood.

Thus when their friends heard that Doug was frequently in Europe alone or, from 1931, in the company of Sylvia née Hawkes, the blonde wife of Lord Ashley, heir to the ninth Earl of Shaftsbury, they thought either that he had gone crazy or the marriage was definitely over. Gossip columnists began hinting the latter to the public. The common belief was that no matter what their personal difficulties the partners in this perfect marriage would not let their public down by divorcing. Inside the industry it was more cynically felt that they would never risk ruining their careers by a formal split.

Mary theorized that her second husband's apparently pointless erratic trips to Europe and his affairs came of the restlessness of middle age, 'the need to prove something to himself rather than to anyone else'. In *Sunshine and Shadow* she wrote: 'Douglas had always faced a situation the only way he knew how, by running away from it. That, I think, was where I served him best. I always preferred to look an issue squarely in the face, and he counted on that. I often had the thankless duty of being his "hatchet man". In the enthusiasm of the moment he would invite someone to stay with us for the summer at Pickfair or promise someone a long-term contract, only to regret his folly the next morning . . . I usually managed [to fix it, but] . . . it always left the bewildered persons liking Douglas and disliking me. They were all convinced that I was the wall between them and him.'

'They separated on taste long before a third person came into it,' said Lillian Gish. 'Douglas liked to travel, Mary liked to stay at home. Douglas wanted to live in the world, she wanted to withdraw from it.' The other main problem, from Mary's point of view, was Douglas's excessive jealousy: 'In the early years of our marriage I adjusted to this fairly well, but it later became a great trial to me. Douglas was even jealous of my mother, I'm afraid, and she of him, which made it a perfect torture for me, loving them both as I did. However, mother controlled herself, which Douglas wasn't always able to do.

'For more than ten years we rarely went to a restaurant or night-club. I had no companionship of people my own age. They were generally older men, older in fact than Douglas himself, who came to spend week-ends with us at Pickfair. One day Rudolph Valentino made an unexpected appearance on the Pickfair lawn, which in the warm months was our outdoor living room. I never saw Douglas act so fast, and with such painful rudeness, as he did in showing Valentino that he wasn't welcome.'

Mary remained publicly silent and took no legal action during a long four years of speculation by the press and public. In June 1932 it appeared to her that Douglas was going to take off on another trip. She asked him point blank if he was going to Europe again. He said no, but she found his steamship tickets from New York. She then took the Santa Fe Chief to New York to consult her attorney. Just after an hour-long stop in Albuquerque, New Mexico, she heard a knock on the door of her compartment. It was a smiling Doug, suitcases in hand, who had been flown to Albuquerque in a friend's private plane. He insisted on moving into her suite, and on the rest of the train trip he swore his love to Mary and disavowed any interest in Sylvia. But once in New York he did sail for England on the *Queen Mary*, ostensibly for a golf tournament, but only after asking Mary if she would wait for him. But Mary returned to Beverly Hills and the unanimous sympathy of her community. The world's sweetheart was losing her husband to another (and married) woman.

Mary made the mistake of confiding the whole story of Douglas's affair with Sylvia to Louella Parsons, the Hearst gossip columnist and a friend of long standing, and even showed her a cablegram from Douglas in London saying he never wanted to return to Pickfair, that Mary could have it alone. Mary begged Louella not to make the matter public and said she did not want to hurt Douglas in any way and had no intention of filing for divorce. Louella agreed to sit on the story and did so for six weeks, until she heard the rival *Los Angeles Times* was going to run the Fairbanks affair, and couldn't resist the full-fledged scoop in Hearst papers all over, and the scandal was public knowledge.

In the aftermath, Mary refused to meet with reporters, but she issued a statement saying that she and Douglas loved each other still, that a divorce was out of the question but that there might be the possibility of a legal separation. Privately, she called Louella 'a disloyal bitch' and never really resumed their friendship, though the columnist insisted to her death in December 1972 at the age of ninety-one that the story was going to be broken anyway and that she was just following her good newspaperwoman's instincts.

\*     \*     \*

Joan Crawford's filing for divorce from Doug Jr, after a stormy four-year marriage, in 1933 curiously helped bring the two Douglases back together again. However, despite their bachelor camaraderie, in Doug Sr's erratic attempts at reconciliation with Mary he felt his son was taking her side, and would temporarily cool toward him. The trip with Tom Geraghty and his step-father to Europe in 1933 brought Douglas Jr into the business of producing motion pictures. Doug Sr was trying to expand United Artists activities by seeking and signing overseas talent and thereby also giving him another legitimate excuse to travel. He contracted Alexander Korda, who once before had failed to crack Hollywood, to become a UA producer-owner, on the basis of his own and his son's enthusiasm for *The Private Lives of Henry VIII*.

In 1934 Doug Sr made his last film, for Alexander Korda, with the almost pathetically apt title *The Private Life of Don Juan*. The picture was shot at Elstree studios outside of London and he rented a 1,100 acre estate, North Mymms Park, in nearby Hertfordshire, for himself and Sylvia. The living quarters were so large its household staff was almost as big as the corps of twenty-six gardeners who took care of the grounds. The house qualified as one of the historic country homes of England, and during Doug's brief tenancy it made history of sorts again. Stories got about concerning the lavish entertaining of his new circle of friends. Doug Jr was never invited to North Mymms Park during his father's stay there.

In January 1934 Mary received a call from Douglas in London saying that he had been named co-respondent in Lord Ashley's divorce suit against Sylvia. Mary did nothing for another year, then finally filed for divorce in Los Angeles during December 1934. Douglas had returned to California to try to prevent the divorce action, but Mary was determined to go through with it and he returned to England.

Interestingly both Mary and Doug turned to Beth Sully Fairbanks Whiting, Doug's first wife, in the intervening time. 'Can you imagine?' Mary asked Beth one day, 'my husband running off with another woman!' Mrs Whiting, who had lost Doug to Mary, could imagine it only too well, but held her tongue. Doug sent Beth a 200-word cablegram asking her to intercede for him with Mary, which Mrs Whiting did. The wire said his leaving had been a stupid mistake he regretted deeply, and that he still loved her. It closed with a request that Mary meet him in New York. Beth, like most of her contemporaries, felt the Pickford–Fairbanks romance was a national monument and she actually asked Mary to take him back. But Mary had been humiliated publicly on the world's front pages, and refused.

The divorce hearing itself, on 10 January 1935, was a surprise and very brief. Mary arrived unannounced in the Los Angeles court of Judge Ben Lindsey—who had often visited Pickfair in happier times—accompanied by her secretary, Elizabeth Lewis, and business manager, N. A. McKay. Mary answered 'yes' to six questions and the three-minute proceeding ended the more than fourteen-year marriage. Her voice was low but audible as she testified to her real name, length of residence in Los Angeles and the truth of her charges against Fairbanks, and acknowledged that 'a fair, just and equitable property settlement' had been made. Miss Lewis, the only other witness, substantiated Mary's testimony. Judge Lindsey granted the divorce, which became final a year later, as was the law in California until recently, and said it was not necessary to go into the details of the action since the charges (that Fairbanks lacked consideration of her feelings and since June 1930 'had absented himself from their home and her society') were well-known to the principals and the court.

Mary's voice broke as she left the courtroom and she looked close to tears. There were few spectators, as the case had not been set or assigned to a court so far as public records showed, until the late afternoon of the 10th, when Mary and her attorney, Lloyd Wright, met at court. She was unable to answer the questions of the reporters who did show up after the decree.

Fairbanks was in St Moritz with Lady Ashley for winter sports. He had not contested the action and when the announcement of the divorce came he shut himself in his hotel room, disconnected his telephone and refused all comment.

The announcement also reactivated the rumors in London and L.A. of the romance between Mary and Buddy Rogers, who was at the time making a film in London, and could also not be reached by the press. His father, in Olathe, Kansas, however, said he was 'just certain it is not so' when asked if Buddy would marry Mary in a year when the divorce became final.

Eleven months into the year of waiting Douglas returned from Europe again and literally begged Mary on his knees not to pick up the final divorce papers. 'She had the satisfaction—if you can call it that—of seeing him come crawling back to her,' commented Colleen Moore to the author. 'I'm sure if she had called after him with one foot on the boat he'd have come back,' said Gloria Swanson in an interview for this book.

But Douglas tried one last time. 'I've never loved anyone but Mary and I never will,' he told Robert. Doug arrived in Hollywood the day after the divorce became final, in January of 1936. Mary had received the final papers from her lawyer but she listened to one more lambent plea. This time he suggested that they run away together since the world had forgotten them anyway—something she was not ready to admit—maybe to Switzerland, maybe just to a ranch they'd build somewhere in southern California.

She was hardly flattered and he fled to New York, despondent. Doug Jr met him there, and watched him pine for days and send Mary lengthy wires that she didn't answer. Finally one morning Doug impulsively left for Europe without even telling his son, having asked Sylvia to marry him the night before. That day, when Doug Jr went to his father's hotel, he discovered that Mary had both called and wired Doug to try to convince him to come back to California, but neither the telephone message nor the telegram had got through. Mary called her newly ex-husband on shipboard and told him she was ready now, at last. 'It's just too late,' he told her. 'It was a tragic thing for them and the public,' said Colleen Moore. 'Douglas begged her to take him back,' agreed Lillian Gish. 'She was the one that said no. Everyone tried to persuade her not to be so stubborn.' Mary was touched by his attempts at persuasion but by now wanted public satisfaction.

Those final papers were issued 10 January and signed by Doug and Mary on 14 January 1936, during a United Artists business meeting, and in Paris on 7 March of that year, he married Lady Ashley, the former Sylvia Hawkes of musical comedy. They moved into the Pickford–Fairbanks Santa Monica beach house, while Mary stayed on at Pickfair, talking briefly and not too seriously about selling it.

Mary began to get telephone calls from Doug asking if he could come up to Beverly Hills and sit by the pool at Pickfair quietly. He and Mary would sometimes sit for hours saying nothing. Once he said 'What a mistake, Mary,' and she said, simply, 'I'm sorry.'

\* \* \*

Shortly after the divorce became final Mary was invited to a cocktail party at Gloria Swanson's home. Miss Swanson had decided she was leaving Hollywood for good, and this party was to be her farewell. She had also invited Douglas and the new Mrs Fairbanks, without telling Mary, and much to the consternation of Norma Talmadge and others who also arrived in all innocence

'Mary blamed me because I introduced her to Sylvia,' remembered Gloria, 'but it was after they divorced. Before that, although Mary was Irish, she didn't drink, but she had a terrific guilt complex that it was her fault and she started drinking.' Mary remembered facing the Sylvia situation head on and walking from the living room of Miss Swanson's home to the dining room, where Douglas and Sylvia were seated. She asked her former husband to introduce his new wife and he refused, Mary recalled, leaving Mary to do it herself. The two women exchanged several sentences, discussing the possible sale of Pickfair among other topics, with an extremely nervous Fairbanks standing nearby.

Soon after this meeting Mary and Sylvia found themselves on the same plane to Washington, D.C., Mary for some reason carrying her fine (second only to Marion Davies') collection of diamond, emerald, sapphire and ruby jewelry in a box on her lap. Sylvia sat down next to her and said, 'Pickey, dear, let me see your jewels.' Mary told Colleen Moore, who recounted the story, that no one had ever called her Pickey and she decided to have Sylvia on. She told her successor that they were all gifts from Douglas—which few of them actually were, Mary having bought most of them herself.

Sylvia was famous for being fond of jewels and got increasingly jealous with each treasure Mary pulled out of the box, particularly at a pair of pear-shaped diamond drop earrings Mary had given her mother and inherited back. Mary innocently asked to see Sylvia's jewels and was shown a single uninteresting pin and given a limp explanation about Sylvia's not having been married very long. If the younger woman ever found out the truth about the 'Fairbanks' jewels, she never let on.

After Doug Sr was finally divorced and remarried and Doug Jr was more established as an actor, they reconciled and began to travel together and became each other's closest friend. 'Dad' and 'Junior' were out of the question for appellations and they decided on Pete and Jayar. 'I settled for this fraternal feeling,' said Doug Jr.

Mary had stayed friends with all the other Fairbankses during the years of separation and attempted reconciliation with Douglas. This was because she liked them, not as a conduit to her estranged husband. Robert, although his brother's confidant, had nothing but admiration for Mary's conduct during the years 1930–5, and yet since he and his daughters had spent a great deal of time with her during this period, he was not at all optimistic about her taking Douglas back.

\* \* \*

With *Secrets* completed, finished as an actress and a graceful retirement decided upon—although not officially announced—Mary had resumed her French lessons, and taken up voice and diction. She stayed active as a producer of movies, making, with

Jesse Lasky, *Gay Desperado* and *Rainy Afternoon*, and by herself, for United Artists, *Sleep, My Love*.

In 1935 she wrote a novel, *The Demi-Widow*, which sold well, as did a spiritual self-help manual, *Why Not Try God?* She did a weekly radio show for an hour on Sunday afternoons and made a personal appearance tour of U.S. movie theaters (sometimes four separate visits a day), and a short run of a stage version of *Coquette*.

To fill the remaining empty hours she began to read the books in the Pickfair library that she hadn't had time for before. But reading remained something of an effort for her with only three months formal education and her favorites were Mary Baker Eddy's *Science and Health* (for she had become 'a student of Christian Science' if not a full convert) and Ludwig's biographies.

With both her mother and Douglas gone there were great time voids, and Mary did her best to fill them. She did not always succeed, and during this period she started drinking to fill some of the lonely hours, beginning with cocktails with whatever girl friend she was having lunch. Even that sort of activity—lunch with the girls—had never been indulged in during her happy years with Douglas: 'I didn't even go to downtown Beverly Hills without first telling him where I was going and promising to call from there or having him call me. Since it was all as complicated as that, I seldom went anywhere.'

Mary remained strict about her appearance in public, particularly during the promotional tour of movie houses, and the stage run of *Coquette*. Her shorter hair was still given a vegetable rinse with every third shampoo to keep its golden light, and dresses and jewelry were selected with the same care as before. The movie star retinue of two maids, two secretaries and a changing complement of management and lawyers continued. For a few years in the mid 1930s she kept talking as if she might make another movie any minute.

Her niece Gwynne Pickford was more and more often with

179

her and, although Mary was usually surrounded, she sometimes solved problems by indulging in out-loud talks with herself, working over a question that previously she would have shared with her mother or Douglas.

'She was never the same after the divorce from Douglas,' said Gwynne. 'A certain sense of direction went out of her life. She tried all things at least once, but she really didn't want to work anymore. They never should have divorced; neither of them survived it, they both lost heart.'

Mary saw Buddy when he wasn't travelling with his band, and other men, even in public after the divorce became final. She had had a brief fling with Leslie Howard during *Secrets*, Gwynne recalled. And one Thursday night when the telephone rang at Pickfair it was Clark Gable, then in his full stardom after *It Happened One Night*, for which he had won an Oscar. 'It's Thursday night, right?' asked Clark. 'The servants are out?' 'Yes,' said Mary. 'I'll be right over,' came the reply. 'No you won't,' said Mary. 'I won't open the door if you do come.' He tried again on a few successive Thursday nights, without luck, and years later Mary would say to Gwynne, 'Here it is Thursday night and still no Gable, you mean I actually turned Clark Gable down?'

\*　　\*　　\*

Once Douglas and Sylvia were actually married and ensconced in the beach house at Santa Monica, the scandal and gossip died down. On their honeymoon in Spain, Douglas had issued a statement to the press saying 'I am through with acting,' and he seemed to mean it. Sylvia made an immediate favorable impression on Hollywood and became a popular hostess and guest.

But Doug, although he was reasonably healthy, still rich despite the extravagances of the past few years and having given Mary most of the contents of Pickfair—the house itself had been

Doug's wedding present to her—and retired from films and hence free to travel, felt bored and neglected. Whereas all his former doings had automatically been pressworthy, the public seemed now not to care about his activities, which was all the more galling since Mary was still basking in the glow of a kind of Queen Mother public affection.

'There's nothing as humiliating as a has-been,' Douglas told one of his close friends at this point. Even his movie-producing company was inactive and his brother Robert had gone to Twentieth Century Fox as studio manager.

Doug's one remaining professional activity was United Artists, and at times he took his attendance at meetings seriously although of course it meant seeing Mary. Once when Mary was sick in bed the meeting was held in her (and of course his former) bedroom. During this particular meeting one UA partner shook his fist at Mary in disagreement.

'How dare you talk to my wife like that?' yelled Doug as he threw the man out of the room. The rest of the UA board ignored this chivalrous anachronism and gut reaction in the house Doug had once been head of.

Junior was invited to stay with his father and Sylvia in Santa Monica, which he happily did until the day when Doug told Kenneth Davenport, his one remaining close friend outside his family and employees (there was only one of the latter, accountant Art Fenn, who lived and worked in a wing of the house) that he wanted Doug Jr out. The young man moved within an hour, and never received an explanation. He and his father weren't to close this breach for several months.

Owen Moore was found dead at his home in Beverly Hills, on the kitchen floor, of a cerebral hemorrhage, 12 June 1939. Mary noted that an Irish maid reading her tea leaves during a visit to London had predicted the death of someone 'close to you and yet not close to you . . . I don't see you crying.' And although Mary denied that she was superstitious, she also noted that Douglas died exactly six months later, 12 December, which was Owen's birthday.

On 11 December 1939 Douglas Fairbanks was stricken with what he took at first to be indigestion, at the house in Santa Monica. He had been doing his athletics as strenuously and obsessively as before, trying to keep up with Sylvia's active social life, and rising early as he had all his life, consequently going without enough sleep. The outbreak of World War II in Europe had curtailed his travelling (Ambassador Joseph Kennedy had strongly urged him and Sylvia to evacuate London and return to California), and so he felt caged.

A heart specialist was called in, on Robert's insistence, and diagnosed a coronary thrombosis. He predicted several weeks or months in bed. Robert and Doug Jr (who had recently announced that he and his new wife were soon to make Doug a grandfather) stayed with him throughout the day, but Sylvia went out to a Red Cross meeting. None of them but Doug himself sensed—or was willing to face—the seriousness of his illness. Shortly after midnight, 12 December, Douglas Fairbanks died alone in bed. Through his brother Robert he had sent one last message to his sweetheart: 'If anything happens to me, tell Mary, "By the Clock".'

It was up to Gwynne to tell her aunt the sad news. Mary was in Chicago with Buddy, who was touring with his band. 'I dreaded calling her, but when I got through I didn't even have to tell her why I'd called,' said Gwynne. 'She was psychic, and there was something in my voice when I said, "Oh, Auntie." She said, "Don't tell me, my darling is gone." "Yes, Auntie, Douglas is dead." '

Douglas's will dated 2 November 1936 named Sylvia as principal beneficiary with a bequest of one million dollars. The total estate, despite his generosity and high living, was in excess of $3 million. Doug Jr received about $600,000. Doug's four nieces and his half-brother Norris Wilcox were left about $50,000 each (the girls' shares were in trust), and his brother Robert, $100,000. Davenport and a few other friends and employees were given trust funds, as was the Motion Picture Actors Relief Fund of Los Angeles, in the amount of $10,000. There was no mention of Mary or of Beth Sully. One of the largest assets of the Fairbanks estate was one-fifth of the outstanding shares of United Artists.

# Chapter Fourteen

DOUGLAS had never, for his own reasons, been able to believe that Mary was actually in love with Buddy Rogers, or might want to marry him. 'She's only pretending, to make me jealous,' he told his brother Robert. 'Why should Mary want to get married again?' he asked. 'She's got money, position, everything that a woman could want.'

A decade of personal and professional reversals had a good deal to do with it, and as Mary delicately put it, 'The attentions of such an attractive young man were naturally a wonderful help during those years of loneliness that followed the final break with Douglas. Although I saw very little of Buddy, since he was travelling with his orchestra, I will say this: more than anything or anyone else, he gave me back my desire to live.'

'Mary kept Buddy waiting ever so long,' recalled Lillian Gish, who knew along with Gwynne and other intimates that Mary was having an affair with Buddy in retaliation against Douglas's escapades. 'She dangled him in front of Douglas,' said Gwynne, 'kept him waiting in the wings, and married him out of spite.'

But Buddy was patient. 'She was the only woman I ever loved,' said Buddy. Whenever he was asked during his lengthy idolization of Mary if he would ever marry, he'd say 'No, the woman I love is already married.'

Anyway Mary finally caved in to Buddy Rogers's ten-year-long devotion to, and pursuit of, her and married him on 26 June 1937.

It was a simple outdoor ceremony on a Saturday afternoon at three at the home of Mr and Mrs Louis D. Lighton in Los Angeles. Only immediate family members and Frances Marion were present. Buddy's father, judge and newspaper editor Bert Henry Rogers and Mrs Rogers came in from Olathe. The Lightons were old friends of Mary's and he was a film producer. His wife, screen writer Hope Loring, was matron of honor, and Buddy's brother served as best man.

Mary changed her mind the night before about her outfit for the wedding. Instead of ice blue crepe she wore ciel (sky) bleu crepe. Her hat was modern empire felt rather than the halo type. And instead of blue gloves to match her dress she changed to gloves of lie de vin (wine dregs), to match her hat. The motif remained empire.

Gwynne remembered that even after this change, Mary was unhappy on her wedding day. 'The dress didn't fit right and had to be pinned. She delayed upstairs in her bedroom at Pickfair and would not come down. She kept stamping her foot and squealing—almost crying—"I don't wanna," like one of the little girls in her films. I'm not quite sure what it was she didn't "wanna" do but Auntie was superstitious and maybe she just felt nobody gets married in a blue dress. If that's what she thought, they've foxed the superstition.'

Mary and Buddy went to Hawaii on their honeymoon, with Gwynne and four of her friends. The Luces were on the same ship, and so were the newlyweds Gene Raymond and Jeanette MacDonald. A crowd of five thousand fans jammed the Honolulu waterfront for the arrival of the two new Hollywood couples.

Buddy had retired from movies after the expiration of his Paramount contract in 1933, to form his own dance band.

'Rudy Vallee told me to do it,' he recalled. 'He said I'd get more girls that way. But when I told the studio, they said "great", they didn't even beg me to stay. But I had more fun in music than in films. I made forty-eight pictures but I was never any good. I couldn't act worth beans.' Most of Buddy's remembered films were attempts at sophisticated collegiate stories, many of them made with Nancy Carroll as co-star. They were very popular with everyone but sophisticated collegians.

'My first piano player was Johnny Green, and my first drummer was Gene Krupa. My girl singers included Mary Martin and Marilyn Maxwell. We toured all over the U.S. and Europe. We held the record for a live stage show at the New York Paramount for fifteen years, until Martin and Lewis came along.'

Buddy virtually stopped working after his marriage to Mary, and almost cheerfully admitted: 'The only years I made any money were during the depression.'

As Mary said to him the day he forgot a comedian's name during a television introduction, 'Don't worry, dear, you don't have to work.'

'That was it,' he said. 'I wasn't lazy but I didn't have to work. I started producing films then and found out I wasn't very good at it, financially at least. So we took our minds off it and travelled and did little things.'

Buddy volunteered as a naval pilot in World War II. After the war he toured with USO troops, leading various bands, did a bit of radio and television, and as late as 1971 did a U.S. tour conducting Fred Waring's orchestra, when Waring took sick.

When they were first married, he at thirty-three for the first time, she at forty-four for the third, Buddy didn't want to live at Pickfair, and for a few months he and Mary thought about moving. As she told an interviewer for the New York *American* in September of 1937, it would be in Bel-Air or Brentwood, not so 'pretentious as Pickfair. Mercy no, only four master bedrooms, and of course tennis courts, swimming pool and things like that.'

'I was a man, you know,' explained Buddy, 'and it was Fair-banks's house and all. Now I think I love Pickfair more than Mrs Rogers does.'

One of the 'little things' Mary piddled at was doing a series of interviews under her own by-line as a special reporter for the New York *Journal* in 1938. Far from being about herself, the series dealt with crime and the streets of New York, and with other important people and topics of the day. She did indulge in one interview with Buddy:

'Wearing a horrible spotted tie, Buddy Rogers, orchestra leader, stepped out of a plane at Newark Airport. His hair is not neat. It looks like a rumpled silver fox,' she wrote.

'He is my husband, but as a reporter it is my duty to be impartial. "Mr Rogers," I say, "you do all the talking and I'll take notes."

' "What a break!" Buddy says with a grin. (That is a dirty crack, because I am usually very talkative and I don't give him a chance.)

'Mr Rogers is a band leader who started out in a little town of Olathe, Kans. He was just a boy with a drum, and when he earned $10 he bought a trombone. By the time he got to Kansas University he was playing many instruments.

' "I play," says my husband, "loud, but not good." (That is not true. He has just come from the South where he and his orchestra have been swinging it with great success.)

' "Which do you prefer, music or the movies?" I ask, because I know he gave up music ten years ago to appear with me in *My Best Girl* and now he is back at music again.

' "I prefer," he says, "a farm."

' "Why a farm?" I pursue the questioning.

' "Well," said Buddy, "you can play the saxophone without the neighbors minding."

'I am in a spot. We are back again where we started, and I am thinking of asking about his ambition to fly and his playing polo, and his third love, the piano. Those are his three loves of which I am jealous. But it is no use. He will not take me seriously. He says:

' "I think you are making history. This is the first time a sob sister has ever interviewed her husband about things other than "what did you do with all the money?" and "where were you last night?"

'So what can you do with a man like that? He is six feet one inch and handsome. He is also clever, as you can see.'

For her *Journal* series Mary also interviewed no fewer than six Kennedys, Mrs Joseph P., Kathleen, Patricia, Bobby, Jean and Ted, as they were sailing to join their father, the new U.S. Ambassador to the Court of St James. Mary snagged twelve-year-old Bobby first and asked him how he thought he would like England.

' "Well," said Bobby, "I've been so excited about it, I couldn't sleep last night. I know I'm going to like it. England is a great country." '

One of Mary Pickford's rare business failures came next, in September 1938 when she launched her own cosmetics company. The headquarters were in New York, with a factory in St Louis. She marketed six rouge colors, four staple and two high fashion, face powder, cold cream, skin freshener and face soap. Mary said, in opening the Mary Pickford Cosmetics line, 'I have put the finest ingredients money would buy into my cosmetics, based upon my own formulas. These I intend to sell at moderate prices, well within the means of the average American woman who wants and should have the best even though her resources are limited.' But the company went out of business after about three years because it required more advertising and promotion than she was willing to finance.

At the World's Fair in New York in the summer of 1939, Mary headlined a tribute to Thomas A. Edison. She lit a replica of his first incandescent lamp, and then re-enacted the 1877 demonstration of the first Edison phonograph, whose records were tinfoil wrapped around a grooved brass cylinder. Mary recorded 'Mary Had a Little Lamb', the same nursery rhyme Edison had used, into the machine, and then it was played back for the audience.

*     *     *

On top of the fortune Mary made in motion pictures, and kept in days of no or little taxation, she made shrewd investments in real estate and other ventures. And much of it was parlayed during this otherwise desperate period for her and Great Depression for everyone else. In 1933 before Prohibition ended she bought in National Distillers at $12 and sold it a few months later—after Repeal—for $120, ten times her investment. She bought some acreage in Beverly Hills at $1.50 an acre, and a series of small parcels in the San Fernando valley on which mortgages had lapsed and were picked up for only the taxes. One piece in particular across from what became the Universal Studios, was sold for $200,000, and she had paid about $3,000 for it.

'She became very very rich buying tracts of land, and build-ings,' said Lillian Gish. 'I was always respectful of her talent for knowing what to buy and apologetic for my own lack of interest. The Gishes could have had Sunset Strip for $500 when it was just a lot of rural land, but we were both non-possessive.'

*     *     *

Because of the accident during her marriage to Owen Moore, Mary was unable to have children of her own. She and Buddy decided to adopt, and in 1943 and 1944, when Buddy was still in the Navy, they selected Ronnie from an orphange at age six, and Roxanne, a six-month-old girl, ten months later. They had investigated the children's backgrounds before adoption and Mary was quoted in *Time* as saying: 'We plan to have at least two more and maybe four when we get out of the Navy.' But Mary was already fifty-one and Buddy forty, and they found parenthood a strain and stopped at two children. In their early years Ronnie and Roxanne were a source of joy and amusement to Mary and Buddy, and they were frequently photographed and brought along to public appearances. But gradually the children proved to be a disappointment and after they reached twenty-one Mary—while providing monetarily for them—would have no contact with them whatsoever. In 1973 both Ronnie and Roxanne were married, he with five children and working as a mechanic, she having moved around the West and worked as a change girl at a Las Vegas gambling casino.

One day in 1942 Mary said to a near-total stranger at Pickfair, seemingly out of context, 'to an alcoholic one drink is too many and fifty aren't enough'. And it was true with the loneliness from Buddy being in the Navy during the war, Mary was drinking more than in earlier days.

'When she'd come visit me after Doug's death she'd like to stay up until five a.m. talking and drinking brandy,' recalled Colleen Moore. 'And on those occasions she'd say, "He was just going through change-of-life, that's all." '

She continued to entertain after the war, and throughout the 1940s she remained the woman with the most overall influence in the movie industry. She and Chaplin maintained their interests in United Artists, neither able to outvote the other and thus engaged in some epic struggles. She owned fifty-one per cent of the Samuel Goldwyn Studio in mid-Hollywood (Goldwyn regained possession in 1955 after a six-year struggle with Mary). As President of Triangle Productions she brought out *Sleep My Love*, with Claudette Colbert, Robert Cummings and Don Ameche. (Buddy was listed as one of two co-producers.) She broadened her charitable activities by giving the film's première in her native Toronto for Unesco.

Mary was also president of Comet Productions, specializing

in low-budget films, and a partner with Lester Cowan in Artists Alliance, which produced *One Touch of Venus*. Mary paid a then-record price of $410,000 to Joseph Chodorov, Sally Benson and Joseph Fields for the movie rights to *Junior Miss*, but she did not go on to produce the film. She also, at various times in the 1940s, owned the contracts of various young, unknown film players, including that of Pedro Armanderez.

At Pickfair in these years they had a governess for the children, entertained about twice a week, and turned the house and gardens —and pool—over to several large charity affairs each year. During the war the pool and gardens were always open to military personnel, and servicemen were still welcome for some years after that.

Buddy, a failure on his own as a producer, worked for Mary's various companies and dabbled in radio.

In late 1943 *Life* ran a picture of Mary and Shirley Temple, referring to them as 'has-beens'. A Hollywood radio commentator broadcast that she was considering suing the magazine.

'Stuff and nonsense,' Mary replied in a letter to *Life*, 'nothing could be further from the truth. As a matter of fact I enjoyed the picture and was highly amused by the caption. How could I resent being labelled a "has-been" when I am placed in the same division as a junior miss of fifteen? (By the way, *Junior Miss* is the title of the picture I am shortly to produce for United Artists.)

'I think the photographer caught a very good likeness. Many of my friends have complimented me on it and there were some who even said I looked like Shirley Temple's sister. Now tell me —after that would I think of suing *Life*? It never entered my head.'

Mary was not deeply involved politically, but her sentiments were visibly super-patriotic and more quietly, ultra-conservative. She disliked Roosevelt, although she met him and Eleanor separately and together several times. The President once encouraged her to run for Congress, and she actually considered it, some thirty years before Miss Temple got around to it. The day after Roosevelt's fourth election, in 1944, Mary wrote to right-wing 'anti-communist' columnist Westbrook Pegler, what she called 'my first fan letter': 'After the defeat of yesterday I wakened in the lowest possible spirits this morning, ready to give up the struggle for decent government, but when I turned to the Los Angeles Examiner and found that you were still there, battling away, it gave me fresh courage and hope.' Ten years later, however, she was on the opposite side from Pegler, defending Charlie Chaplin, whom she felt shouldn't be condemned as a Communist without his day in court.

Toward the end of World War I Mary had headed a committee to raise $40,000 for ambulances as a gift to the war effort from the motion picture industry. The war ended with only $13,000 spent and Mary suggested the balance become the start of the Motion Picture Relief Fund, 'to care for our own people who need help' and build a country home for aged and ill actors and other workers in movies.

The studios asked their employees to donate one half of one per cent of their salaries, and a benefit radio show raised $10,000 a week for a time in the 1920s and 1930s. The Motion Picture Country Home, complete with screening room to preview all the latest Hollywood products, was built in the San Fernando Valley and a hospital was added later. Mary Pickford is still widely credited—particularly by those indigent retired studio employees living there—as the founder of the Home.

In the 1940s, after an invitation from Ida Mayer Cummings (L. B. Mayer's sister) to speak at a luncheon of an organization aiding Orthodox Jewish aged in the Boyle Heights section of Los Angeles, Mary became involved in building a 100-bed five-story housing unit for the elderly Jews. At Mayer's insistence the building was named for Mary Pickford. She remained active in the Jewish Home for more than thirty years. She credited her initial involvement to an anti-Semitic remark she had made to the

Jewish actress Carmel Myers; others attributed it to Douglas's Jewish blood.

In the summer of 1949, forty blind World War I veterans from the Sawtelle Veterans Hospital in western Los Angeles came to a party on the Pickfair lawn that was so successful it became an annual event.

In 1952, twenty years after the making of *Secrets*, Mary announced her movie comeback as an actress. The project was *The Library*, a Daniel Taradash-Elick Moll script based on a newspaper account of a small-town librarian who was fired after refusing to remove a controversial book from her charge. Pickford would play the librarian whose influence on young people leads them to true Americanism. After two decades of turning down scripts she accepted *The Library*, she said, 'because this is a picture which stands for everything we Americans hold dear. It is the most important subject in the world today and the one nearest my heart.'

1952 also found Chaplin hard at work as writer-director-star of *Limelight*, and the old rivalry found Pickford in a competitive spirit. She wasn't to produce this film, but did have approval of cast and director. Stanley Kramer, a specialist in the topical type of commercial film—and this was the 'anti-Communist' McCarthy era—was the producer, and Irving Reis was signed as director. At Mary's insistence the picture would feature practically the only aspect of movie-making she hadn't experienced previously in her career—Technicolor.

Kramer had originally planned to make the movie (for Columbia) in black and white, but Mary wanted her comeback in color and, after a highly successful color screen test (her first screen test since the one for Griffith on her first day at Biograph), Kramer agreed to make the change.

However, in those days of still-prosperous box-office but limited color ability, Technicolor was backed up in its commitments to film companies and couldn't promise anything for *The*

*Library* for several months. Kramer's schedule wouldn't permit that kind of postponement on the movie, briefly renamed *Circle of Fire*, and three weeks before actual production was to begin Mary withdrew, reluctantly. (She had attended some line-reading and run-through rehearsals at Columbia Studios.)

Her letter to Kramer said in part:

'Since the decision not to make *Circle of Fire* in Technicolor I have been very unhappy and very much disturbed. I do feel that after so long an absence from the screen my return should not be in black and white. That is why I insisted in the beginning that the picture be made in color. I realize . . . that you cannot, because of your other commitments, postpone the production further. Under the circumstance I am asking to withdraw from this picture.

'You know of my enthusiasm for the story from the beginning and, therefore, you will understand my deep regret over the circumstances which have arisen.'

She indicated her high regard for Kramer and said that she hoped when she did return to the screen it would be in one of his productions. Kramer for his part was equally sorry. He said, 'She is a great star. Her rehearsals promised a bombshell performance.'

But in fact Pickford was never again to seriously consider an acting 'return', and *The Library* (for so it was quickly renamed again) was apparently an ill-fated project from the start. Barbara Stanwyck was briefly involved as the replacement for Mary but during another delay in production Irving Reis died and Kramer split with Columbia, leaving the studio with the rights to the property. The picture was finally made with Taradash début-directing Bette Davis in the lead—and in black and white—and was an unqualified disaster in 1956, under yet another title, *Storm Center*.

\* \* \*

In 1954, Mary produced a once-over-very-lightly memoir, *Sunshine and Shadow*, by dictating to Louis Biancelli over a six-month period. The book, which came out in 1955 under her name only, was just too late for her as a movie star, and too early for nostalgia and history. It was kind to the cast of characters, herself especially, and provoked only a minimal if polite public response.

*       *       *

Marion Davies, a one-time screen star herself but perhaps at least as well-known as the long-time mistress of William Randolph Hearst, was a great chum of Mary's until her death in 1963. (Marion introduced Mary to friends as 'my illegitimate daughter by Calvin Coolidge'.) Hearst and Marion had of course entertained Doug and Mary many times at San Simeon, but the girls stayed reasonably close even after Mary's divorce from Doug, and the publisher's death in 1951. Marion was married only ten weeks later to Captain Horace Brown, an aging playboy sometimes known in the press (but never by Miss Davies) as 'Hossie Wossie', but the girls would frequently meet for lunch or drinking in the afternoon and the Browns and the Rogerses were sometimes a foursome.

It was on one such double-date that Captain Brown accidentally injured Mary by shooting two bullets from a new gun he was demonstrating to Buddy. The Rogerses and the Browns had been to a party given by designer Tony Duquette to unveil his new interior decorating salon, on a Saturday night in late May of 1956. Champagne and most other forms of alcohol had been free-flowing at the Duquette party, and it was well into Sunday morning when the two couples found themselves on the driveway at Pickfair. Captain Brown insisted on showing Buddy his new pearl-handled pistol, a Belgian .38. It accidentally discharged when, according to all four principals, the captain slipped on an oilslick in the driveway. Mary was grazed on the forehead by a richocheting bullet and a piece of slug or a piece of stucco hit her on the back of the head, causing it to swell. She was treated by a doctor for the minor abrasion and pronounced, gratefully, 'God was good to me, he really blessed me.'

Captain Brown did not fare so well. Beverly Hills Police Chief Clinton Anderson took away the gun and Brown's permit for using it, and his deputy sheriff's card and badge. The involved parties, and of course there were no witnesses, continued to insist he had slipped on an oil spot, on the ordinarily immaculate Pickfair driveway.

Marion Davies, in her retirement, was the one lady star whose wealth rivalled Mary's, although much of Marion's had come from Hearst while Mary made all of hers. Both women were also equally charity-minded in the 1950s. And while they had been good friends for thirty years, there was at times a slightly competitive spirit to these good works, especially when it came to the matter of billing. Once a movie star, always a movie star.

On one occasion when Marion went to the University of Southern California at Los Angeles to give $1.5 million to the children's wing of the hospital, Captain Brown suggested to her, 'Mommy, wouldn't it be nice if we got somebody like Mary Pickford to build a second floor?'

'What?' Marion snapped. 'I'll not have her name on top of mine!'

The Dean of the Medical School was compelled to intervene with assurances that it wouldn't happen.

In 1956 Mary hosted a garden party at Pickfair for more than 200 silent film stars, including Edwin August, the Biograph Boy, who was suitably kissed for photographers by the Biograph Girl, Ramon Navarro, Antonio Moreno, Clara Kimball Young, and Doug's former leading lady, Eileen Percy. 'I was a talkie victim,' said Miss Percy at the party. 'I got smart, married and settled down.' The assembled stars, who also included Pat O'Mally, an Edison Player in 1907 and still supporting himself from television which in 1956 had taken much of the work opportunity away from Hollywood films, were said to be more than $1,000 million worth of talent at their top career contract prices. *Life* went to the party held on Easter Sunday, 1 April 1956, but it got April Fool's weather, with thunder, lightning, hail and cold rain. The participants had to be moved indoors and crowded into the main hall, living and dining rooms.

The ostensible occasion was the publication of Daniel Blum's book, *The Pictorial History of the Silent Screen*, and most of the people still alive who had made that history were there. Bill Boyd, 'Hopalong Cassidy', made it, as did Hedda Hopper, Frank Borzage, Anna Q. Nilsson, Harold Lloyd, Zasu Pitts, Annette Kellerman (the Esther Williams of her day), Frances Marion, Marion Davies, Buster Keaton and Francis X. Bushman. There was general disapproval of Ronald Colman, Norma Shearer, Micky Nielan, and Joan Blondell for not showing up, the presumption being that they didn't want to be bunched with the old-timers, since all were in town that day.

Everyone who did come found a gracious Mary Pickford in a rare burst of total extrovert behavior, not only welcoming all her colleagues from the past but allowing the *Life* photographers the run of her home and even to take her picture with her feet up and her shoes off after the party was over.

* * *

One day in the mid-1950s Mary drove alone in her big white Cadillac up to the front gate of United Artists. There was a severe strike on and the picketing workers combined to lift the whole car, with Mary, whom they didn't recognize, in it. 'Put me down, you idiots,' she shouted, 'I own this whole damned studio.'

'Auntie was good with the four-letter words when she was angry,' said Gwynne. 'She always said it was the Irish in her acting up. Most of the time she was a lady.'

Throughout the 1950s Mary stayed very active in charities.

With President and Mrs Eisenhower she launched a major United States savings bond drive, the first for her not involving a war. And in 1961 she went to Washington as a delegate from Beverly Hills to the White House Conference on Aging. At sixty-eight, she looked very Beverly Hills and not very aging, and for one of the last few times, stole the show.

Socially, however, her day was past. She almost never gave parties and almost as rarely ever went to them.

By the time of the visit of U.S.S.R. Premier Nikita Khruschev on 19 September 1959, Mary was so outside of the Hollywood social scene that, not only was there no thought of entertaining Khruschev at Pickfair, but, when all the stars in Hollywood assembled at the Twentieth-Century-Fox studio commissary for a chicken and peas lunch in his honor (even Elizabeth Taylor and Marilyn Monroe were on time), Mary wasn't even invited.

In 1960 the city of Beverly Hills, in one of the industry's very rare attempts at commemorating its own heritage or cultural contributions to the lifestyle of the continent, unveiled a bronze statue of eight film greats of the past: Pickford, Harold Lloyd, Tom Mix, Will Rogers, Fairbanks, Conrad Nagel, Fred Niblo and Rudolph Valentino. Griffith, Chaplin, Swanson and dozens of others at least as important as the two cowboys were ignored. Mary and Harold Lloyd, and Conrad Nagel, the only three of the eight still living, attended the elaborate dedication.

The monument, at the intersection of Olympic Boulevard and South Beverly Drive, was really more for the work of the eight honorees in fighting to keep Beverly Hills independent from Los Angeles in 1923.

In 1961 Mary Pickford received an honorary degree of Doctor of Humanities from Middlebury College for 'her lifelong dedication to causes and actions of benefit to her fellow man'.

And the following year Emerson College in Boston gave her an honorary doctorate in humane letters, at their November Founders Day Convocation. The citation read in part:

'MARY PICKFORD PIONEER CINEMA ACTRESS, QUEEN OF THE SILENT SCREEN, BELOVED FRIEND OF HUMANITY:

'IN THE LONG HISTORY OF THE THEATER THERE HAVE BEEN A FEW INDIVIDUALS WHO, COMBINING SKILLS OF THEIR PROFESSION WITH A SENSITIVE PERCEPTION OF LIFE, HAVE BEEN ABLE TO SPEAK TO THE HEARTS AND MINDS OF THEIR FELLOW MEN. THESE FEW GREAT INTERPRETORS OF THE THEATER HAVE TAUGHT MEN TO SEE VISIONS AND DREAM DREAMS. TO MILLIONS OF YOUR CONTEMPORARIES YOU SYMBOLIZE THE WORLD AS THEY WOULD HAVE IT BE AND, BECAUSE YOU PROVIDE INSPIRATION, THEY COULD BELIEVE THAT THEIR DREAMS AND VISIONS COULD COME TRUE.

'AS ONE OF THE MOST POPULAR AND BEST LOVED WOMEN OF HISTORY YOU HAVE THOUGHT NOT OF YOURSELF BUT HAVE DIRECTED THE GREAT WEIGHT OF YOUR INFLUENCE TOWARD THE PROMOTION OF COUNTLESS HUMANITARIAN CAUSES. IN THE SUPPORT OF YOUR COUNTRY IN TIME OF NATIONAL STRESS AND CRISIS YOU HAVE GIVEN US PHYSICALLY OF YOUR ENERGY AND TALENTS: IN THE MIDST OF A BUSY LIFE YOU HAVE FOUND TIME TO SHARE YOUR RICH PERSONAL INSIGHTS THROUGH THE WRITING OF SIGNIFICANT BOOKS: AND NOW, LATERALLY, IN THE RELATIVELY NEW FIELD OF GERIATRICS YOU ARE PROVIDING IMPORTANT LEADERSHIP, ESPECIALLY IN YOUR WORK WITH HOUSING FOR SENIOR CITIZENS AND THE WHITE HOUSE CONFERENCE ON THE AGED.'

She had sold her last block of stock in United Artists in 1956 —after Chaplin had sold his without telling her. But for a few more years Mary Pickford remained an important symbol of the industry. In 1963 she was the highlight of the International Film Festival in Mar Del Plata, Argentina.

That same year she took her last trip to Toronto, where she presented a tapestry made by Queen Mary to the Toronto museum. Asked to pose for photographers with a glass of whiskey in her hand, she said: 'Not me, I'm a hypocrite.' She told reporters she wouldn't let her daughter Roxanne, then eighteen, see movies like *Never on Sunday*. 'No, and never on Monday, either,' said Mary. She also said she would bar the release of her films to TV. 'If I were very poor I might reconsider. But in my day there were only sixteen apertures to a second, now there are twenty-five, causing a jerky effect when they are shown. The young laughed at Valentino when they saw his old movies. People have illusions that are very precious to them, let them keep them.'

Her last public appearance was in Paris in 1965 for the French Government's Mary Pickford Retrospective at the Cinemateque.

'The French never forget an artist who has pleased them,' Mary said the morning after the first showing. 'I have received many honors in my life and have had audiences with kings and queens and the world's great. But this tribute touches me most of all. Last night my heart sang.'

Henri Sauget, the celebrated French composer, played the piano accompaniment to her films at the Cinemateque Française. Buddy went along on the trip, which also included London.

The success of *The Taming of the Shrew* in Paris encouraged Mary to re-release the film commercially in the U.S. the next year, with a re-recorded sound-track, new music and sound effects. Matty Kemp, a former silent-screen actor himself, was retained to refurbish *The Taming of the Shrew*, and stayed on with the Mary Pickford Company to preside, with Buddy, over the subsequent re-releases of her films. Mary declined to attend the première of her new-old movie, which had cost $1.6 million to produce in 1929. The opening, coincidentally, took place five months before the Burton–Taylor remake of the same Shakespeare play. Both versions failed.

\* \* \*

In 1970 she gave fifty-one Biograph shorts to the American Film Institute collection in the Library of Congress; she appears in forty-seven of them. The Institute paid for refurbishing them and presented a Mary Pickford retrospective in Washington in November of 1970, including showings of nine of the Biograph shorts. Pickford festivals followed in Los Angeles, New York, London, Benalmadena in Spain (where Gwynne lives) and other cities. Mary attended none of them, only occasionally talking to reporters on the telephone from each city.

More and more she refused to leave her bed, and each day began to resemble the one that went just before it. She got up anywhere from eleven a.m. to twelve-thirty p.m. She read a little, watched TV—*Bonanza* was a favorite, partly because 'Lorne Greene looks like my Buddy'. She saw only a very few people and refused to try to wear the contact lenses that she was advised to wear. She was excessively religious, a believer in ESP, ghosts and other forms of the occult. She had long been a devotee of astrology—an Aries who had visited Evangeline Adams in New York regularly in the 1920s.

Her butler Tony DeVos started her days, with the excised newspaper and her breakfast-lunch about noon; 'a fried-egg sandwich, cottage cheese and stewed fruit, about all she eats,' said Tony. Her dinner is at about six–six-thirty and is almost always something 'very spicy', like enchiladas, Chinese chop suey, and vegetables, with white fluffy cake for dessert.

Mary was depressed by the Vietnam war, the Sharon Tate murders, and the deaths, in the 1970s of so many of her contemporaries, Harold Lloyd, Bebe Daniels (one of her brother Jack's old girlfriends) and Zasu Pitts and others. She stopped screening movies because she thought they got so dirty and, although a founder of the Motion Picture Academy, she didn't vote in the Oscar competition for several years.

When Chaplin came home to America in April of 1972 for his special Academy Award, Mary was not in a conciliatory mood towards him either.

'I think they should ask some of his wives what they think of him,' she snarled. 'As Sam Goldwyn would say, "I can tell you in two words what it was like to do business with Chaplin: im—possible." ' She hadn't seen Charlie since 1951 and didn't plan to again.

*　*　*

Even visitors to Pickfair are now asked to talk to Mary on the telephone from downstairs, and she issues most of her orders through that device. Interviews, rarer and rarer, are also almost all telephonic. The Merv Griffin Show in 1971 did two special tributes to silent films, and for one of them Mary allowed a taped telephone interview, but it was so incoherent the producers quietly dropped it and let Buddy on live to substitute for her.

Mary Pickford has perhaps too much time for reflection, and reflect she does; on her movies she said:

'My career was planned. There was never anything accidental about it, it was painful, it was purposeful. I'm not exactly satisfied, but I'm grateful, and that's a very different thing. I might have done better, I don't know. There are unexpected circumstances that hinder us, and we just have to put up with them. We have to do the best we can under pressure.'

And on Hollywood in general she said, 'Hollywood now is like the rest of the world—disturbed and frightened. In the old days Hollywood was young and the country was young. They are both mature now.'

Mary remains a staunch admirer and friend of Douglas Fairbanks Jr thirty-four years after his father's death. He is always welcome at Pickfair, and she tells him repeatedly it is still his home. To Tony the butler he is still 'the young master' of the house. 'She keeps saying she wants to give me some of my father's things from the house,' said Fairbanks, 'but so far all she's given me are a couple of his walking sticks.' He stayed at Pickfair when he was in Los Angeles, and many times she let him give parties there. At one of them, in 1971, Pearl Bailey requested to go up and see Mary, and Mary, a long-time admirer of the singer agreed, to everyone's surprise. Pearl went up alone and on entering Mary's bedroom asked about 'the doll'. 'What doll?' Mary demanded. 'The one I dreamed about, with the broken head,' responded Pearl. Mary, astonished but a fellow believer in ESP, pointed to the doll Belasco had given her for *The Warrens of Virginia*, the china doll with a broken head.

Pearl offered to take the doll to a dolls' hospital and have it fixed, but only after admonishing Mary for being like her doll, with her spirit defeated and broken. 'When this doll is mended, you will be too,' said Pearl. 'You've got to pull yourself together and get up and get out again, and you will.'

Mary agreed, and urged Pearl to sneak the doll out under her coat so Buddy and Doug Jr and the others wouldn't see it. She wanted her doll fixed, and for a brief time at least Pearl thought Mary wanted herself to be well again.

# *Appendix*

## THE FILMS OF MARY PICKFORD

### *1909 Releases*
(All Biograph, directed by D. W. Griffith)

1. *Her First Biscuits;* location, New York Studio; Cameraman G. W. 'Billy' Bitzer; contemporary farce; cast also included Florence Lawrence, Owen Moore, Harry Salter, Mack Sennett.
2. *The Violin Maker of Cremona;* N.Y. Studio; Bitzer; costume melodrama; John Compson, David Miles, Moore.
3. *The Lonely Villa;* Fort Lee, New Jersey; Arthur Marvin; contemporary chase melodrama; scenario by Mack Sennett, based on an item in a newspaper, as he claimed, or perhaps on a play by Andre deLorde, *At the Telephone;* Adele deGarde, Marion Leonard, Moore, Sennett.
4. *The Son's Return;* N.Y. Studio, Leonia and Coytesville, N.J.; Bitzer, Marvin; contemporary melodrama.
5. *The Faded Lillies;* N.Y. Studio; Marvin, Bitzer; contemporary melodrama.
6. *The Peach Basket Hat;* N.Y. Studio; Fort Lee, N.J.; Bitzer, Marvin; chase farce; Linda Arvidson (Mrs D. W. Griffith), Compson, Lawrence, Leonard, Moore.
7. *The Way of Man;* N.Y. Studio, Edgewater, N.J.; Bitzer, Marvin; contemporary tragedy.
8. *The Necklace;* studio; Bitzer, Marvin; contemporary melodrama; Lawrence.
9. *The Mexican Sweethearts;* studio; Bitzer; romance.
10. *The Country Doctor;* Greenwich, Connecticut; Bitzer; contemporary melodrama.

11. *The Cardinal's Conspiracy;* Greenwich; costume (17th century) romance; Lawrence.

12. *The Renunciation;* Shadyside, N.J.; Bitzer, Marvin; western comedy; James Kirkwood, Billy Quirk.

13. *The Seventh Day;* studio; Bitzer; contemporary drama; Egan, Kirkwood, Moore, Frank Powell, Sennett.

14. *A Strange Meeting;* studio; contemporary religious melodrama.

15. *Sweet and Twenty;* Greenwich, studio; Bitzer; contemporary adolescent comedy; Kirkwood, Lawrence, Quirk.

16. *The Slave;* studio; Bitzer; Roman melodrama; Lawrence.

17. *They Would Elope;* Little Falls, N.J.; Bitzer, Higgins; contemporary chase comedy; Kate Bruce, Kirkwood, Quirk, Sennett.

18. *The Indian Runner's Romance;* Cuddebackville, N.Y.; Bitzer; Indian melodrama.

19. *His Wife's Visitor;* studio; Bitzer; contemporary romance; Kirkwood, Moore, Powell.

20. *Oh, Uncle;* studio; Bitzer; farce; Kirkwood, Quirk.

21. *The Sealed Room;* studio; Bitzer; Renaissance melodrama.

22. *1776, or The Hessian Renegades;* Cuddebackville; Marvin, Bitzer; American Revolution melodrama.

23. *The Little Darling;* Cuddebackville, studio; farce; Robert ('Bobby') Harron, Arthur Johnson, Lottie Pickford, Quirk, Henry B. Walthall.

24. *In Old Kentucky;* Cuddebackville; Bitzer; Civil War melodrama; Bruce, Moore, Walthall.

25. *Getting Even;* Edgewater, N.J.; Bitzer; contemporary comedy; Compson, Kirkwood, Quirk, Sennett.

26. *The Broken Locket;* Edgewater; Bitzer; contemporary temperance melodrama.

27. *What's Your Hurry?;* Fort Lee; Bitzer; contemporary comedy; Bruce, deGarde, Egan, Lottie Pickford, Quirk, Sennett, Dorothy West.

28. *The Awakening;* Edgewater; Bitzer; contemporary romance.

29. *The Little Teacher;* Greenwich, Leonia; Bitzer, Marvin; contemporary comedy; A. Johnson.

30. *The Gibson Goddess;* Highlands, N.J.; Bitzer; contemporary comedy.

31. *In the Watches of the Night;* Edgewater; Bitzer; melodrama.

32. *His Lost Love;* studio, Bitzer; melodrama.

33. *The Restoration;* Little Falls, N.J.; Bitzer; romance; Kirkwood, Leonard, Moore.
34. *The Light That Came;* studio; Bitzer; contemporary romance; Bruce, Johnson, Kirkwood, Leonard, Sennett.
35. *A Midnight Adventure;* studio; Marvin; contemporary comedy; Dorothy Bernard, Bruce, Quirk, Sennett.
36. *The Mountaineer's Honor;* Cuddebackville, N.Y.; Bitzer; Kentucky Mountain romance.
37. *The Trick That Failed;* studio; Bitzer; romance; Johnson, Gertrude Robinson, Sennett.
38. *The Test;* Coytesville, N.J.; Bitzer, Marvin; contemporary comedy; Compson, Johnson, Leonard, Lottie Pickford, Quirk.
39. *To Save Her Soul;* Fort Lee, N.J.; Bitzer, Marvin; based on the novel *The Christian*, by Sir Hall Caine contemporary religious romance; A. Johnson, Lottie Pickford.

### 1910 Releases
(All Biograph, all directed by Griffith
except 40, directed by Frank Powell;
all filmed by Bitzer except as noted.)

40. *All On Account of The Milk;* director Frank Powell; Fort Lee; Marvin; comedy-romance; Bruce, Johnson, Sennett, 'Mrs Smith', Blanche Sweet.
41. *The Woman From Mellon's;* studio; romance; Verner, Clarges, Kirkwood, Moore, Lottie Pickford, Quirk, Robinson, Sennett.
42. *The Englishman and the Girl;* studio; contemporary comedy; Bruce, Nicholls, Tony O'Sullivan, Robinson, Sennett.
43. *The Newlyweds;* N.Y. Studio, Los Angeles Studio, Los Angeles exterior; Bitzer and Marvin; contemporary comedy; Florence Barker, Bernard, Bruce Egan, Johnson, Nicholls, O'Sullivan, Jack Pickford, Sennett, Walthall, Charles West.
44. *The Thread of Destiny:* A Story of the Old South-west; San Gabriel Mission, California (Pickford's first Californian location film); scenario by D. W. Griffith.
45. *The Twisted Trail:* A Story of Fate in the Mountain Wilds; Sierra Madre, California; contemporary melodrama.
46. *The Smoker;* Glendale, California and L.A. Studio; contemporary

comedy; Compson, Frank Opperman, Jack Pickford, Lottie Pickford, Quirk.

47. *As It Is In Life;* California Pigeon Farm; contemporary drama; Bruce, Gladys Eagan, Leonard.

48. *A Rich Revenge:* A Comedy of the California Oilfields; Edendale, California; William J. Butler, Nicholls, O'Sullivan, Quirk.

49. *A Romance of the Western Hills;* Sierra Madre, Pasadena, California; Indian melodrama.

50. *May and December;* Verdugo, California; by Frank Powell; Marvin; romantic comedy; Bruce, Charles Hill Mailes, Quirk; screenplay by Mary Pickford.

51. *Never Again!;* Brentwood, Venice, California; Marvin; love comedy; Quirk, Sennett.

52. *The Unchanging Sea;* Santa Monica, California; Marvin, Bitzer; romance based on Charles Kingsley poem 'The Three Fishes'; Arvidson.

53. *Love Among the Roses;* Hollywood, California; Marvin, Bitzer; romance; Leonard.

54. *The Two Brothers;* In the Days of the Padres; San Juan Capistrano, California; Bitzer and Marvin; 18th-century Mexican romance; Leonard.

55. *Ramona;* A Story of the White Man's Injustice to the Indian; Peru, California, Camulos, Ventura County, California, L.A. studio; romance; Bruce, Frank Grandin, Walthall—adapted from novel by Helen Hunt-Jackson; the first long shots.

56. *In the Season of Buds;* Stamford, Conn.; Marvin, Bitzer; comedy.

57. *A Victim of Jealousy;* N.Y. Studio; melodrama.

58. *A Child's Impulse;* Westfield, N.J., N.Y. Studio; Bitzer, Marvin; contemporary melodrama.

59. *Muggsy's First Sweetheart;* Westfield, N.Y. Studio; contemporary comedy; Flora Finch, Quirk.

60. *What the Daisy Said;* Delaware Water Gap, N.J.; romance; Bruce, Moore, Nicholls, Robinson, Sennett, West.

61. *The Call to Arms;* Lambert Castle, Paterson, N.J., N.Y. Studio; medieval melodrama; Arvidson, Dell Henderson, Moore, Sennett.

62. *An Arcadian Maid;* Westfield, N.Y. Studio; melodrama; Sennett.

63. *Muggsy Becomes A Hero;* Cuddebackville, Coytesville; Marvin; comedy romance (series); Bruce, Jack Pickford, Quirk, Sennett.

64. *The Sorrows of the Unfaithful;* Atlantic Highlands, N.J., N.Y. Studio; contemporary melodrama.

65. *When We Were in Our Teens;* Coytesville, N.J.; Marvin; romance; Joe Graybill, Quirk, Sennett.

66. *Wilful Peggy;* Cuddebackville, N.Y. and N.Y. Studio; 18th-century Irish romance; Bruce, McDowell, Robert (Bobby) Harron, Walthall, Clarges; based on *The Country Cousin.*

67. *Examination Day at School;* Westfield, N.J., N.Y. Studio; contemporary comedy; Bruce, Clarges, deGarde, Harron, Jack Pickford, Lottie Pickford, Robinson, Sennett, Dorothy West.

68. *A Gold Necklace;* Cuddebackville, N.Y. Studio; Marvin; contemporary comedy; Bruce, Eddie Dillon, Florence LaBadie, Lottie Pickford, West.

69. *A Lucky Toothache;* Westfield, N.J. ;Marvin; comedy; Arvidson, Bruce, Dillon, Claire McDowell, Walter Christie Miller, Quirk, Sennett.

70. *Waiter No. 5;* N.Y. Studio; anti-Czarist melodrama, including scenes of starving poor in Russia.

71. *Simple Charity;* Fort Lee, N.J., N.Y. Studio; Bitzer, Marvin; melodrama.

72. *The Masher.*

73. *The Song of the Wildwood Flute;* Fishkill, N.Y., Fort Lee, N.Y. Studio; Indian drama; Dark Cloud.

74. *A Plain Song;* Westfield, N.J., N.Y. Studio; contemporary melodrama.

*1911 Releases*
Biograph, (Griffith Director, Bitzer
Cameraman)

75. *White Roses;* N.Y. Studio; Marvin; romantic comedy; Edwin August, Bruce, Dillon, Joe Graybill, Miller, Jack and Lottie Pickford.

76. *When A Man Loves;* Westfield, N.J., N.Y. Studio; comedy romance; Dillon, O'Sullivan, C. West.

77. *The Italian Barber;* Fort Lee, N.Y. Studio; contemporary comedy; Sennett.

78. *Three Sisters;* N.Y. Studio; contemporary romance. Vivian Prescott, Sennett, Marion Sunshine.
79. *A Decree of Destiny;* N.Y. Studio; contemporary romance; Joseph Graybill, Jack Pickford, Sunshine.


### The IMP Company
(Thomas H. Ince directed most of the films, about twelve of which were made in Cuba.)

80. *The First Misunderstanding.*
81. *The Dream;* scenario by Mary Pickford.
82. *Maid or Man.*
83. *At the Duke's Command.*
84. *The Mirror.*
85. *While the Cat's Away.*
86. *Her Darkest Hour.*
87. *Artful Kate.*
88. *A Manly Man;* Cuba.
89. *The Message in the Bottle;* Cuba.
90. *The Fisher-maid;* Cuba.
91. *In Old Madrid;* Cuba.
92. *Sweet Memories of Yesterday;* Cuba.
93. *The Stampede.*
94. *Second Sight.*
95. *The Fair Dentist.*
96. *For Her Brother's Sake.*
97. *Back to the Soil.*
98. *In the Sultan's Garden;* N.Y. Hudson River; Turkish melodrama.
99. *The Master and the Man.*
100. *The Lighthouse Keeper.*
101. *For the Queen's Honor.*
102. *A Gasoline Engagement.*
103. *At a Quarter of Two.*
104. *Science;* adapted from *A Dog's Tale*, by Mark Twain (unacknowledged); with King Baggott.
105. *The Skating Bug.*
106. *The Call of the Song.*
107. *The Toss of A Coin.*

108. *The Sentinel Asleep.*
109. *The Better Way.*
110. *His Dress Shirt.*
111. *'Tween Two Loves* (The Stronger Love): camera Irvin V. Willat with William E. Shay.
112. *The Rose's Story.*
113. *From the Bottom of the Sea.*

### The Majestic Company

114. *The Courting of Mary;* directed by George Loane Tucker.
115. *Love Heeds Not the Showers;* directed by Owen Moore.
116. *Little Red Riding Hood;* Owen Moore.
117. *The Caddy's Dream;* Owen Moore.

### 1912 Releases
### The Majestic Company

118. *Honor Thy Father;* Owen Moore.

### The Biograph Company
(all except 124 directed by Griffith, and all but 124 shot by Bitzer, 124 unknown.)

119. *The Mender of Nets;* Santa Monica, California; romance; Charles West.
120. *Iola's Promise;* California; Indian romance; Johnson.
121. *Fate's Interception;* California; Indian romance; Lucas.
122. *The Female of the Species;* California desert; melodrama; Mac-Doweth, Bernard.
123. *Just Like a Woman;* California Oil Fields; romance; Lucas, Mailes.
124. *Won By a Fish;* Santa Monica Pier, California; directed by Mack Sennett; comedy; Bruce, Dillon, Del Henderson, Grace Henderson.
125. *The Old Actor;* California; contemporary drama; August, W. Christie Miller, Frank Opperman, Charles West.
126. *A Lodging for the Night;* California; Mexican romance.

# CLAIR'S

Marble Arch W.1.

*Hair & Beauty Salon*

All Beauty Treatments
Suntanning &
Hair Straightening

157, Shepherds Bush Precinct
London, W.12
01-743 4748

CLOSED
MONDAYS

127. *A Beast at Bay;* California; contemporary automobile-train melodrama; Mailes, Alfred Paget.

128. *Home Folks;* L.A. Studio; drama; Bruce, Harron, Mailes.

129. *Lena and the Geese;* California; Dutch romance; screenplay by Mary Pickford; McDowell, Mailes, Marsh.

130. *The Schoolteacher and the Waif;* California; comedy; Edwin August, Bruce, Harron, Claire McDowell, Mailes, Mae Marsh, Frank Opperman, Paget, Jack Pickford.

131. *An Indian Summer;* California; contemporary romance; scenario by George Hennessy; Bernard, Bruce Marsh Miller, Jack Pickford.

132. *A Pueblo Legend* (2); Isleta, New Mexico; Indian romance—the first Biograph two-reeler and only Pickford two-reeler; Harron, Wilfred, Lucas.

133. *The Narrow Road;* New York; contemporary melodrama. Elmer Booth, Henry Hyde, Mailes.

134. *The Inner Circle;* N.Y.C.; Mafia melodrama; Adolph Lestina.

135. *With the Enemy's Help.*

136. *Friends;* Coytesville, N.J., N.Y.C.; romance; Lionel Barrymore, Harry Carey, Harron, Walthall; the first close-up.

137. *So Near, Yet So Far;* N.Y.C.; romance; scenario by George Hennessy, L. Barrymore, Booth, Harron, Walter Miller, Antonio Moreno.

138. *A Feud in the Kentucky Hills;* Palisades, N.J.; romance; Bruce, Curey, Walter Miller, Walthall, Jack Pickford.

139. *The One She Loved;* Fort Lee; contemporary romance; L. Barrymore, Lillian Gish, Walthall.

140. *My Baby;* N.Y.C.; Lillian Gish, Walthall, Miller, L. Barrymore.

141. *The Informer;* N.Y.C.; Civil War melodrama; L. Barrymore, Carey, Lillian Gish; scenario by George Hennessy.

142. *The Unwelcome Guest;* N.Y.C.; Carey, Lillian Gish, MacDowell, Miller, Jack Pickford.

143. *The New York Hat;* Fort Lee; contemporary romance; original screenplay by Anita Loos (her first); L. Barrymore, Dorothy Gish, Lillian Gish, Harron, Mae Marsh, Mailes.

*1913 Releases*
*Feature Films*
Famous Players
(Later Paramount and Paramount Artcraft)

1. *In the Bishop's Carriage* (4); director and camera Edward S. Porter; based on the novel by Miriam Nicholson; N.Y.C.; David Hall, House Peters, J. Searle Dawley.
2. *Caprice* (4); J. Searle Dawley; based on the play starring Minnie Maddern Fiske; N.Y.C.; Louise Huff; Owen Moore, Ernest Truex.

*1914 Releases*
(Famous Players—Paramount)

3. *A Good Little Devil* (5); Porter, director-cameraman; from the David Belasco Broadway production of the play by Maurice Rostand (in which Mary Pickford also played); Edward Connelly, William Norris, Truex (also from Broadway company) Belasco appeared in a prologue.
4. *Hearts Adrift* (4); Edwin S. Porter director-cameraman; from Cyrus Townsend Brady's story, *As the Sparks Fly Upward* California Studio—first billing in electric lights; Harold Lockwood.
5. *Tess of the Storm Country* (5) (first version); from the novel by Grace Miller White; L.A. Studio; director-cameraman Porter; Olive Fuller Gordon, David Hartford, Lockwood.
6. *The Eagles' Mate* (5); director-cameraman James Kirkwood; Southern mountain romance from the novel by Anna Alice Chapin; Kirkwood, Ida Waterman.
7. *Such a Little Queen* (5); Hugh Ford; from the play by Channing Pollock; Carlyle Blackwell, Russell Bassett, Arthur Hoops, Lockwood.
8. *Behind the Scenes* (5); Kirkwood; Bassett, Kirkwood, Lowell Sherman, Waterman.
9. *Cinderella* (4); Kirkwood; classic fairy tale; Moore, Georgia Wilson.

10. *Mistress Nell* (5); Kirkwood; Restoration-set historical romance from the novel and play by George C. Hazelton, Jr; Ruby Hoffman, Hoops, Moore.

11. *Fanchon, The Cricket* (5); Kirkwood; based on a George Sand story; Adele Astaire, Fred Astaire, Gertrude Norman, Jack Pickford, Lottie Pickford.

12. *The Dawn of Tomorrow* (5); from a story by Frances Hodgson Burnett; Kirkwood; Robert Cain, David Powell, Forest Robinson.

13. *Little Pal* (5); Kirkwood; Alaska Indians' story; George Anderson, Bassett.

14. *Rags* (5); Kirkwood; from a story by Edith Barnard Delano; J. Farrell MacDonald, Joseph Manning, Marshall Neilan.

15. *Esmerelda* (4); Kirkwood; from a story by Frances Hodgson Burnett; Hoops, Waterman.

16. *A Girl of Yesterday* (5); Allan Dwan; story by Mary Pickford; Donald Crisp, Frances Marion, Neilan, Norman, Jack Pickford. Mary Pickford becomes first actress to fly in a movie.

17. *Madame Butterfly* (5); Sidney Olcott; camera Hal Young; from the John Luther Long story, not the Puccini opera; Neilan, Olive West.

18. *The Foundling* (5); John B. O'Brian; camera H. Siddons; Marcia Harris, Edward Marindel, Mildred Morris, Maggie Weston.

19. *Poor Little Peppina* (7); Sidney Olcott; camera Emmet Williams; W. T. Carleton, Edwin Mordant, Eugene O'Brien, Jack Pickford, Edith Shayne.

20. *The Eternal Grind* (5); J. O'Brien; camera Emmet Williams; Loretta Blake, John Bowers, Cain, Dorothy West.

21. *Hulda From Holland* (5); J. O'Brien; camera Emmet Williams; from a story by Edith Barnard Delano; Bassett, Bowers, Frank Losee.

22. *Less Than the Dust* (7); John Emerson; Mary Alden, Basset, Powell.

23. *The Pride of the Clan* (7); Artcraft; Maurice Tourneur; Massachusetts coast; adapted by Elaine Stern and Charles E. Whittaker; photographed by John Van der Broek and Lucien Andriot; sets by Ben Carre; Scottish melodrama; Matt Moore, Kathryn Browne Decker, Warren Cook, Ed Roseman, Joel Day.

24. *The Poor Little Rich Girl* (6); Tourneur; N.Y.C.; Van der Broek and Andriot; scenario Frances Marion; from the Eleanor Gates novel; sets Ben Carre; child-fantasy social comment comedy; Frank Andrews; Charles Craig, Madelaine Traverse, Charles Wellesly.

25. *A Romance of the Redwoods* (7); Cecil B. De Mille; camera Alvin Wycoff; Elliot Dexter, Raymond Hatton, Tully Marshall, Charles Ogle.

26. *The Little American* (5); Cecil B. De Mille; San Pedro, California, L.A. Studio; Wycoff; scenario by Jeanie MacPherson, based on the sinking of the Lusitania; melodrama; Ben Alexander, Hobart Bosworth, Hatton, Jack Holt, Walter Long, James Neil, Guy Oliver. Ramon Novarro was an extra.

27. *Rebecca of Sunnybrook Farm* (6); Marshall Neilan (début as director); photographed by Walter Stradling, scenario by Frances Marion from the play by Kate Douglas Wiggins and Charlotte Thompson; Pickford classic little girl comedy; Wesley Barry, Marjorie Daw, Mayme Kelso, Eugene O'Brien, Charles Ogle, Zasu Pitts (début), Toncray, Frank Turner, Violet Wilkey.

28. *A Little Princess* (5); Neilan; Stradling, Charles Rosher, Norman Kerry, Pitts, Theodore Roberts, Anne Schaefer.

29. *Stella Maris* (6); Neilan; photography Walter Stradling; scenario by Frances Marion based on the novel by William J. Locke; art direction Wilfred Buckland; social comment-tragedy; Joseph Crowell, Conway Tearle, Ida Waterman. Pickford played two parts for the first time, those of Unity, the cockney girl and the well-born Stella Maris.

30. *Amarilly of Clothes-Line Alley* (5); Neilan; Stradling; Barry,

Norman Kerry, Kate Price, Herbert Standing, William Scott, Waterman.

31. *M'Liss* (5); Neilan; Stradling; Monte Blue, Tully Marshal, Thomas Meighan, Ogle, Theodore Roberts.

32. *How Could You, Jean?* (5); William Desmond Taylor; Rosher; Spottiswoode Aitken, Casson Ferguson, Pitts, Herbert Standing.

33. *Johanna Enlists* (5); Taylor; Rosher; Wallace Beery, Blue, Fred Huntley, Emory Johnson, Douglas MacLean, Schaefer.

### 1919 Releases
#### (Paramount-Artcraft)

34. *Captain Kidd, Jr* (5); Taylor; Rosher; Aitken, Robert Gordon, MacLean.

#### (First National)

35. *Daddy Long-Legs* (7); Neilan; photography by Charles Rosher and Henry Conjager; scenario Agnes Johnson; social comment comedy; Betty Banton, Barry, Milla Davenport, Mahlon Hamilton, Lillian Langdon, Fay Lemport, Neilan. Pickford's début as producer.

36. *The Hoodlum* (6); Sidney Franklin; Rosher; scenario by Frances Marion; Andrew Arbuckle, Dwight Crittendon, Max Davidson, Ralph Lewis, Buddie Messenger.

37. *The Heart O' the Hills* (6); Kenneth Harlan; Franklin; Rosher; John Gilbert, Claire MacDowell; Kentucky Hills melodrama-romance based on story by John Fox.

### 1920 Releases
#### (United Artists)

38. *Pollyanna* (6); Paul Powell; photography Charles Rosher; scenario Frances Marion from the novel by Eleanor Porter; child comedy; George Berrell, William Courtleigh, Helen Jerome Eddy, J. Wharton James, Herbert Prior, Howard Ralston.

39. *Suds* (5); John Frances (Jack) Dillon; Rosher; William Austin, Lavender (horse), Roberts.

### 1921 Releases
### (United Artists)

40. *The Love Light* (7); Frances Marion; Rosher; Raymond Bloomer, Evelyn Dumo, Fred Thompson.
41. *Through the Back Door* (6); Alfred E. Green and Jack Pickford; Rosher; script by Mary Pickford; Gertrude Astor, Elinor Fair, John Harron, Peaches Jackson, Wilfred Lucas, Adolph Menjou.
42. *Little Lord Fauntleroy* (10); Green, Jack Pickford; L.A. Studio; photographed by Rosher; scenario by Bernard McConville, based on book by Frances Hodgson Burnett; art direction Stephen Gooson; child fantasy drama; Rose Dione, Joseph Dowling, Claude Gillingwater, Colin Kenny, Emmett King, James A. Marcus, Frances Marion, Kate Price.


### 1922 Release
### (United Artists)

43. *Tess of the Storm Country* (remake) (10); John S. Roberts; Rosher?; Jean Hersholt, Gloria Hope, Lloyd Hughes.


### 1923 Release
### (United Artists)

44. *Rosita* (9); Ernst Lubitsch; L.A. Studio; Rosher; based on *Don Cesar de Bazan*; Holbrook Blinn, George Periolat, Irene Rich, George Walsh.


### 1924 Release
### (United Artists)

45. *Dorothy Vernon of Haddon Hall* (10); Neilan; L.A. Studio, San Francisco; Charles Rosher; Elizabethan drama; Clare Eames, Allan Forrest, Marc MacDermott, Lottie Pickford, Estelle Taylor, Anders Randolph.

46. *Little Annie Rooney* (10); William Beaudine; L.A. Studio; Rosher,
Hal Mohr; child fantasy melodrama based on the song; Gordon
Griffith, William Haines, Carlo Schipa, Vola Vale.

47. *Sparrows* (9); Beaudine; L.A. Studio; photographed by Rosher
and Karl Struss and Hal Mohr; original story by Winifred Dunn;
adaptation by C. Gardiner Sullivan; settings Harry Oliver;
Southern swamp, social comment, horror-thriller melodrama;
Mary Louise Miller, Charlotte Mineau, Gustav von Seffertiz,
Roy Stewart, Lloyd Whitlock.

48. *My Best Girl* (9); Sam Taylor; L.A. Studio; Rosher; contemporary comedy-satire; screenplay by Allen McNeil, Tim Whelan,
from the story by Kathleen Norris, adaptation by Hope Loring;
art director Jack Schulze; Charles 'Buddy' Rogers, Hobart
Bosworth, Carmelita Geraghty, Evelyn Hall, Sunshine Hart,
Lucien Littlefield.

49. Sound
*Coquette* (9); Taylor; L.A. Studio; Karl Struss; based on the
Broadway play by Anne Bridgers and George Abbott and
starring Helen Hayes; Louise Beavers, John Mack Brown, George
Irving, Matt Moore.
Academy Award for Mary Pickford, Best Actress—her first
talkie, first sound Oscar.

50. Sound (also 7-reel silent version)
*The Taming of the Shrew* (8); Taylor; L.A. Studio; Struss;
scenario by Taylor based on the play by William Shakespeare;

Douglas Fairbanks, Joseph Hawthorn, Clyde Cook, Dorothy Jordan, Edwin Maxwell, Geoffrey Wardwell. First Shakespearean talkie.

*1931 Release*
(United Artists)

51. Sound
   *Kiki* (10); Sam Taylor; L.A. Studio; Struss; Reginald Denny, Margaret Livingston.

*1933 Release*
(United Artists)

52. Sound
   *Secrets* (9); Frank Borzage; California; camera Ray June; Leslie Howard, Bessie Barriscale, Ethel Clayton, Blanche Federici. C. Aubrey Smith, Ned Sparks.

Note—1918, a one-real propaganda film for War Bonds; *One Hundred Percent American*; director Arthur Rossen; camera Hugh McClurg; Glen MacWilliams; Henry Bergman, Monte Blue.

Note—1927, walkon as The Madonna in Douglas Fairbanks film *The Gaucho* with Lupe Valez, directed by Richard Jones.

# Bibliography

ASTOR, MARY. *A Life on Film*, W. H. Allen, 1973.

BLUM, DANIEL. *A Pictorial History of the Silent Screen*, Grossett & Dunlap, Los Angeles, 1955.

—— *A Pictorial History of the American Theatre 1860–1970*, Crown, 1971.

BROWNLOW, KEVIN. *The Parade's Gone By*, Sphere, 1973.

CONNELL, BRIAN. *Knight Errant, A Biography of Douglas Fairbanks, Jr.*, Hodder & Stoughton, London, 1955.

FAIRBANKS, LETITA and HANCOCK, RALPH. *Douglas Fairbanks: The Fourth Musketeer*, Davies, 1953.

GISH, LILLIAN. *The Movies, Mr. Griffith and Me*, W. H. Allen, 1969.

GOODMAN, EZRA. *The Fifty-year Decline and Fall of Hollywood*, Simon & Schuster.

GRIFFITH, LINDA ARVIDSON. *When the Movies Were Young*, Dover.

HENDERSON, ROBERT M. *D. W. Griffith: The Years at Biograph*, Secker & Warburg, 1971.

*Ladies Home Journal.* 'My Story', July, August, September 1923.

MOORE, COLLEEN. *Silent Star*, Doubleday, 1968.

NIVER, KEMP R. *Mary Pickford Comedienne*, Locare, Los Angeles, 1969.

PICKFORD, MARY. *Why Not Try God?* Methuen, 1935.

—— *My Rendezvous With Life*, H. C. Kinsey & Co., 1935.

—— *Sunshine and Shadow*, Heineman, London, 1955–6.

SPEARS, JACK. *Hollywood, The Golden Era.*

TALMEY, ALLENE. *Doug and Mary and Others*, Macy-Masius (Vanguard Press), 1927.

WAGENKNECHT, EDWARD C. *The Movies in the Age of Innocence*, Norman, University of Oklahoma Press, 1962.

WALKER, ALEXANDER. *The Celluloid Sacrifice*, Michael Joseph, 1966.

WINTER, WILLIAM. *The Life of David Belasco*, Moffat, Yard & Co., 1920.

# Index

221

225